That Beautiful Little Post

The Story of Fort Missoula

Published by the

Friends of the Historical Museum at Fort Missoula

and

Big Elk Books

ISBN 978-0-9838390-2-6

Library of Congress Control Number: 2012915105

Published by the
Friends of the Historical Museum at Fort Missoula
and
Big Elk Books

Acknowledgments

That Beautiful Little Post is dedicated to the many volunteers who have worked to preserve the history, buildings, and artifacts of Missoula's fort over the years. Fort Missoula would have faded into obscurity long ago were it not for those citizens who rallied together to protect the historic post from closure or redevelopment.

The title of the book was inspired by Col. Andrew S. Burt, the fort's commander from 1892 to 1898. Interviewed by a reporter on the day his battalion of the 25th Infantry Regiment left Missoula on the way to the Spanish-American War, Colonel Burt remarked that, "nothing would please me better than to come back to Missoula sometime and spend the rest of my days, and were it not for the impending war that threatens this country, I would that this train and regiment would be ordered back to that beautiful little post on the banks of the Bitterroot."

I would like to thank the Friends of the Historical Museum at Fort Missoula for their generous support in publishing this book. I would also like to thank the staff members of the Historical Museum. The museum's executive director, Dr. Robert M. Brown, as well as curator Nicole Webb, and former development director Diane Sands deserve particular credit for their contributions to this book. I am also indebted to the many scholars who have studied Fort Missoula. A partial list includes Wallace Long, Capt. A.E. Rothermich, Stan Cohen, Carol Van Valkenburg, Linda Bailey, George N. Sorensen, Tate Jones, James Habeck, Dale Johnson, Marcia Porter, Sharon Garner, and an unknown captain who left an early history in the adjutant's desk at Fort Missoula. In addition to those previously mentioned, Walter M. Johnson, M.Y. "Bo" Foster, Hayes Otoupalik and many others have played a major role in preserving Fort Missoula's history. The author would also like to thank Greg Siple, Donna Gaukler, Kris Crawford, Mark Fritch, Mac Palmer, and Kelsey Glynn for their contributions.

About the Author

Gary Glynn served on the board of the Friends of the Historical Museum at Fort Missoula from 1995 to 2001, and on the Missoula County Board of Trustees for the Historical Museum from 2001 to 2010. He received the Lt. James Moss Award for outstanding service to the museum in 2011. He has been writing about military history, Montana history, and Fort Missoula for 30 years. Recent works include *Montana's Home Front During World War II, 2nd ed.* (Big Elk Books, 2011) and *Historic Photos of Montana* (Turner Publishing, 2009). He is currently working on the *Brink of War*, the story of the United States' intervention during the Mexican Revolution.

Photo Credit Abbreviations:

HMFM - Historical Museum at Fort Missoula
LC - Library of Congress
NARA - National Archives
UM - University of Montana

MHS - Montana Historical Society
USGS - United States Geologic Survey

Uncredited color photos are by the author

Table of Contents

1

Missoula Has Got That Post at Last

"...the great advantage will be in the partial breaking down of our isolation, improvement of our social condition, the increase in population, and the more rapid development of our resources"
Chauncey Barbour, editor of the *Weekly Missoulian*

The Missoula Valley lies in a bowl surrounded by glacier-sculpted mountains and defined by the Clark Fork River. It sits at the hub of the upper and lower Clark Fork, the Bitterroot, the Blackfoot, and the Mission valleys. The surrounding mountains bear the horizontal marks of the ancient shoreline of Glacial Lake Missoula, which repeatedly filled the valleys of western Montana with hundreds of feet of water during the Ice Ages, then emptied suddenly in cataclysmic floods. A natural crossroads, the valley was home to the Salish (or Flathead), Kootenai, and Pend d'Oreille (or Kalispel) tribes. The Nez Percé, who lived near the junction of Oregon, Washington and Idaho, routinely traveled through the valley on their way to the buffalo hunting grounds of central Montana. They had generally good relations with the Indians of western Montana, and many were related by marriage.

Meriwether Lewis led the first white party into the valley in 1806, having separated from William Clark at the mouth of Lolo Canyon just a few miles south of the Missoula Valley. Lewis named the river that passed through the Missoula Valley the Clark Fork after his partner, although early settlers often referred to it as the Hellgate or Missoula River.

British explorer David Thompson briefly surveyed the valley from a hill near the present day Missoula airport in 1812, but for the next few decades only a few fur trappers dared to pass through lands occupied by the Indians of western Montana. The eastern entrance of the Missoula Valley was a narrow canyon cut by the Clark Fork River. The Blackfeet were known to ambush the Salish and Nez Percé as they traveled east through this canyon on their way to the buffalo grounds of eastern Montana, and this ancient battleground, littered with the bones of long-dead warriors and horses was described by French trappers as *Porte de l'Enfer*, or "the Gates of Hell."

Iroquois Indians, who often accompanied French trappers, told the Salish of the powers of the Black Robe (Catholic) priests, and the local Indians invited Jesuit priests to establish missions in the Bitterroot Valley (south of Missoula) in 1841 and the Mission Valley (north of Missoula) in 1854. Isaac Stevens, the Governor of Washington Territory led an expedition into western Montana (then part of Washington Territory) in 1853. His party included C.P. Higgins and John Mullan. Both men would have a major impact on the development of western Montana. Stevens returned in 1855 to negotiate the Hellgate Treaty at Council Grove with the Salish, Kootenai and Pend D'Oreille. Stevens' goal was to entice the Indians to relinquish their claims to the Bitterroot Valley and much of western Montana and Idaho as well, all in return for $120,000. A treaty was signed (despite the fact that according to Father Adrian Hoecken, "not a tenth of what was said was understood by either side," and was ratified in 1859.

Governor Stevens was also the powerful patron of a plan to build an overland road across the Rocky Mountains, and Captain John Mullan and 200 men embarked on an expedition to construct a military road from Walla Walla, Washington to Fort Benton, Montana, on a route through the Missoula Valley. Construction began in 1858 and, despite Indian troubles and repeated flooding, continued until 1862.

The first white settlers in the valley adopted the name Hellgate after a small town grew up around a trading post built by Frank Worden and C.P. Higgins, staffed by Frank Woody. Missoula County (still part of Washington Territory) was established in 1861. While small amounts of gold dust had been found at Gold Creek as early as 1854, miners were not interested in Montana until 1862 when the town of Bannack appeared during a major gold rush at Grasshopper Creek. By 1863 the placer works at Alder Gulch soon spawned Virginia City, while the diggings at Last Chance Gulch grew into the town of Helena.

Montana became a territory in 1864, and that year the construction of a flour mill and lumber mill near Rattlesnake Creek prompted many of the residents of Hellgate to move a few miles east to the new community of Missoula Mills. Leading citizens of the new community included C.P. Higgins, Frank Worden, Frank Woody, and David Pattee.

The move to build a military fort in western Montana can be traced to the Red Cloud War of the Sioux during the late 1860s. Although the residents of Missoula were far from the fighting, they still felt threatened by the Lakota, Northern Cheyenne, and Arapaho warriors who drove the US Army from the Powder River country of southeastern Montana and northern Wyoming from 1865 to 1868. The war created panic throughout the state as the Native Americans, alarmed by the intrusion of whites into their traditional hunting grounds, effectively shut down the Bozeman Trail used by gold-seekers hoping to reach the boomtowns of Montana. Attacks against Fort C.F. Smith in Montana and Fort Kearney in Wyoming resulted in more panic among the white residents of Montana, and Acting Territorial Governor Thomas F. Meagher requested troops. When that request was refused Meagher formed a state militia which accomplished little except for running up a bill of more than one million dollars, of which the US government eventually paid about half.

Martin Maginnis, Montana Territory's representative to Congress, was instrumental in gaining approval to construct Fort Missoula, even if he had to bypass regular Congressional appropriations to do so. He was said to possess, "keenness of wit, vibrant utterances, and commanding presence."[1] McGinnis worked to open much of Montana to white settlement, lobbied for land grants to build railroads and for construction of the state Capitol and the university system, and opposed reducing the size of the Army.
LC-BH832-159

During this period local residents first began lobbying for a military post in the Missoula Valley to protect the settlers of Missoula, as well as the Mullan Road, from Indian attack. While the local Native Americans had a long history of living peacefully with the whites, the Indians were known to rustle the occasional horse or cow. Soldiers in the area, it was reasoned, would not only discourage the thievery but prevent more serious violence as well.

The Cedar Creek gold rush near present-day Superior brought thousands of prospectors to the area in 1869 and 1870, and helped establish Missoula as a regional trade center.

As part of the US Indian Reservation Policy established in 1871, President U.S. Grant finally ordered the Salish to vacate the Bitterroot Valley in 1874 and move to the Jocko Reservation north of Missoula under the terms of the 1855 Hellgate Treaty. However, Chief Charlo refused to move from his ancestral lands, and local settlers feared that violence would erupt if the Salish were pushed too hard.

Businessmen in Missoula recognized the financial bene-

The Bitterroot Salish and the Hellgate Treaty

Council Grove State Park west of Missoula marks the location where the Hellgate Treaty of 1855 was negotiated between Governor Isaac Stevens of Washington Territory (which included western Montana at the time) and the Salish, Kootenai, and Pend d'Oreille tribes. Stevens wanted to open much of western Montana to white settlement in exchange for establishment of the Flathead Indian Reservation, often referred to as the Jocko Reservation. The Salish insisted that a reservation be established in the Bitterroot Valley as well, but on that point Stevens slipped a condition into the treaty. While article I of the treaty spelled out the lands the Indians were ceding, and Article II defined the lands that would become the Flathead Reservation, mention of the Bitterroot Valley did not appear until Article XI, near the end of the treaty. It read that if the Bitterroot Valley, "in the judgment of the President, to be better adapted to the wants of the Flathead tribe than the general reservation provided for in this treaty, then such portions of it as may be necessary shall be set apart as a separate reservation for the said tribe." Rather than guaranteeing the Salish ownership over their ancestral homeland, the treaty instead gave the President of the United States final say over whether their lands would be open to settlement by whites. This clause was agreed to by Chief Victor only because, "not a tenth of what was said was understood by either side,"[2] The Hellgate Treaty was ratified by the US Senate on March 8, 1859, and for the next dozen years the Salish lived peacefully in the Bitterroot Valley, believing it to be theirs forever. Chief Victor was determined to stay, as was his son Charlo.

White settlers began to illegally intrude into the Bitterroot Valley, and in 1867 the Indians met on Lolo Creek to discuss ordering the settlers from the valley. Major John Owen at Fort Owen wrote to Indian Agent John W. Wells in March 1868 to ask the valley be opened to white settlement because he did not believe the Salish would ever leave on their own. The government then began to cut down on the food aid sent to the non-reservation Salish.

Chief Victor died in 1870, and the following year President Ulysses Grant found that the Bitterroot had been surveyed for settlement and that in his opinion the Salish would be better off on the Flathead Reservation. Having met the deceptive terms of the Hellgate Treaty, on June 5, 1872 Congress passed a bill mandating the removal of the Salish from the Bitterroot. Future President James A. Garfield was appointed by the Secretary of Interior to convince the Flatheads to sign a treaty that obligated them to move. Chief Charlo never agreed to the Garfield Treaty, but the printed version of the treaty indicated he had signed, although the original copies clearly showed he had not. Senator G. G. Vest and the Honorable Martin Maginniss, Montana's Delegate to Congress traveled to the Bitterroot to meet Charlo, who told them that Garfield had placed his name on a document he never signed, and that he had no faith in white men. Charlo's claim was backed up by Father Ravalli and by a copy of the document held by Indian Agent Peter Ronan. Chief Arlee did sign the treaty, and he and a majority of the Salish moved to the Jocko Reservation. Arlee thereafter was recognized as chief of the Salish by the government, but Charlo never spoke to Arlee again. When Peter Ronan became Indian Agent in 1877, he discovered 50 patents for land allocated to the Bitterroot Salish in his predecessor's office, where they had languished for a year since they were issued. After the death of Arlee, Peter Ronan again tried to persuade Charlo to move to the Jocko Reservation, but the chief had lost all faith in the white men his tribe had befriended seventy years before. In the conclusion to an eloquent speech in 1876, Charlo spelled out why the whites could never be trusted, "His laws never gave us a blade of grass nor a tree, nor a duck, nor a grouse, nor a trout. No, like the wolverine that steals your cache, how often does he come? You know he comes as long as he lives, and takes more and more, and dirties what he leaves."[3]

Council Grove State Park west of Missoula marks the spot where Governor Isaac Stevens negotiated the Hellgate Treaty with the Salish, Kootenai, and Pend d'Oreille tribes in 1855.

fits of having a military post nearby, especially during the economic downturn following the Panic of 1873 when the isolated town began to lose population. Local farmers and businessmen suffered, and the prospects of a nearby military post seemed the fastest way to boost the economy. Leading citizens repeatedly asked Governor Benjamin Potts and Martin Maginnis, (Montana's Territorial Representative to Congress from 1873 to 1885) for help.

The Territorial legislature also weighed in, and on February 5th, 1874 voted to ask Congress to establish a military post at the mouth of the Bitterroot River. Chauncey Barbour bought the *Weekly Missoulian* in 1875 and soon became the most outspoken proponent of the fort. He wrote, "To be sure, the few thousands of dollars that will be added to the general circulation will be of advantage; but the great advantage will be in the partial breaking down of our isolation, improvement of our social condition, the increase in population, and the more rapid development of our resources." Barbour's newspaper also exaggerated every incident between Indian and white, and regularly referred to the peaceful Salish as "savages" and "barbarous."

Frank Woody, one of the first white residents of the valley, had a more realistic view. "If surrounding tribes occasionally donned their war paint their excursions were not in the direction of the valleys named, hence there never really existed any cause for the quartering of any soldiers here in the settlement of the country."

Tensions rose once more when Missoula resident Jack Allen was killed by an Indian north of Flathead Lake in 1875, and Barbour whipped up a frenzy with his fears of a general uprising by the Indians. He put out a special edition claiming three whites were dead and five missing. Allen was killed in retaliation for his murder of a Kootenai man, but the incident ended there. Nevertheless, Barbour was very effective at arousing fears in the white population of western Montana, and in response to public pressure, the US Army sent Lt. Col. Wesley Merritt of the 9th Cavalry Regiment to Missoula in January 1876 to determine if a fort was needed. Local residents presented Merritt with at least three potential sites, one at the Blackfoot Bridge near present-day Bonner, one at the mouth of Grant Creek, and a location adjacent to the Bitterroot River (the mouth of Pattee Canyon may also have been considered). The Grant Creek site was favored by local businessmen who felt they would profit more from a fort close to town. Numerous parties and banquets were held by local townsfolk trying to in-

Colonel Wesley Merritt

Lieutenant Colonel Wesley Merritt arrived in Missoula to eveluate the prospects of locating a military post in the valley. His decision was complicated by the eager citizens of the valley, who wined and dined him without relief. Merritt recommended a small military post be built in the Missoula Valley, and declared all of the locations advocated by local citizens were suitable. Merritt was an 1860 graduate of West Point. Just days before the Battle of Gettysburg in 1863 the Army appointed both Captain Merritt and Lieutenant George Armstrong Custer as brigadier generals in the Union Army, although both men reverted to their pre-war rank after the hostilities ended. Merritt served with the 9th Cavalry from 1866 to 1876, and soon after his visit to Missoula he took command of the 5th Cavalry Regiment. He served on the Court of Inquiry that investigated Major Marcus Reno after the Battle of the Little Big Horn in 1879. He was sent to the Philippines during the Spanish-American War, where he became the military governor. He served for five years as Superintendent of West Point, and was buried there after his death in 1910. Camp Wesley Merritt, which was built near Lame Deer in 1884 was named for him, as was Camp Merritt, a World War I-era post in New Jersey.

fluence Merritt's decision, and Merritt was so well entertained by the citizens of Missoula that he not only supported building a fort, but "had the banquet lasted much longer it is not improbable that the worthy colonel would have advocated the establishing of three forts, one on each site."[4] On February 8, 1876 Merritt recommended establishing a post in Missoula garrisoned by one or two infantry companies.

The annihilation of Lt. Col. George A. Custer and five companies of the 7th Cavalry at the Little Big Horn after a reckless attack on a combined village of Lakota and Northern Cheyenne warriors on June 25, 1876 prompted immediate calls for the construction of several new forts in Montana. Representative Maginnis was a principal force behind getting Congressional approval for Forts Keogh and Fort Custer in 1876. Less than a month after Custer's death, Congress appropriated $200,000 for the construction of Fort Keogh at the mouth of the Tongue River near present-day Miles City, and construction began the following month. By 1877 Fort Keogh boasted 30 buildings and housed five infantry companies and six cavalry companies, with Col. Nelson Miles in command. By early June of 1877 four companies of the 11th Infantry were hard at work building Fort Custer at the intersection of the Big Horn and Little Big Horn Rivers near present-day Hardin. It was soon considered one of the finest cavalry posts in the world.

Missoula resident's became concerned that the appropriations for construction of Fort Keogh and Fort Custer would harm their chances of having a fort built in the Missoula Valley, and Washington J. McCormick of Missoula traveled to Washington to help Representative Maginnis lobby for a fort near Missoula as well. After Congress appropriated money for Forts Keogh and Custer in 1876, Maginnis decided Congress was unlikely to send any more money to Montana Territory, and so he convinced the Quartermaster General of the Army to set aside $20,000 from his general fund for construction of a one or two company post in the Missoula Valley as recommended by Lt. Col Merritt. The fort was to be constructed by the soldiers stationed there using money from the Quartermaster's general fund, thereby bypassing Congressional approval. Chauncey Barbour, editor of the *Weekly Missoulian* reported, "Too great credit in this post matter can not be accorded to our efficient Delegate, Major Maginnis, who has labored in our behalf with such importunity as almost at times to render himself disagreeable."

Barbour went on to say that, "Without the intelligent co-operation of Governor Potts, and the strong recommendations of Colonel Medary, in this behalf, we could have had no post. The press and the people of Deer Lodge and Lewis and Clarke counties have given us valuable and material assistance…"

The Colonel Medary mentioned by Barbour was controversial Indian Agent Charles S. Medary of the Jocko Reservation. Agent Medary was not popular with the local chiefs, and after they threatened to eject him from the reservation in December 1876, Medary called for and received a detachment of troops from Fort Shaw. The 20 soldiers under Lieutenants Scofield and Fuller stayed at the Agency until March 1877. Even editor Barbour stated, "The danger was probably magnified, and agent Medary, in his zeal to assist the people of this region to a military post, may have gone beyond what was really necessary; but the fact remains that Charley S. Medary did more to hasten the establishment of a military post than any official ever located here..." Missoula resident Will Cave also credited this dispute with hastening construction of the fort, although Cave agreed that the threat was overblown. The unpopular and alcoholic Medary was replaced by a much more capable Indian Agent, Peter Ronan in mid-1877.

Choosing the final site of what was then called "the post on the Missoula," fell to Lt. Col. Charles C. Gilbert and 2nd Lt. Charles A. Worden, acting engineer of the 7th Infantry. They arrived in July 1876 with orders to choose a location close to Cold Springs Ranch near the Bitterroot River. Perhaps hoping to avoid the hoopla that had accompanied Col. Merritt's visit months before, the two officers proceeded directly through town towards the present-day site of Fort Missoula, which they found a suitable location. However, before deciding on the current location they took the time to climb McCauley Butte (in the company of Major McCauley himself) to examine the Grant Creek site by binoculars. The two officers had already examined the proposed location near the mouth of the Blackfoot River just before arriving in Missoula, but decided the location closest to the Bitterroot River provided the best defensive position, and Lt. Col. Gilbert planted a flag in the middle of where he determined the parade ground of the new fort should be.

Lt. Worden and the county surveyor determined the borders of the military reservation, which they defined as Section 31, township 13 N, R. 20 W. Unfortunately, due either to bad maps or a surveying error, they miscalculated the location of the flag that Gilbert had planted. Rather than being comfortably within Section 31 as they assumed, the flag and many of the buildings that would eventually be built around the parade ground were actually located in the adjacent Section 36, which had already been transferred to Montana Territory to provide income for public education. This surveying error would cause no end of grief for the commanders of the new post, would threaten the very existence of the fort, and would not be rectified for almost 30 years.

President Ulysses S. Grant officially set aside Section 31, Township 13 N., Range 19 W. for the establishment of a fort on Feb. 19, 1877. By June 1, 1877 the Quartermaster of the Army had set aside $20,000 for construction of a post near Missoula, with the final location up to Col. John Gibbon at Fort Ellis. Even so, the citizens of Missoula still worried that the fort would never be built.

The prospect of a fort in the Missoula Valley was met with great enthusiasm. Editor Barbour wrote that, "A military post in this section of the country has been a pleasant dream from the time when the first dwellers attempted to reclaim the wilderness and make it blossom and bear fruit for civilization. The dream began to furnish hope of realization a little over a year ago. Our plucky Delegate, in the face of discouragements, procured an order specially detailing General Merritt to visit us and inspect and report upon the necessity for military protection. His report was of the most favorable character, leading us to believe that the advent of troops could not be long delayed."

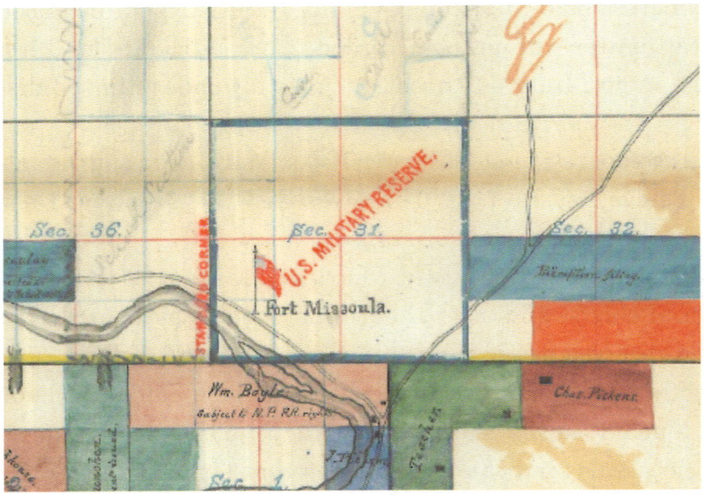

This 1877 hand-colored map of the Fort Missoula Military Reserve shows the flagpole that Colonel Gilbert planted on the original parade ground of the fort, as well as the boundaries of Section 31 that Congress set aside for the fort. Due to a surveying error, the flagpole was actually located a few hundred yards west of what was indicated on this map. As a result much of the parade ground, and many of the buildings constructed around the parade ground were actually located in Section 36, land set aside by statute to fund public education. This surveying error ultimately threatened the very existence of Fort Missoula.

There were 1,100 soldiers stationed in Washington and Idaho in early 1877, but only 450 soldiers in Montana, located primarily at Fort Shaw, Fort Ellis, and Fort Benton, with a few soldiers detailed to the fledgling forts Keogh and Custer. The shortage of men was such that Major Guido Ilges, the commanding officer of Fort Benton, complained that, "Escorts and expeditions of the utmost importance have to be refused and delayed on account of scarcity of officers and enlisted men."[5] He noted that the daily sentries at his post rarely exceeded three men.

The shortage of men and money delayed construction of Fort Missoula, leading editor Barbour to complain, "The proverbial dilatoriness of red tape and a combination of infelicitous circumstances have put off the long-looked-for event. Hope deferred has sickened the heart of many, and they declare that they will not believe in it until they see the boys marching down the canyon, the pendants and guidons floating in the air, the chug of caissons, the clang of military trappings and the band advancing into the Garden Spot to the music of 'Girl I left behind me.'"[6]

The *New Northwest* paper in Deer Lodge was

more optimistic. "Missoula has got that post at last, and a two-company one at that. But as infantry companies are to be reduced to thirty-five men each, the number will still be small. It will be sufficient, however, to exercise a salutary influence over any evilly disposed Indians and to inspire a feeling of security throughout the entire region."

Several companies of the 7th Infantry had been stationed at Fort Shaw since 1872. Colonel John Gibbon on June 5, 1877 ordered the regiment's senior captain, Charles C. Rawn to march his Company I and Captain William Logan's A Company, 44 men in total, to the Missoula Valley. Captain Rawn's company was to garrison the fort while Captain Logan's men were to leave once the buildings were constructed. They left Fort Shaw on June 9, 1877, accompanied by the wives and children of the officers and non-commissioned officers, as well as the company laundresses. They marched 217 miles from Fort Shaw in 17 days, enduring rain and muddy roads for much of the last week.

Rawn and Lt. Johnson left the command at a place they called "Frenchwoman's" on June 12, and hurried on to Helena, where Lt. Johnson would spend more than two weeks negotiating contracts for construction materials and other supplies to be sent to Missoula. Rawn hurried on to Missoula and arrived June 19, where he began soliciting local businessmen for services that would be needed by the soldiers.

On June 25, 1877 a drummer and fifer led the men of the 7th Infantry in two columns into Missoula. Corporal Charles N. Loynes wrote, "On a beautiful June day we entered the struggling village of Missoula, composed at the time of a gristmill, about twenty log houses, and a camp of two or three hundred friendly Indians under an old chief about eighty years of age by the name of Big Canoe." Loynes neglected to mention Worden's store, the hotel, bank, the courthouse built six years before, and the ongoing construction of the Eddy and Hammond store, which would become better known as the iconic Missoula Mercantile. Lieutenant Edward E. Hardin of F Company, who arrived a month later, would declare it simply a, "nice little place." The men proceeded through Missoula, crossed the Clark's Fork River on the new bridge, and made their way to the site of the proposed fort, where they pitched their tents. Within a day or two lumber was being delivered to the fort, and the men of the command spent their first week in Missoula, "making camp comfortable, erecting tool shop and shed for carpenters, lime house, and other necessary preliminary work." Unbeknown to the men of the 7th Infantry, their construction efforts were about to be delayed by circumstances beyond their control.

Captain Charles C. Rawn, the first commander of Fort Missoula, was a Civil War veteran with 16 years service in the 7th Infantry Regiment. Just one year before marching into Missoula the men of his company had helped transport the wounded survivors of Custer's 7th Cavalry Regiment to safety at the Little Big Horn.

Family Albums of Harrisburg

Several hundred angry and well-armed Nez Percé warriors, along with their families and everything they owned, including thousands of horses, were on the way over Lolo Pass into Montana, pursued by troops under the command of General Otis O. Howard. Their ultimate destination was the Bitterroot Valley, only a dozen miles south of the new fort.

Catholic missionaries had been ministering to the Salish in Montana for more than twenty years by the time St. Michael's Church was built in Hellgate in 1863. Local Superior Father U. Grassi planned the church and bought the land, which was located at the top of a hill near the north bank of the Clark's Fork River. William Claessens of the Hellgate Brothers built the church out of hand-hewn logs. Father J. Caruana, a Catholic priest who stopped at Hellgate on his way to the Coeur d'Alene Indians in 1863, was the first superintendent.

Father L.B. Palladino, author of *Indian and White in the Northwest*, a history of Catholic missions, credited Father Anthony Ravalli with being the first resident priest. Ravalli lived there for three years, and baptized Mrs. Sims, his first recruit, in the church on October 1, 1866. Acting Territorial Governor General Thomas Francis Meagher and his wife served as her sponsors. During the winter of 1866-67 Father Ravalli is believed to have subsisted mostly on muskrats shot by a supporter from a nearby slough.

Eventually a government surveyor ruled that the church and a local settler both occupied the same 40-acre tract. Although the church was located at Hellgate several years before the settler arrived, Father Menetrey agreed to relinquish claims to the tract as long as the church was allowed to occupy its small space. Once the settler received title to the entire parcel, he reneged on the agreement and ordered Father Menetrey to vacate the land. The church and priest's house were disassembled. The priest's house became firewood, but the church was carted by wagon to Missoula and reassembled in about 1874. St. Patrick's Hospital already had a chapel, so St. Michael's church became a school for boys. It was damaged by fire early on, and was covered by lumber siding for a while. It was later moved behind Sacred Heart Academy, where it served as an emergency infirmary for school children. It was moved back to Hellgate in 1962, then moved to its present location at the Historical Museum at Fort Missoula in 1981.

2

The Most Extraordinary of Indian Wars

General William T. Sherman - 1877

The Flight of the Nez Percé

The Lolo Trail has been used for thousands of years by the Nez Percé tribe to access the buffalo hunting grounds in Montana. It was also familiar to Montana Indians who traveled west to the salmon runs of Idaho, Oregon and Washington. Lewis and Clark took the trail to the west in 1805, which nearly proved fatal for the 32 hardened frontiersmen of the Corps of Discovery. Hungry and exhausted, they were assisted by the Nez Percé when they reached Idaho, beginning a long and friendly relationship between the tribe and the whites. The Nez Percé (they call themselves the Nimi'ipuu, or the real people) lived in an area that included parts of Oregon, Washington and Idaho. In 1855 several bands of Nez Percé signed a treaty that gave them rights to some 12,000 square miles of their traditional home in Idaho. Other bands, collectively known as the non-treaty Nez Percé, ignored the treaty and continued to live in their traditional homeland even as white settlers began to intrude on their land.

Tensions between the white settlers and the Nez Percé began as early as 1858, leading to fears in western Montana that the Mullan Road from the west would be cut off if hostilities broke out. The situation escalated when gold was discovered on Nez Percé land in 1860, and by the following year thousands of miners had illegally entered tribal territory. American authorities tried to convince Joseph's band of non-treaty Nez Percé to give up their claims to the Wallowa Valley in 1863, and instead move to a smaller reservation near Lapwai, Idaho. This plan was repeatedly rejected by Old Joseph, the chief of the Wallowa band, and later by his son Chief Joseph, as well as by four other bands of non-treaty Nez Percé. Nevertheless, white settlers kept arriving, seeking the gold in the hills, the rich farmland, and the unbranded cattle belonging to the Indians. President Ulysses S. Grant finally issued an executive order in 1873 granting half of the Wallowa Valley to the Nez Percé, but he rescinded the order two years later. Joseph's band still refused to leave their home. In the next year at least three Nez Percé men were murdered by whites, all of whom were eventually acquitted by white juries.

After seventy years of peace, the US Army sent General Oliver O. Howard to remove several bands of non-treaty Nez Percé from the Wallowa Valley in 1877. Howard believed the Nez Percé had a legitimate claim to their land, but his orders were to move them to the Lapwai Reservation, and no Army officer who valued his career wanted to be labeled an “Indian lover.” After trying unsuccessfully to convince the Indians to move, Howard eventually told them they had 30 days to gather their stock and move to Lapwai. Joseph asked to postpone the move until fall, when the rivers would be low enough to ford with their livestock, but Howard maintained that they must leave within the month. Five bands of non-treaty Nez Percé met at Tolo Lake on June 3, 1877 to decide what to do.

Many of the young men of the tribe wanted to fight, but Joseph counseled peace, and his band began to move towards Lapwai. As Joseph had predicted, a portion of the tribe's cattle were swept away during a river crossing, and after white men stole part of the remaining herd, a band of warriors slipped away and took their revenge. On June 14, 1877, Wahlitits and two other warriors killed four white men, the worst violence between the Nez Percé and whites in 70 years. News of the killings emboldened other young men of the tribe, and by the following day 11 more whites had been killed, including a three-year-old girl. The murders caused panic among the settlers in the area. That evening 99 US soldiers left Fort Lapwai in pursuit of the murderers. The elders were angry at both the whites and the hot-headed young men of the tribe. The separate bands of Nez Percé were divided on how to proceed, but the chiefs agreed to negotiate with the soldiers in an effort to avoid war. They then split up.

On June 17, 1877 Joseph and White Bird's bands were camped at White Bird Canyon when two companies of mostly inexperienced soldiers and a small group of civilians approached. Although the Indians sent out a small party with a flag of truce, they were fired on by a civilian. In the resulting melee, the Nez Percé led by White Bird and Joseph's brother Ollokot killed 34 soldiers, while the Indians suffered only a few wounded.

Embarrassed by the loss incurred by his soldiers at White Bird Canyon, General Howard sent a detachment to arrest Chief Looking Glass, who had remained neutral and had already moved his band to the Lapwai reservation. Gunfire broke out during the botched arrest attempt, and the Indians fled their lodges. When they returned later, they found that soldiers had destroyed all of their belongings. Looking Glass and his people, peaceful up this time, then joined the other bands of non-treaty Nez Percé.

Eagle of Light (left) and 11 lodges of Nez Percé (perhaps 50 people) lived with Chief Charlo in the Bitterroot Valley during the summer of 1877. They reluctantly accompanied the fleeing Nez Percé when they passed through. The figure in the center was not Chief Joseph as indicated in the caption, but his younger brother Ollokot, who was killed at the Bear's Paw Battle. The man on the right is Middle Bear.
LC-USZ62-126380

The non-treaty bands crossed the Salmon River on July 2. On the following day they clashed again with some of Howard's troops at Cottonwood, Idaho. A dozen soldiers were killed, and 200 Army troops were besieged for two days by the Indians. Three civilians who attempted to help the soldiers were also killed before the Nez Percé once again slipped away.

Four bands of non-treaty Nez Percé joined forces on July 6. Looking Glass, White Bird and Toohoolhoolzote decided the safest course was to head for Montana, where they had good relations with both the Salish Indians and the whites in the Bitterroot Valley. Chief Joseph at first opposed moving into Montana, but then reluctantly agreed. He told the others that he would supervise the movement of the women and children on the journey, and would leave the fighting to the other chiefs.

The cautious and slow-moving General Howard finally caught up with the Nez Percé on July 11 when he surprised them at the battle of the Clearwater. Howard shelled the Indian camp from a mile away, forcing the Indians to abandon some of their lodges and belongings. After fighting for two days, the Nez Percé withdrew. By the time the soldiers reached the village, the Nez Percé were gone, and the soldiers wasted valuable time looting the Indian's possessions while the Indians headed east towards the Lolo Trail and Montana. Eight hundred Nez Percé, men, women and children set off over the difficult trail in a desperate quest for freedom.

Howard followed slowly behind them with 14 companies of infantry and cavalry, some 700 officers and men. The expedition also had Indian scouts and civilian packers in charge of 350 mules.

Residents of western Montana had been following the news

from Idaho, and from the beginning were worried that the Indian trouble would soon spill over the mountain passes. The nearest telegraph line to Missoula was in Deer Lodge, and couriers on horseback made the 80–mile trip to Missoula six days a week. By late June the white citizens of western Montana, from the Jocko Agency in the north to Darby in the south, were in an uproar. Word had arrived that the Nez Percé were on their way west, towards Montana.

Governor Benjamin Potts wrote to President Rutherford Hayes, Secretary of War George McCrary, and General Irvin McDowell at the Department of the Pacific in San Francisco, appealing for troops to defend the state and asking for authority to form a citizen's militia, which was denied. General McDowell told Potts to arrest the Nez Percé. Potts replied that was impossible since he did not have the authority to form a militia.

When no help appeared to be forthcoming from out of state, Potts, who had neither the authority nor the funds to do so, called for the formation of local militia companies and ordered the state armory in Helena to send 160 rifles to Missoula and another 100 to Deer Lodge. (These were obsolete military weapons given to state governors for the protection of the citizens.)

Local men formed several militia companies, and the rifles were distributed to the captains of each militia by the sheriffs of Missoula, Deer Lodge, and Beaverhead counties. The men, who provided their own horses and equipment, practiced drilling with the new guns.

When the soldiers building the new fort were advised of the approach of the Nez Percé, Corporal Loynes at Fort Missoula reported, "we at once commenced to fortify our camp as best we could by throwing up rifle pits, cutting away the brush that would shelter the Indians, and piling up sacks of grain in such a position as to give protection to the wives and children of officers and the laundresses of the companies."[1] On June 27th, just two days after Captain Rawn's men arrived in the Missoula Valley, 32 residents of Stevensville sent a letter to Rawn asking for arms from the Army. Lt. Johnson, writing on behalf of Rawn, replied on June 30th that they had no spare arms, nor the authority to transfer them if they had, but he reported that the residents of Missoula had just received 100 rifles from Governor Potts, and they needed to appeal to the governor.

Rawn wrote, "The people of the Bitterroot being in dread (causelessly I think) of incursions from Nez Percé Indians, now at war, are stampeding from the valley, and though one of the Mill men who lives in the valley, with whom contract for lumber has been made, still remains, he may leave at any time, in which case the building of the post will be greatly retarded."[2]

The Nez Percé, even though they appeared to exhibit little haste, traveled much faster than the Army, and by August 6 the Nez Percé were 150 miles in front of General Howard. The Nez Percé seemed to feel that the fighting with General Howard's troops was strictly a local affair, and were sure that once they reached the Montana side of Lolo Pass they would be safe. The Indians assumed that if they tried to join the Salish or Crows, passing quietly through land where they had friendly relations with the whites, they would not be bothered.

They had routinely camped in the Missoula and Bitterroot Valleys without any problem from the white settlers

William H. Jackson photographed this Nez Percé camp in Montana in 1871.
LC-DIG-stereo-1s00437

there. Looking Glass had even visited a doctor in Missoula the summer before. The Indians did not understand that a conflict with one group of soldiers meant that other soldiers would come from hundreds of miles away to support their brothers in arm. The Nez Percé knew they had to avoid the soldiers stationed at Fort Shaw and Fort Ellis, but seemed to believe that they would be allowed free passage through most of Montana. Under ordinary circumstances, they may have been right, but they were unaware of the apprehension felt by the settlers in western Montana. James Thompson, the Missoula under-sheriff wrote on July 10, "There is a manifest feeling of uneasiness among our citizens not before exhibited. A general opinion seems to prevail that we will have more or less trouble before it ends."

Captain Rawn received word of the continuing hostilities in Idaho, and on July 8 he traveled north to the Jocko Reservation to confer with Indian Agent Peter Ronan, as well as with Chief Andrea of the Pend d'Oreille, and Chief Arlee of the Salish. By 1877 there were 1,500 Kootenai, Pend d'Oreilles, and Salish living on the Jocko Reservation to the north of Missoula, and approximately 350 Salish and 50 Nez Percé living in the Bitterroot Valley to the south. The chiefs assured Rawn that they intended to remain friendly to the whites, and would not join with their old friends the Nez Percé in any hostilities. In a letter to the adjutant at Fort Shaw, Rawn remarked that, "I am not disposed to take the word of an Indian in relation to such a matter. Yet in this case I do for the reason that I saw that their interest required that they should maintain friendship." Rawn asked the Indian police force to send ten scouts to keep watch for the Nez Percé on Lolo Pass and near Elk City, Idaho. The police chief asked for uniforms and pay for the designated scouts, and while Rawn could provide uniforms, he was not authorized to pay the scouts. The Indians then declined to scout for Rawn, understandably unwilling to risk their lives without compensation.

After returning to the "Post on the Missoula," Captain Rawn then traveled thirty miles up the Bitterroot Valley to speak with Chief Charlo of the non-treaty Salish. Charlo told Rawn that he would not fight the Nez Percé due to his long friendship with them, and mentioned their help in fighting the Blackfeet. Charlo warned that even though a few young men of his tribe might join the Nez Percé, most would remain peaceful and would not harm the whites. Charlo did agree to send scouts up the Lolo Trail to locate the Nez Percé and gather information on their intentions.

The one-armed General Oliver O. Howard was relentless in his pursuit of the Nez Perce from Oregon through Idaho and Montana.
Harper's Weekly, from a photograph by Gardner, Washington

Rawn declared "...with all my prejudice against Indians and my belief that all of them are treacherous, I am inclined to think that they are in earnest and that they intend to remain friendly."

Rawn returned to his post, where on July 16 he reported that work on the fort "has so far made steady and acceptable progress." In the meantime Chief Charlo's scouts located the Nez Percé near Lolo Pass. When Rawn learned of this on July 18th he sent a five-man scouting party under 2nd Lt. Francis Woodbridge up the Lolo Canyon (which Rawn spelled as Loo Loo or Lou Lou) to determine the location of the Nez Percé. The soldiers had orders to find a vantage point where they could see the Indians approaching from several miles away.

On July 20, Colonel John Gibbon at Fort Shaw ordered the commander at Fort Ellis to send one infantry company and as many mounted men as possible to Missoula, with contract wagons to follow along with the tents and gear. Other companies were dispatched from Fort Benton and Camp Baker.

On that same day Lt. William English, on behalf of Rawn, wrote Indian Agent Ronan warning that Angus McDonald, the Jocko Reservation trader, was about to receive a shipment of 4,000 rounds of ammunition, and that three Nez Percé men hoped to acquire some of this ammunition. English asked Ronan to make sure the ammunition was locked up so the Indians could not purchase it.

Lt. Woodbridge and his men rode over the summit of Lolo Pass without encountering any of the hundreds of Nez Percé and their thousands of horses. The Lolo Pass area is a maze of ancient trails that wind through thick timber, and a handful of soldiers had no hope of completely covering a massive and unfamiliar territory that the Indians knew well. Looking Glass and White Bird, on the other hand, were soon aware that soldiers were scouting the trail ahead of them.

When no word had been received from Lt. Woodbridge by July 21, Rawn sent 1st Lt. Charles A. Coolidge, with one soldier and several civilians, to locate the missing men. On the following day Coolidge encountered Woodbridge and his scouts as they returned from Idaho.

Delaware Jim Simonds, who lived with a Nez Percé woman, informed the soldiers on the 23rd that the Nez Percé had reached Lolo Hot Springs in Montana, and Woodbridge sent a courier back to town with the news. According to Rawn, this "spread such alarm in Bitter Root Valley that companies were organized to repel the Indians. The people of Missoula also formed volunteer associations for the purpose of protecting themselves."

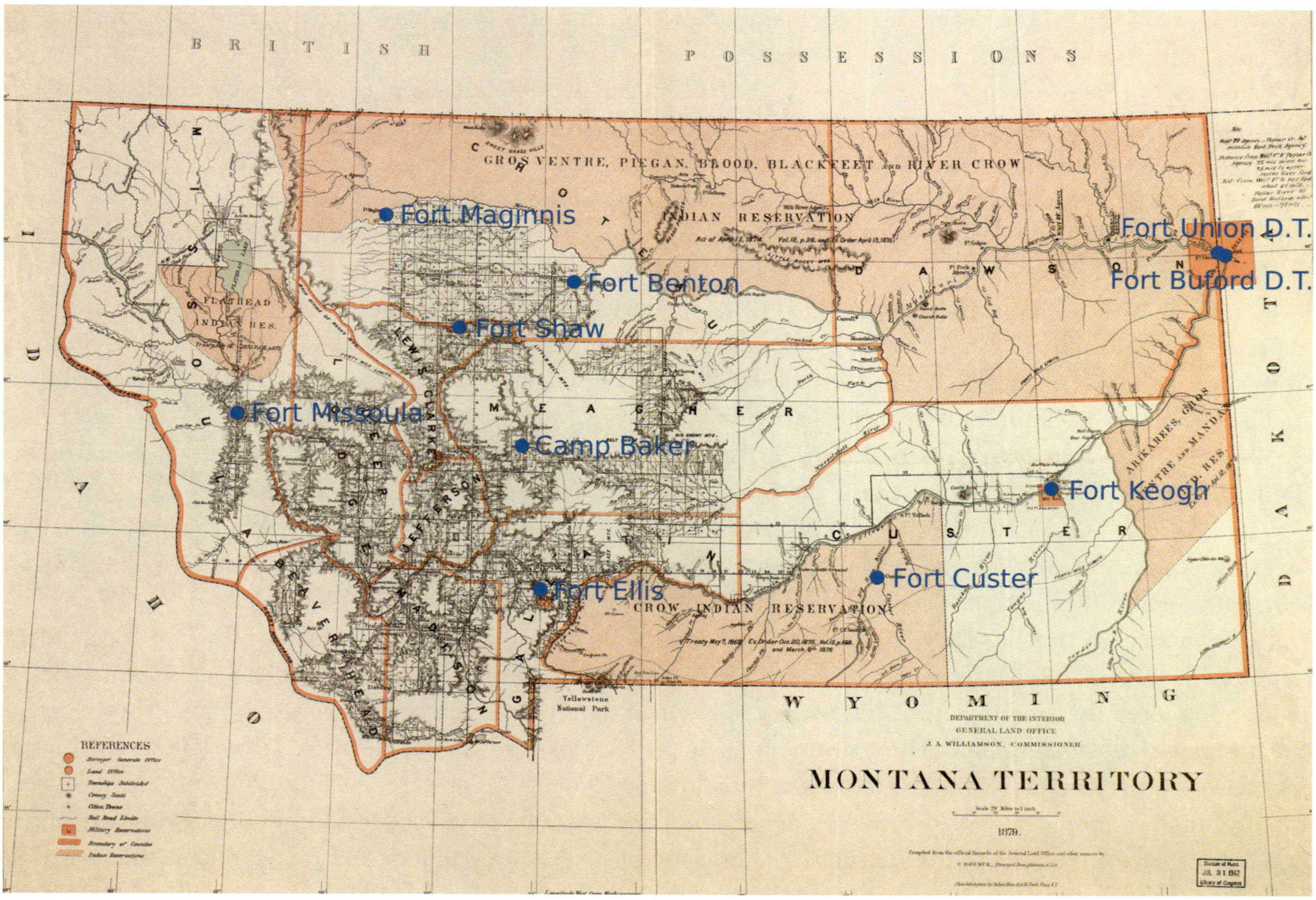

Significant portions of Montana Territory had been opened for white settlement by 1877, but Native Americans still occupied much of their traditional homeland (shown in pink). Soldiers at several isolated and undermanned forts were expected to keep the peace.
Map from General Land Office, Department of Interior 1879

The families of farmers and ranchers moved to town, and work began to fortify various building to protect the women and children. Many of the residents of Frenchtown moved to Missoula for the crisis, while several families from the Nine Mile area occupied an old grist mill in Frenchtown. Missoula residents planned to shelter in the courthouse and Worden's store, while the construction site of the Hammond and Eddy store, now known as the Missoula Mercantile, was designated a defensive position to repel any Indians who attempted to cross the wooden bridge across the Clark Fork river in the heart of the city.

Stevensville's Fort Owen was reinforced with new adobe bricks, and makeshift fortifications for the defense of women and children were built at Corvallis and Skalkaho.

Stalemate at Fort Fizzle

Captain Rawn received orders to prevent any armed Nez Percé from entering the Bitterroot Valley, and was informed that General Howard's slow-moving column was on the march from Idaho. Rawn prepared to march to the mouth of Lolo Canyon.

E.A. Kenney, the captain of a company of civilian volunteers from Missoula, arrived in the canyon on July 24th with four men, and was one of the first to make contact with the Nez Percé. He camped that night just below Woodman's ranch, where the Nez Percé warriors were camped (the women and children camped further up the canyon at Graves Creek).

John Hill, a Delaware Indian who lived with the Nez Percé, came into Kenney's camp voluntarily on July 25 and reported the Indians wanted to confer. Kenney soon found himself surrounded by a "formidable force of painted savages," but the warriors told the settlers no harm would come if they were allowed to pass peacefully through the Bitterroot Valley. Kenney told them he had no authority to bargain, but indicated Captain Rawn would be there on the following day, and scheduled a meeting at that date. He sent word back to Rawn in Missoula.

The July 25th special edition of the *Weekly Missoulian* carried the banner headline, "Help! Help! White Bird Defiant! Come Running!" That morning Captain Rawn left the partially constructed "Headquarters Post at Missoula" with 25 men. Each soldier carried four days of rations and 100 rounds of ammunition apiece. Rawn had hired a dozen pack mules from local contractor Alfred Cave to ferry supplies from the fort. (While returning to Missoula three days later, this pack train caused a panic when it was mistaken for a column of mounted Indians.) The soldiers marched south along the Bitterroot River to the mouth of Lolo Canyon.

By this time at least 50 volunteers from both the Missoula and Bitterroot Valleys had attached themselves to Rawn's command, and they advanced up the canyon in a skirmish line for three miles. The 75 men, many on foot, with a mixture of weapons, were no match for the 250 to 300 well-armed and well-mounted Nez Percé warriors they expected to face. They had gone a few miles when warning shots were heard, although the soldiers kept advancing until Rawn located a suitable defensive position in a narrow part of the canyon. Rawn called a halt and ordered the men to dig in. He instructed his men to fall trees across the bottom of the narrow canyon. Each company of soldiers and volunteers built their own segment of the fortification. They laid several large logs down on the ground to block the canyon, then dropped smaller trees perpendicularly across the base logs. Finally, another large tree was dropped on top of, and parallel to the base logs, leaving a slit between the upper and lower logs for the men to fire through. The breastworks were three to four feet high, and the soldiers used their trowel bayonets to dig rifle pits behind the line, with the dirt piled in front of the logs. A few rifle pits were dug on high ground to either side and back from the main line as well, in order to provide some protection on the flanks, however Rawn had barely enough men to defend the valley floor, and had no hope of controlling the steep hillsides that rose hundreds of feet above him to the north and south of his position. Had the Nez Percé wanted to attack Rawn's small force, they would have had little trouble outflanking the soldiers and firing down upon the rear of the breastwork from the surrounding hills.

That afternoon Rawn reported his position to Lieutenant Levi Burnett, the District Adjutant at Fort Shaw, 230 miles away, and asked for more troops. Delaware Jim Simonds met with the Indians on the 25th, and reported his meeting to Rawn, who wrote that "White Bird will go through peaceably, if he can, but will go through. This news is entirely reliable." Couriers on horseback carried the message nearly 100 miles to the telegraph line in Deer Lodge.

In the meantime, a steady stream of visitors and additional volunteers arrived at the makeshift breastworks. Rawn would eventually have five officers and 30 US regulars, a small contingent of Salish Indians (personally led by Chief Charlo and his son), and approximately 160 white citizens. By the evening of July 27 there would be 216 men behind "Rawn's Breastworks". Most of the civilians were from the Bitterroot Valley, although there were also companies from Missoula and Frenchtown. Leaders of the volunteers included C.P. Higgins, Henry Buck, and E.A. Kenney. As they prepared to defend the breastworks on July 26, many of the men wrote letters to loved ones. John H. Hammer of Missoula later recalled that he wrote out a three-page will, leaving his assets to his sister and brother.

Governor Potts, who had been active in the effort to organize and arm citizen militias in western Montana, arrived in Missoula on the 25th, and immediately sent a courier to Deer Lodge asking for reinforcements. Potts then headed for the breastworks, which he reached early in the morning on the 26th. He told Rawn it was madness to fight the Indians with an inadequate force, to which Rawn replied he had his orders to keep the Indians from the Bitterroot Valley.

Captain Rawn, William Baker, Amos Buck, and Cole B. Saunders rode up to Woodman's Prairie, a few miles up the canyon under a flag of truce late on July 26. At a point just out of rifle range from the Indian camp, they met with Looking Glass and White Bird. Rawn and his companions were alarmed when a growing force of warriors, some 75 in all, arrived to support their chiefs. Rawn reported that the chiefs hated the one-armed General Howard and would fight him wherever they found him, but they would not fight if they were allowed to proceed peacefully through the Bitterroot Valley. Rawn replied that he had orders to prevent them from entering the Bitterroot, and the Indians would have to give up their weapons and all of their horses if they wanted to proceed. Of course, these conditions were unacceptable to the Nez Percé, and some accounts indicate the Indians said the only way they would give up their ammunition would be through the barrel of a gun. Nevertheless, the two parties agreed to meet the next day. Chief Joseph arrived at the end of this meeting.

On July 27 Captain Rawn, accompanied by the same group as the day before plus Governor Potts, Captain Logan, Chief Charlo, three other Flatheads, and interpreter Delaware Jim, rode to within a half mile of the Indian camp at 2:00 p.m. Backing them was an escort of 100 soldiers and volunteers who stayed to the rear. As they approached the Indian village in a skirmish line, Tom Andrews, the manager of the grist-mill in Missoula, stumbled across two Nez Percé guarding a small horse herd. Guns were leveled on both sides, but the Indians had only a few cartridges between them, and quickly surrendered. They were identified as John Hill, (who had met with Kenney two days before) and an old man named Honan or Kannah. Another prisoner was taken when Thunder Eyes (sometimes known as Amos) approached the breastworks, seeking peace for the small band of Nez Percé living in the Bitterroot. All three were taken prisoner, bound hand and foot and escorted to the rear, where they would become the first of many prisoners held at Fort Missoula.

Rawn sent one of the Salish men to the Nez Percé camp. Upon his return the Salish man reported that Looking Glass and an interpreter would meet with Rawn and an interpreter halfway between the opposing lines. At that meeting Rawn again told Looking Glass he needed to turn over his horses, guns, and ammunition before proceeding. Looking Glass offered to turn over ammunition at this meeting, but refused to relinquish horses or guns, which Rawn insisted on. Looking Glass eventually told Rawn he would need to confer with the other chiefs, and asked to meet again at 9:00 the following morning. Rawn declared that any further meetings would have to be under a flag of truce at the breastworks.

Captain Rawn returned to his fortification fully expecting the Nez Percé to attack. Governor Potts then returned to Missoula, where he sent word to Butte and Deer Lodge, "that he desired every fighting man at Missoula." Potts claimed he intended to use these reinforcements for a surprise attack on the Indian village from the flanks.

The men of Deer Lodge and Butte heeded the call, and 150 Butte men, including future Copper King W.A. Clark, were among the contingent that headed for Missoula. "Men were frantic for guns, horses, equipments[*sic*], and as quickly secured they were off for Missoula as fast as they could go. Organization was impossible; 'We will organize at Missoula, or wherever we strike Indians,' was the universal response."[3]

Rawn discovered that while some volunteers were still arriving, many of the Bitterroot volunteers decided to leave, believing the Nez Percé's promise to not harm the settlers in the Bitterroot Valley. Rawn was angry when the volunteers refused his orders to stay, and a junior officer was heard to threaten to shoot one of the volunteers.

The Nez Percé had been playing for time, and had located an escape route that ran over the steep hills on the north side of the canyon. The Indians spent the night striking their camp and preparing to travel. Early on a bright summer morning, they rode down to within a mile of the entrenchment before ascending the hills to the north, out of sight of the breastworks.

Some of the civilians reported that the civilian pickets stationed west of the breastworks were pulled back by Captain Rawn because he had cut a deal with the Nez Percé when the Indians promised to not harm settlers in the Bitterroot Valley. The absence of those scouts allowed the Nez Percé to make their way up the ridge without being discovered.

The main column of the Nez Percé climbed far above the canyon floor and bypassed the soldier's position about half a mile to the north on the morning of July 28. By 8:30 a.m. the soldiers reported seeing a long column of mounted Nez Percé riding high above them and headed for the Bitterroot Valley. The Indians fired a few warning shots, and a civilian named August Gird returned fire from the breastworks, but was reprimanded by Rawn. John Martens from Victor colorfully wrote, "Exspected [*sic*] an attack from the Indians but they like senscible falows found a way aroun us and let us alone."

Men of the Nez Percé tribe in traditional dress posed for this July 4th, 1906 photo commemorating their flight to freedom in 1877.
Photo by Major Moonhouse

According to some accounts, Captains Rawn and Logan shared a bottle of whiskey the night before the Nez Percé escaped. Volunteer Wilson Barber Harlan claimed that both Rawn and Logan were incapacitated by drink by morning, and refused to believe the Nez Percé had escaped. Other accounts reported all men were awake and alert at dawn as they expected an attack.[4]

The Nez Percé stayed on the high ground until they were safely past Rawn's "corral," and at Sleeman Creek they dropped down to the valley floor and headed for the mouth of Lolo Creek, where they easily brushed aside a small rearguard Rawn had established to round up any deserters.

The Indians encountered other groups of civilians leaving the breastworks, as well as fresh volunteers on their way up the canyon, all without serious incident. Twenty men from Philipsburg, who had heeded the call for volunteers to protect Missoula, actually passed close by the Indian column on their way to the breastworks, seemingly unaware that these were the hostile Indians that the fuss was all about.

Peter Scheffer of Frenchtown reported "I can remember seeing the Indians cross the ridge when they came down the Lolo Canyon and they could have wiped out all the whites in an hour, but they passed peaceably and went up through the Bitterroot."

Rawn abandoned his defensive position in early afternoon and headed downstream until he reached the mouth of Lolo Creek, where he found a strong force of warriors occupying a timbered ridge guarding the approach to the Bitterroot. Rawn tried to establish a skirmish line across the canyon, "with my regulars and such of the volunteers as I could control and advanced in the direction the Indians had gone."

At the sight of the Nez Percé, many of the remaining civilian volunteers decided it was a good time to head for home, some at a rapid gait. By the time Rawn reached the mouth of the canyon all but 10 or 20 of the citizen volunteers had scattered, leaving him with at most 55 men he could rely on, most of them on foot.

Rawn realized that further pursuit of a mounted and numerically superior force was not only futile, but dangerous. He ordered a return to Fort Missoula, where his small garrison was reinforced the next day (July 29) by Company G of the 7th Infantry.

Missoula residents were in a near panic through the morning, with families fleeing toward the Deer Lodge Valley. The women and children who remained were quartered in the town's few brick buildings. A visibly nervous Governor Potts coordinated the defense of Missoula, since most of the able-bodied Missoula men were with Rawn. Potts had only a small company of volunteers from Frenchtown, Deer Lodge, and Bearmouth to defend Missoula. He sent most of the men to O'Brien Creek to guard the bridge over the Bitterroot River, leaving only a handful of civilians, mostly exhausted men who had just ridden 80 miles from the Deer Lodge Valley, to defend Missoula itself.

A chain was stretched across the Higgins Bridge and a defensive position was established in the half-built Eddy & Hammond store a block away. (Potts' focus on defending bridges ignored the fact that the water level was low in late July, and the Nez Percé were familiar with numerous fords across the Bitterroot and Clark Fork Rivers.) Duncan McDonald, the son of the reservation trader Angus McDonald, was half Salish and knew the Nez Percé well. He skeptically examined the feeble defenses in Missoula, and warned the citizens that if the Nez Percé arrived, their best hope was to treat them cordially.

A forest fire consumed the remains of the breastworks at Fort Fizzle in 1934. Today the site is a National Forest picnic area with modern interpretive signs and a reproduction of the breastworks.
Stan Cohen Collection

Rawn received much criticism for not stopping the Indians, and some of the weekend soldiers from Deer Lodge and Missoula felt they had been cheated out of a fight. The ever-colorful Chauncey Barbour of the *Weekly Missoulian*, who was overjoyed to see soldiers arrive five weeks before, at first declared Rawn to be incompetent and a coward, while his soldiers were, "useless as boys with popguns."[5] He asked Governor Potts to, "wipe out the disgrace that has been put upon us, and never let any regular officer again command Montana Militia."[6] (Barbour's anger had cooled somewhat by the time the next issue of his newspaper came out.)

The New Northwest, a weekly newspaper in Deer Lodge, reported "Capt. Rawn was at first very severely censured for his course. As yet there is no explanation of it, but the heat of public feeling has cooled and there is a disposition to await his report and give fair judgement [*sic*]... Capt. Rawn's record of fifteen years is that of a good fighting officer and it entitles him to a suspension of adverse expression until all the facts are known."[7] Corporal Loynes on the other hand said of Rawn, "a better officer never lived."[8]

The Nez Percé credited Rawn with acting wisely at the "corral," as did Duncan McDonald, who was convinced that if fighting had broken out in Lolo Canyon, the young men of the Salish, Kootenai, and Pend d'Oreille would have joined the Nez Percé, who would have then turned north toward Missoula, instead of south through the Bitterroot Valley. The presence of Chief Charlo and his Salish at the breastworks also was credited with helping prevent an attack by the Nez Percé.

The Battle of the Big Hole

For his part, General Howard was not pleased that the Nez Percé had escaped into the Bitterroot, and would later claim that the Indians negotiated their way past Rawn. Chief Joseph would also state that there was a "treaty" to let the Nez Percé pass if there was no violence, a claim backed up by John Humble, captain of the pickets that had been pulled back to the breastworks.

In any case, the Nez Percé reached open country and, seemingly in no haste, camped not far from the mouth of the canyon at the J.P. McClain ranch. The residents of the Bitterroot were just as alarmed as the citizens of Missoula. W.B. Harlan reported that 263 women and children were at Fort Owen, under the care of 14 men armed with two needle guns and a few shotguns and rifles. Harlan's letter to *New Northwest* stated "Looking Glass told us he would not hurt any persons or property in the valley if allowed to pass in peace, and we could pass through his camp to our homes. We decided it would be silly to uselessly incite the Indians to devastating our valley; and I do not think our critics would have done otherwise had they and their families and homes been situated as ours. If they want Indians for breakfast they are still within reach, and have been ever since the fiasco at Fort Fizzle on the Lolo."[9]

Colonel John Gibbon, commander of the 7th Infantry Regiment, ordered the attack on the sleeping Indian camp at the Big Hole, and was wounded in the leg during the ensuing fight.
LC-B8172-1464

After the Nez Percé entered the Bitterroot, Henry Buck hurried home from the newly christened Fort Fizzle in time to watch the Indian column pass by Fort Owen. He reported the procession took an hour and a quarter to pass by, with no gaps in the line, and estimated the Indians had 3,000 horses. Most settlers in the Bitterroot congregated at Fort Owen, and the makeshift defenses at Corvallis and Skalkaho, but in one of the more bizarre episodes of the Indian Wars, some of the Nez Percé rode into Stevensville and went shopping, seemingly unaware that US soldiers from Oregon, Idaho, Montana, and Wyoming were marching towards them. The small number of white men remaining in Stevensville recognized the volatility of the situation, as did the 15 armed Salish Indians who had shown up to help protect the community. Chief Looking Glass also recognized the danger, and during the visit he sat on his horse, keeping a close eye on his hot-headed young men to ensure that there was no trouble. Several of the young men of the tribe bought whiskey from two merchants in town, until other residents of Stevensville forcibly removed the barrels of whiskey in order to keep the peace. Henry Buck particularly remembered a very large Nez Percé woman who bought a bolt of cloth from him. Days later, at the Big Hole battlefield, he would recognize her body, wearing the new dress made from the cloth he had sold her. The Indians paid for their purchases with gold coin, and moved on without serious incident.

The merchants of Stevensville were widely criticized for selling goods to the Indians, although many of the citizens were acquainted with members of the tribe, and the Nez Percé could easily have taken the goods rather than pay for them.

On July 31 the Nez Percé column moved slowly south, looting a few cabins along the way, then turned east towards Sleeping Child and the Sapphire Mountains. Captain Rawn had asked two civilians who knew the Nez Percé to scout for him. They rode all the way to Skalkaho with the tribe, and later reported the Indians were in possession of several hundred rifles, many of them repeaters. They also had adequate ammunition, and from two to three thousand horses.

Looking Glass was in charge of the column through the Bitterroot, while Joseph oversaw the camp of the women and children. The Nez Percé proceeded at a slow pace over the Continental Divide, and didn't reach the Big Hole Valley until August 7. Looking Glass wanted to rest the horses and cut new lodge poles to replace the tipis lost at the Clearwater. He was unaware that soldiers under Gibbon and Howard continued to follow, although Howard's progress had been slowed by the rough terrain of the Lolo Trail.

Lt. Col. John Gibbon, on his way to Missoula from Fort Shaw, asked Governor Potts to raise a force of 300 volunteers to prevent the Nez Percé from leaving the Bitterroot Valley. Despite Gibbon's plea, the Army denied Potts the authority to pay for the militia, and the companies from Butte and Deer Lodge were quickly disbanded. Gibbon left Fort Shaw on July 28 with Companies D, F, and K, with 76 men and 8 officers, and by August 1st Captain Rawn knew that Gibbon was just a few days march away. Gibbon and his men marched into Fort Missoula on August 3rd, joining the three companies already there. Gibbon now had men from Fort Missoula, Camp Baker, Fort Ellis, Fort Benton, and Fort Shaw, and yet still had only 17 officers and 149 men when he left Fort Missoula. Leaving approximately a dozen men at Fort Missoula, the soldiers left for the Bitterroot Valley on August 4th, with the infantrymen riding in mule-drawn wagons. The column was accompanied by a 12-pound howitzer pulled by mules.

Chief Joseph is usually considered the leader of the Nez Percé, but it was Looking Glass (above) who advocated for the trip to Montana, and led the column to the Battle of the Big Hole.
William Henry Jackson 1871 - National Park Service

At least 75 civilians joined the column along the way, although Gibbon had little use for the civilians, and half dropped out before the column reached the southern part of the valley. The Indians were traveling leisurely, and the soldiers in wagons quickly caught up, arriving in the southern part of the Bitterroot Valley by August 6. By this time General Howard's force had emerged from the Lolo Canyon, and learned that Gibbon was hot on the trail of the Nez Percé. Over the next three days Howard and his 200 weary men on horseback covered 75 miles in an effort to catch up with Gibbon.

Lt. James Bradley led a mounted detachment consisting of 11 infantrymen mounted on horses obtained locally, and the eight men of the 2nd Cavalry who had accompanied the troops from Fort Ellis. They were accompanied by the 38 mounted civilian volunteers from the Skalkaho area led by Capt. John B. Catlin, a former major during the Civil War. The mounted detachment rode ahead of Gibbon's infantry column and soon determined the Indians were heading for the Big Hole Valley. The trail to Ross Hole from the Bitterroot was very rough, and the wagons and artillery had a great deal of trouble crossing the Continental Divide, but by August 8 Bradley knew he was close to the Indian camp. Leaving the rest of the men concealed, Bradley and Lt. Jacobs crept up to the Indian village, where they could see women cutting lodge poles. The Nez Percé had left a few scouts behind, but were unaware of the approach of Gibbon's column.

Gibbon decided to approach the village on foot late that night. He left 12 soldiers of Captain Logan's company and four civilians with the wagons. The other soldiers and Catlin's volunteers successfully infiltrated between the camp and the Indian horse herd on the night of August 8. These soldiers were just across from the sleeping camp, separated by a swampy area in the river bottom. Gibbon's plan was dependent on attacking the village on a broad front, in order to prevent the Indians from regrouping. Some of the civilians were detailed to stampede the Indian ponies once the fighting began.

Bradley's dismounted detachment and Catlin's civilians were on the left of the line, with the two companies from Fort Missoula on the right, and the other six companies in the center.

The attack began at 4:00 a.m. on August 9 when an elderly Nez Percé man went to check on the horse herd. He stumbled on several of Catlin's volunteers, and was killed by a hail of bullets.

Firing broke out all along the line. The soldiers and civilians fired indiscriminately into the camp of sleeping Indians, killing women, children and warriors alike. Most of the Indian casualties were killed in the first panic-stricken moments as bullets tore through the lodges. Many of the non-combatants fled for the willow bushes and the riverbank, where they suffered more casualties. Some women and children were killed deliberately, while soldiers allowed others to escape once they realized they were not warriors. Catlin maintained that some of the women were using rifles with as much skill as the men, which is why so many were shot.

The soldiers of D Company and K company in the center of the line charged across the swampy, brushy bottom land and entered the camp, firing as they ran. On the north end of camp Lieutenant Bradley and the civilians had to advance through a hundred yards of thick willows and a swamp full of waist-deep brackish water before they reached the village. This delay allowed White Bird a few precious moments to rally a defense. There were several instances of vicious hand-to-hand fighting, and Bradley was killed almost immediately. Seeing their commander killed, the men on the left were unwilling to advance further into the village. They halted to form a firing line, with some men drifting towards the center of the line. Once the attack on the left faltered, the Indians began to regroup, led by White Bird, who had been on his way to the horse herd when the firing broke out. Some of the soldiers stopped to burn the damp lodges, burning to death children who were hidden under buffalo robes inside. Occupied with pillaging the village, the infantrymen failed to press the attack, allowing the Nez Percé warriors to reach cover in thick willow bushes and on the high ground on either side of the village.

On the other side of the village Looking Glass organized a defense against Captain Logan's Company A. Logan rushed into the village and shot a Nez Percé warrior, perhaps Wahlitits, one of the hot-headed young men who had helped ignite the violence almost two months before. The warrior's sister grabbed a revolver from his dead hand and shot Logan in the head before falling mortally wounded over her brother's body.

The troops held the upper end of the village, but the warriors had by this time recovered from the surprise attack, and began to fight back. They regrouped on the high bluffs, where thick brush gave them cover, and began picking off the soldiers, while Chief Joseph and another man stampeded the horse herd before the civilians and soldiers could run them off, saving their 2,000 to 3,000 horses.

Gibbon rode down to the village, and was hit by a bullet that passed through his leg and broke his horse's foreleg. As the Indian fire increased, the wounded Gibbon soon realized he needed to pull his men back to a more defensible position, and he ordered a retreat to the hill they had attacked from. As the soldiers moved through an open area, they came under intense fire. Several fell from accurate rifle fire.

In order to give the majority of soldiers time to escape, Gibbon ordered Captain Rawn to attack the brush where the worst fire seemed to be coming from. Rawn's I Company advanced in a skirmish line toward the Indians firing from the brush, while the rest of Gibbon's troops withdrew the way they had come. Under withering fire, Rawn's men were soon forced to pull back as well, leaving several wounded men begging not to be left behind. Rawn ordered Corporal Loynes, Corporal Daniel McCafferey, and Sergeant Michael Hogan to retreat. McCafferey was immediately wounded, and Loynes and Hogan tried to help him to the rear. A shot killed Hogan, and Loynes abandoned McCafferey and ran for his life. The soldiers retreated to a high spot half a mile south of the camp, and dug in as best they could. They had but one wounded horse belonging to Lt. Woodruff, which was soon killed.

With the soldiers besieged, the Indians were able to retake the village and retrieve some of their tipis. The soldiers could hear the screams of the women mourning their dead, and the angry cries of the warriors seeking vengeance. Colonel Gibbon wrote, "Few of us will soon forget the wail of mingled grief, rage, and horror which came from the camp four or five hundred yards from us when the Indians returned to it and recognized their slaughtered warriors, women, and children."[10]

The Indians, who had lost at least 89 family members, hurriedly buried their dead as best they could, many in a mass grave under a bank. Chief Joseph supervised as the women and children broke camp and cared for the wounded, then he led them to a camp a dozen miles away, where several of the wounded passed away. While the non-combatants were hitting the road, the warriors renewed the attack on the pinned-down soldiers.

The howitzer, guarded by six soldiers from three companies (with only one man trained in its operation) finally arrived at a point overlooking the village. The crew managed to fire two shots at maximum range, then were overwhelmed by 30 Nez Percé. One of the lead mules was killed, immobilizing the gun, and the soldiers were quickly overrun in a sharp little battle. One soldier was killed, two were wounded, and the remaining men

Captain William A. Logan

Along with Captain Rawn, Captain Logan is considered one of the founders of Fort Missoula. He was born in Ireland, emigrated to America, enlisted as a private in the 7th Infantry in 1851, and quickly rose to sergeant. He served throughout the Civil War and was promoted to lieutenant in 1864. By 1869 Logan was the commander of Camp Baker, near the Smith River in Montana Territory. He was a "brave and sagacious" officer according to Lt. James H. Bradley, and was known to his colleagues as "Sagebrush Bill." During the 1876 Sioux war Logan commanded Company A (2 officers and 23 men) as part of the Montana Column under Col. John Gibbon. His oldest son William A. Logan served as a scout during this expedition. After his death Camp Baker was renamed Fort Logan, and a bronze plaque commemorating Logan was installed at the site. The small town of Logan in Gallatin County is also named for him. Logan had a Masonic ring and a seal ring that had been in his family for generations. After his death, Mrs. Logan advertised widely for return of the rings, both of which wound up in the possession of two Nez Percé warriors who were later killed by the Blackfeet in separate incidents. The seal ring was eventually bought from a Blackfeet man by a trapper. Some time later, a friend of Captain Logan recognized the ring on the finger of the trapper, and bought it. Captain Logan's son William recognized the worn Masonic ring on the finger of a Blackfeet woman in 1900. He purchased it and returned it to his mother 23 years after the death of his father.

Captain William A. Logan, a 26-year veteran, was killed at the Battle of the Big Hole.
MHS

fled. The Nez Percé stripped the wagon of its wheels, tools, and anything else they could remove, rendering the cannon inoperable. At the same time they captured a pack mule carrying 2,000 rounds of rifle ammunition.

The movement of the Indians towards the howitzer allowed the soldiers in the siege area a few precious minutes to secure their position, however other Indians soon began firing into their defenses, killing and wounding more soldiers. Lt. English was standing next to Gibbon watching the men prepare defenses when he was struck in the back by a long-range shot. Private Philo Hurlburt of I Company carried English inside the defenses and was shot in the shoulder for his trouble. The soldiers by this time had no water, no food other than the single dead horse, no medical supplies, and their ammunition was running so short that there were doubts they could withstand one more determined attack (the men had gone into the battle with 90 rounds apiece). The wounded, many with more than one injury, suffered horribly. Dressed in damp clothes, they had no medical attention, food or water. The 7th Infantry had no surgeon present, or even bandages. Civilian doctor Emil Cooke was listed as the Fort Missoula physician, but he didn't accompany the troops to the Big Hole. Lt. Charles Coolidge of A Company (who had been sent on the second scouting party up Lolo Canyon) was the only officer with medical experience, but he was among the badly wounded.

The Nez Percé set the grass and brush on fire, using the smoke and flames as cover. Lt. Woodruff, in a letter to his wife, said "their idea was to follow up the fire and charge us when it reached us. I began to fear I should never see you again. Some of the wounded covered up their heads and expected to be killed, I got my two revolvers said my prayers thought of you and Bertie, and determined to kill a few Indians before I died."[11] Fortunately for the desperate soldiers, the vegetation was too green to carry a fire, and a shift in wind kept it from reaching the siege area.

Once night fell, civilian Billy Edwards volunteered to carry a message to Deer Lodge. He crawled through the Indian lines, hiked all night until he could find a horse, and arrived at the telegraph office in Deer Lodge (80 miles away) the next morning, with messages from Gibbon requesting "food, clothing, medicines and medical attendance." Physicians and wagons from Butte and Deer Lodge set out to bring the wounded back to the hospital in Deer Lodge.

Most of the warriors also left that night, leaving only a handful of young men to keep the soldiers pinned down in misery throughout the following day. The soldiers received a parting volley of shots from the Indians sometime after dark on August 10, and the remaining Indians faded away. Late on the 10th an escort of 25 men managed to bring the wagon train into the siege area, providing blankets and food (hardtack, bacon and coffee). During that night, seven of the civilian volunteers slipped out of the siege area to return home, and they soon stumbled into General Howard's camp.

General Howard, accompanied by 20 of his best men and 17 Bannock Indian scouts camped at Ross Hole, some 20 miles from the Big Hole on the evening of August 10, where he learned from the fleeing civilians of the battle and Gibbon's plight. Howard left early the next morning for the scene of the battle, and arrived at mid-morning on August 11.

Gibbon had lost 23 soldiers and 6 civilians killed in action, plus 34 soldiers and five civilians wounded. Two of the wounded, including Lt. English would eventually die of their wounds. Of the troops who had founded Fort Missoula six weeks before, A Company had lost Captain Logan and Pvt. John B. Smith, while Lt. Coolidge and four privates from the company had been wounded, three of them seriously. Three men from Company I, Michael Hogan, Daniel McCafferey, and Herman Broetz, had been killed during Captain Rawn's attempt to cover the retreat of the rest of the force. (All three men were immigrants, from Ireland, Canada, and Germany respectively.) Company I also had five men wounded, with Lt. English the most serious of the cases. Catlin's Bitterroot volunteers lost five dead and five wounded in the fight, and a civilian guide from Fort Shaw was also killed. Once Howard's advance party arrived at the battlefield, Gibbon told the civilian volunteers they were no longer needed and could return home. (John Catlin and Henry Buck, leaders of the civilians, felt that Gibbon's subsequent report on the battle did not give adequate credit to the citizens who fought bravely at the Big Hole, and seemed to blame them for selling supplies to the Nez Percé at Stevensville.)

The wounded were cared for and the dead were buried with the few shovels belonging to a civilian packer. Captain William Logan was buried by his son-in law Captain Richard Comba of D Company. The regimental surgeon and assistant surgeon arrived at the battlefield with medical supplies on August 12, and the rest of Howard's cavalry arrived that afternoon. They found "a horrible state of affairs." The wounded had their injuries dressed, then were carried by travois (made from poles and the hides of the dead horses) and wagons on a three-day journey to Deer Lodge, where the Sister's of Charity had built Montana's first hospital four years before. Captain Rawn was in charge of the hospital train when the column marched toward Deer Lodge on August 12. Gibbon and the wounded were met by spring wagons, Concord wagons and ambulances sent by the citizens of Deer Lodge, Butte, and Helena. On the final day of the march Mrs. English arrived from Fort Missoula. Married only four months and pregnant, she had rushed to Deer Lodge to comfort her dying husband. The column reached Deer Lodge on August 16, and the most seriously wounded were sent to St. Joseph's Hospital, while the walking wounded were treated in another building. Lt. English died on August 20, and was accorded a Masonic burial and full military honors. Nine days later, Private John B. Smith of Company A also died in the hospital.

Soon after arriving in Deer Lodge, Gibbon's companies returned to their respective stations, taking the walking wounded with them. The wounded who could not travel were left at St. Joseph's hospital, some for months afterward. Companies A, D, G, and I arrived back at Fort Missoula on August 21, nearly two weeks after the start of the battle. The Congressional Medal of Honor was eventually awarded to six soldiers of the 7th Infantry for their part in the battle. Four of them were men who had marched into Fort Missoula in June (see page 25).

The Nez Percé had once again defeated the US Army and evaded capture, but at a terrible cost. They headed to Skinner Meadows, crossed into southern Idaho and headed for the Yellowstone area, which had been designated as the world's first national park five years before. By now the Indians regarded all white men as enemies who would not keep their word, and more settlers were killed.

Howard and his cavalry continued to pursue the Nez Percé, accompanied by 50 volunteers from Gibbon's command. The column's supplies were carried by numerous mules and wagons rented from residents of Missoula and Stevensville. On August 20 a group of Indians made off with 150 of Howard's horses, including 20 pack mules belonging to Fort Missoula contractor Alfred Cave, as well as a mare belonging to his step-son Will. "These animals, I think, constituted the finest pack train that I ever saw. These animals were entrusted to the care of Dick Johnson, a packer who handled the train for Mr. Cave."[12]

The Nez Percé were still intending to reach the Crow Reservation, but word reached them that while the Crows would allow them to pass through their land without trouble, they were not welcome to stay. The Nez Percé decided their only choice was to head north, towards safety in Canada. After exiting the northeastern edge of Yellowstone National Park near Cooke City, the Nez Percé followed the Clark Fork of the Yellowstone downstream, and fought a running skirmish with Colonel Samuel Sturgis and the 7th Cavalry at Canyon Creek, just west of present-day Billings. After escaping through the Rimrocks, they headed north towards the Musselshell River with Sturgis on their heels and General Howard not far behind. They crossed the Missouri River at Cow Island, engaging in a skirmish with soldiers guarding supplies there, and camped northeast of the Bear's Paw Mountains, forty miles from Canada. It was Col. Nelson Miles and the 7th Cavalry, riding hard from the new post on the Tongue River (Fort Keogh) who finally caught up with Nez Percé. Miles and his 600 men mounted a cavalry charge on September 30, killing several of the tribe's respected chiefs, including Joseph's younger brother Ollokot, and more women and children. Nevertheless, Miles suffered very heavy casualties during the charge, and decided the best course was to persuade the Indians to surrender. The arrival of General Howard's command on the evening of October 3 convinced Joseph and others that further resistance was futile. Looking Glass and White Bird wanted to flee to Canada, but Looking Glass was killed by a long distance shot. White Bird and other warriors did manage to escape to Canada, but Joseph and the majority of surviving Nez Percé surrendered on October 5, ending a remarkable 1,170 mile retreat. Despite Miles's promise to send them back to Idaho, Joseph and most of the Nez Percé were marched to Fort Keogh, then on to Fort Leavenworth, Kansas, and eventually to Oklahoma, where many died of fever, neglect, and homesickness. It wasn't until 1885 that Joseph and the remaining Nez Percé were allowed to return to the Nez Percé reservation in Idaho and the Colville Reservation in Washington.

For several years after the surrender, small groups of Nez Percé who had fled to Canada or otherwise escaped capture passed through Missoula as they tried to make their way home, and troops from Fort Missoula were frequently called out to escort them back to Idaho.

On September 20, after Rawn heard reports that the bodies of the soldiers buried at the Big Hole were being dug up by bears and other predators, he sent Lieutenant J.T. Van Orsdale (another son-in-law of Captain Logan) and seven enlisted men of D Company to the Big Hole by way of Deer Lodge to rebury the dead. They found 14 disinterred bodies, including Capt. Logan and Lt. Bradley. The bodies were temporarily reburied in the siege area, except for Captain Logan. Van Orsdale carried his father-in-law's body to Deer Lodge, where he was given a proper burial. Logan's body was moved from Deer Lodge to the cemetery at the Little Big Horn Battlefield in 1892. A friend of Lt. Bradley who visited the battlefield site in late 1878 was unable to recover Bradley's remains as they had been scattered by animals.

Duncan McDonald, who interviewed many of the Nez Percé after the battle, wrote, "The gallant Seventh Infantry! It should be called the cursed Seventh! They were not satisfied in killing Indians whom they found asleep. They must kill women and children too."

Almost 40 years later, when Col. John B. Catlin of the Bitterroot volunteers was asked to help commemorate the battle, he retorted, "I don't know what we'd celebrate. The Indians licked hell out of us."[13]

The Powder Magazine

The fort's powder magazine was built near the banks of the Bitterroot River in 1878 at a cost of $435. It was close enough to the fort so that soldiers could keep an eye on it, but far enough away from inhabited buildings to minimize any danger from explosion. The stones for the two-foot-thick walls were quarried from nearby McCauley's Bluff. The wooden door is covered with sheet metal. The ceiling was built of nine-inch thick larch logs, covered with a foot-and-a-half of sand to minimize the effects of an explosion. At one time rifles may have been hidden in this sand.

Besides small arms ammunition, the magazine was used to store target frames and other equipment. The name of Sgt. Horace Bivins, a buffalo soldier who served as post ordnance sergeant, is scratched inside the building. He had previously served with the 10th cavalry in the Apache wars and Spanish-American War before he was appointed ordinance sergeant. He retired in Billings, but when World War I broke out he volunteered, and was appointed a captain of infantry and served at Fort Dix, N.J.

The powder magazine was still in use by the National Guard to store ammunition as late as 1967. One of only three original structures remaining at the Fort, Building T-334 is now owned by the Northern Rockies Heritage Center, and leased to the Rocky Mountain Museum of Military History, which has plans to install an exhibit inside.

Fort Missoula's Medal of Honor Winners

- **Private Lorenzo D. Brown** of Company A, 7th Infantry. Battle of the Big Hole. "After having been severely wounded in right shoulder, continued to do duty in a most courageous manner." Medal issued May 8, 1878.
- **Musician John McLennon** of Company A, 7th Infantry. Battle of the Big Hole. "Gallantry in action." Medal issued December 2, 1878.
- **Sergeant Patrick Rogan** of Company A, 7th Infantry. Battle of the Big Hole. "Verified and reported the company while subjected to a galling fire from the enemy." Medal issued December 2, 1878. Rogan was married to John McLennon's sister and the two men are buried next to each other in Wyoming.
- **Sergeant Milden H. Wilson** of Company I, 7th Infantry. Battle of the Big Hole. "Gallantry in forming company from line of skirmishers and deploying again under a galling fire, and in carrying dispatches at the imminent risk of his life." Medal issued December 2, 1878. Wilson, a Civil War veteran, volunteered to help Lt. Bradley locate the Indian camp, and was sent to Deer Lodge on the morning of August 11th with messages and letters from the officers. He remained in the army until at least 1912, and lived with John McLennon's other sister.
- **Hospital Steward Harry Garland** won two Medals of Honor in 1877. After a battle in May he was cited for "Gallantry in action with hostile Sioux, at Little Muddy Creek, Mont." His second medal was earned in August while pursuing the Nez Percé. "Having been wounded in the hip so as to be unable to stand, at Camas Meadows, Idaho, he still continued to direct the men under his charge until the enemy withdrew." His remains were moved from Fort Ellis to the Fort Missoula Cemetery in 1887.
- **Private Michael Himmelsback**, Company C of the 2nd US Cavalry, was cited for "gallantry in action" for his actions on May 15, 1870 at Little Blue, Nebraska. He was one of a party of five men who were searching for missing horses when they were surrounded by 50 hostile Indians. They successfully fought off an attack, but were forced to withdraw on foot. Rescuing a settler's family of two women and a child, they successfully returned to their command late that night. All five men received the Medal of Honor. Himmelsback died at Fort Ellis in 1881 at age 32 and was reinterred at Fort Missoula in 1887.
- **Sergeant George Ernest Veuve**, a native of Switzerland and a Civil War veteran, was awarded the Congressional Medal of Honor for the, "gallant manner in which he faced a desperate Indian on 3 November 1874, while serving with Company A, 4th US Cavalry, in action at Staked Plains, Texas." Veuve arrived at Fort Missoula with the 3rd Infantry in 1877, and as the fort's quartermaster sergeant was responsible for the goods stored in the storehouse, the first building to be completed. He is credited with being the first soldier to sleep under a roof at Fort Missoula. Veuve was discharged from the army in January 1880, and was married a week later. He settled down in Missoula with a contract to haul firewood for the fort's quartermaster. Veuve and his family continued to live on the 600 block of East Pine Street until his death in 1916. In 1957 the fort's Army Reserve Center was dedicated Veuve Hall in his honor, and in 2006 a bronze plaque was placed on his grave at the Missoula Cemetery to commemorate his status as a Medal of Honor recipient.
- **Major Gaines Lawson** served with the Union Army in Tennessee during the Civil War. Thirty years after the war he was awarded the Congressional Medal of Honor for an incident that occurred in 1865. His citation read, "Went to the aid of a wounded comrade between the lines and carried him to a place of safety." Lawson served for several years as a company commander with the 25th Infantry at Fort Missoula.

Four of the men stationed at the 'Post on the Missoula' were awarded the Medal of Honor for their actions at the Battle of the Big Hole. Shown above is the medal awarded to Army soldiers from 1862 to 1895.

The Army Heritage Museum

The Fort Missoula Cemetery

The cemetery, platted in 1877, is slightly less than one square acre in size and is located several hundred yards north of Officer's Row. A wooden fence was built around the cemetery in 1879. The first burial was Private William Gerick, on September 26, 1878. The second man interred was 1st Lieutenant Edward A. Belger, who died of dysentery while working on the Mullan Road in 1879. Lieutenant Thomas S. Wallace died of hypothermia after his horse threw him into the Clark's Fork River during a hunting trip in December 1878. Mrs. Matilda Judge Clinchey Tatje, age 45, a laundress for the 3rd Infantry Regiment, died in November, 1879 and was the fourth person buried at Fort Missoula.

When Fort Ellis was closed, the cemetery there was emptied in 1887, and 36 men of the 2nd Cavalry Regiment were re-interred at Fort Missoula, including Medal of Honor recipients Harry Garland and Michael Himmelsback (see page 25). Sgt. William Baker, who commanded the escort for the first military expedition to Yellowstone National Park, is also buried at Fort Missoula. He was accidentally shot to death at Fort Ellis on March 31st, 1874 during a fight between two other soldiers. His remains were moved to the Fort Missoula Cemetery in 1887.

After a period of neglect a wrought-iron fence was built around the cemetery in 1905, and wooden grave markers were replaced with marble ones. The cemetery is the last resting place for veterans of every war from the Mexican-American War to Vietnam. Three generals are buried there, including one lieutenant general. More than 40 black soldiers of the 25th Infantry are buried at Fort Missoula, with one stone marked simply "US Soldier." Most of the soldiers buried at the fort died from accidents and disease. One was killed by a jealous husband, another by a fellow soldier during a hunting accident, two died in train accidents during training exercises, two drowned, two overdosed on drugs, and a few died of diptheria and flu. A World War I draft evader named Aati Tryvanien starved himself to death at the fort, and his body was never claimed by relatives. A few civilian employees of the Army were also buried in the cemetery.

At least 60 children are buried at the fort. A dozen of them were babies who died prematurely, including a grandchild of Gen. John C. Fremont, the famous explorer and presidential candidate. Most of the other children died of influenza or Rocky Mountain Spotted Fever. Burials at the Fort Missoula Cemetery are now restricted to active duty or retired military personnel and their dependents. Today it is an active Class IV National Cemetery, and has room for more than 400 grave sites. The cemetery is divided into four sections, labeled A, B, C, and D. There were 239 headstones and 251 individuals buried at the fort by 2007. Twelve stones have more than one family member buried underneath. There was an unsuccessful effort in 1995 to add six acres of land owned by Missoula Public Schools to the cemetery. In 2008 a 23-acre Western Montana State Veteran's Cemetery was dedicated on former fort land about a half mile north of the Fort Missoula Cemetery.

3

Building The Fort

"Four hundred men here will equal a thousand at any point within 400 miles."

General William T. Sherman

After the Big Hole Battle, four understrength companies (A, D, G & I) of the 7th Infantry, 120 men in all, returned to Fort Missoula, but remained on the lookout for scattered bands of Nez Percé. By mid-September there were four Nez Percé prisoners held at the fort, and others were soon picked up. Capt. G.S. Browning and four enlisted men traveled to Stevensville to pick up Nez Percé chief Persicho. Lieutenants Jones and Bloom of the 4th Artillery captured two Nez Percé "in the pass, and [they] are supposed to have been in the Big Hole fight."

Accounts differ as to the fate of the first prisoners. John Hill, captured at Fort Fizzle, was ordered released by General William T. Sherman. Others were released after the surrender of the Nez Percé near the Bear's Paw Mountains. Amos, who was captured at "Lou Lou," on September 19, 1877 was held for almost two years, and may have been one of the two Nez Percé men who were sent to Fort Leavenworth in June 1878. Two other Indian prisoners apparently escaped from the post guardhouse in a driving rainstorm while being guarded by a young musician.

With winter approaching, the soldiers quickly resumed construction work. Captain Rawn polled the men to identify any who had experience as carpenters, stonemasons, or blacksmiths. Building sites were laid out, stones for foundations were hauled from a makeshift quarry on the nearby slopes of McCauley Butte, while timber, particularly long, straight larch logs, were cut in Pattee Canyon, several miles to the east. Sergeant John L. Reynolds of Company A served as Chief Carpenter.

One month after the Battle of the Big Hole, General William T. Sherman, the commander-in-chief of the Army, visited the fort and liked what he saw. He was impressed with the location, and recommended enlarging it to a battalion size post. He declared Missoula was, "a strategic point that will remain so forever, made so by the conformation of the rivers and mountains. These will force all roads to converge here, and four hundred men here will equal a thousand at any point within 400 miles."[1]

Sherman also noted that the surrounding area was rich in hay, oats, flour, beef and timber. He observed that food was cheaper than in Pennsylvania, with beef selling for four cents a pound, while oats sold for about three cents. On the downside, civilian workers made an average wage of $40 per month, higher than the rest of the country.

Sherman found that Rawn had made "fair progress" on the post, with the quartermaster and commissary warehouse storehouse "of sawed logs 6 x 8 inches" completed and roofed in, one set of officer's quarters constructed but not yet roofed, and work had started on the company quarters. Sherman was accompanied by General Orlando M. Poe, his engineering aide-de-camp, and they carefully examined the plans. Sherman noted the fort was based on, "the old stereotyped plan of a square, of 250 feet - good enough and large enough for one company, but this cannot remain a one-company post. Had there been four companies here last year the Nez Percé would not have dared to revolt." Sherman himself modified the plans, allowing Rawn to complete the plans for the winter, but then to begin to construct a four-company post in the spring based on the existing buildings. Congress was asked to appropriate an additional $20,000 for the expansion.

By the end of September Rawn could report, "The officer's quarters and the company quarters are under good headway, and the commissary and quartermaster storehouse has already been used for storing supplies. A large cellar is being dug for the purpose of preserving such articles of subsistence stores as might be injured by being frozen. A corral has been partly completed, in fact, considering the hardships the troops have undergone, the Indian campaigns, and the skeleton strength of the companies, I am well-pleased with the progress made in the construction of the new post."[2]

The storehouse, the first building completed, was built to protect perishable supplies and food from the elements. The storehouse's location had been determined when Fort Missoula was supposed to be a one company post, and when General Sherman ordered the construction of a four-company post, the storehouse was located right in the middle of the proposed parade ground. A larger storehouse was soon built to the northwest, and the fort's first building was used as a temporary company barracks during the first few years of the fort's existence, and then was removed in the 1880s. One set of company quarters was completed in 1877 and a set of officer's quarters, built of squared logs, was finished during the winter of 1877-78, with two more sets, built of sawn lumber, completed in 1878. The buildings were very similar in shape and construction to the buildings at Fort Shaw, where the officers and men of the 7th Infantry had previously been posted.

Much of Captain Rawn's time was spent doing routine paperwork and sending reports and correspondence to the Department of Dakota and the War Department. He had to ask written permission for all expenditures, including buying such mundane items as axe handles and saws. Maj. H.L. Chipman, one of Rawn's successor's, was compelled to write a letter to regimental headquarters at Fort Shaw explaining his unauthorized purchase of iron bolts to repair wagons, the purchase of candles for the office, and repair of a clock.

Fort Missoula was constructed according to an open plan, with no fortifications. Instead, the Army units were expected to patrol the surrounding territory aggressively. There were 11 military forts built in Montana between 1866 and 1892, and only four were fortified. The flaw in this plan was that the Army units stationed at these forts, and in particular the infantry regiments, were so understrength and lacking in mobility that they could not effectively patrol the vast territory surrounding them, and indeed would have had a difficult time defending the wide-open fort had a determined Indian force decided to assault it. Nor were there enough troops to adequately defend surrounding communities.

By the fall of 1877, tensions were rising between the United States and Canada, and General Sherman decided that the Army needed to increase its presence in Montana, Idaho, and Washington. He felt the West was not adequately garrisoned and envisioned a chain of forts south of the Canadian border from North Dakota to the Pacific Ocean. The forts at Coeur d'Alene, Boise, and Lapwai in Idaho, as well as Forts Missoula, Ellis, and Shaw in Montana would be vital links in the defense of the country. After his visit to Fort Missoula, General Sherman travelled to Spokane via the Mullan Road, which he found to be in poor repair. He ordered that troops from Fort Missoula and Fort Coeur d'Alene begin work to repair the Mullan road in 1879.

Arrival of the 3rd Infantry

The 3rd Infantry Regiment had been stationed in the deep south in previous years, but early in 1877 had been ordered north to quell labor riots in Indiana, Ohio, and Pennsylvania. The regiment, commanded by General John R. Brooke, received orders to proceed to Montana on September 3, 1877, with one battalion to take up station at Fort Missoula.

Accompanied by wives, children, and the unit's laundresses, the regiment crowded into rail cars for the long journey to Corrine, Utah. There they made camp and arranged to hire local Mormon teamsters to drive oxen-teams and covered wagons with trailers for the journey north to Montana. The Army also had their own army wagons hitched to mules. The column followed a route known as the old stage route, at first through Mormon settlements, and then along a new road being built to Dillon. The road generally followed the route of what is now Interstate-15 through southeast Idaho and into Montana. The road was long and the dust was suffocating. "One small boy was heard to remark, "I want to go home." His sister replied, "Home! You have no home except under your hat."[3]

For most of the soldiers, their first glimpse of a Native American came when they encountered a friendly band of Bannock Indians, led by Buffalo Horn, (who would be killed by the Army the following year after he led his starving people off the reservation in search of food).

Once they reached Ryan's station on the Beaverhead River, the party split, with the headquarters and six companies bound for Helena, and eventually Forts Shaw and Logan. The First Battalion, consisting of the 130 men of companies B, D, H and I turned towards Missoula. Many of the soldiers enjoyed fishing for their supper, and experienced their first snowstorm in the Deer Lodge valley (many of the soldiers had never seen snow before). They found the Hell Gate River (better known as the Clark Fork) muddy and polluted from the placer mining on Gold Creek, and had trouble fording both the Hell Gate River and the Blackfoot River. On November 13th they camped on the banks of the Big Blackfoot River, and arrived at Fort Missoula the next day after a journey dubbed, "Fourty days in the wilderness."[4]

The officers found Missoula to be, "attractive but by no means imposing." Perhaps it was the officer's wives who noted that, "The principal, if not the only stores were those of Higgins and Worden, and of Eddy and Hammond."[5]

Four miles later they arrived at the collection of half-completed buildings that Congress had just designated Fort Missoula. (The Headquarters Post on the Missoula was officially renamed Fort Missoula on November 8, 1877.) "Great was the rejoicing, the hardships of the long trek across the country were forgotten, in anticipation of the new life about to begin."

The new arrivals found that Captain Rawn's men were still living in tents, but had partially completed one set of NCO barracks, one officer's barracks and a few cabins. The only completed buildings were the storehouse and two log buildings constructed by the post trader William "Billy" Logan, a son of the lieutenant recently killed at the Big Hole. Once their replacements arrived, Rawn's men immediately returned to Fort Shaw.

The men of the 3rd Infantry pitched their tents while the building continued. Building shelter was the regiment's sole concern during the winter, and some of the officer's wives were commissioned to draft plans for the buildings. A hospital, barracks, store houses, officer's quarters, and stables were completed in a "marvelously short time." Some of the officer's families lived in tents for weeks, then were jammed into quarters built for one family. The tents were heated with Sibley stoves but the Montana winter was fast approaching. Most of the men managed to squeeze into the mess hall and squad room by December 31. The senior officers rented rooms in Missoula until their quarters were completed in mid-summer 1878, however they were required to receive written permission from the Department of Dakota before doing so. General Brooke was soon transferred to Helena, and Colonel Henry L. Chipman took command of Fort Missoula.

A Chinook wind melted the snow in the spring and as the flowers bloomed, "Bird life appeared, and everyone felt that they were occupying one of the loveliest spots on earth."[6]

Missoula had only a few hundred residents when the soldiers who built Fort Missoula arrived in 1877. This brick building at the corner of North Higgins and Main was the commercial heart of Missoula at the time, although the rival Missoula Mercantile was under construction just a block away.
UM - 70.0112

Building the Fort

Construction of the fort's original seven major buildings continued unabated through 1878 until April 1879 when funds and material were exhausted. One of the original buildings, a duplex housing the families of two lieutenants, burned in 1878. Three other buildings were complete by the spring of 1879, and work continued on three others. In addition to barracks and officer's quarters, the fort also had a powder magazine, lime house, ice house, carpenter shed, dry kiln, blacksmith shop, wagon shed, mule shed, and fire engine shed. Lt. Col. Chipman appealed for more money, but the Secretary of War decided, "No more money will be authorized for the erection of buildings at this post."

A frustrated Chipman asked his superiors if the post was to be left in an unfinished condition. He declared there was "insufficient accommodations" for officers, several of whom were living in quarters designed for laundresses and the ordnance and commissary sergeant's quarters. He suggested building comfortable log structures at much less cost than the frame buildings originally called for, and stated it was impossible for families to live in tents most of the year due to the "severe climate." While waiting for instructions and funds, Chipman directed his soldiers to practice drilling and target shooting, although the shooting had to be curtailed when ammunition ran low. They practiced company and battalion drills until August 1879 when, "the garrison was so reduced as to render them impossible."

During the fall of 1879 the fort received orders to replace the officer's quarters accidentally burned the previous November, and to build a new forage house. The soldiers later completed a row of houses on the south side of the post, from lumber sawed at Pattee Canyon. In the 1920s it was reported, "These same buildings are still in use. One houses post headquarters, and the rest are inhabited by junior officers and married non-coms."[7] By August 1881 six officers quarters had been completed and the foundation of the commander's house was laid.

Chipman left the post for other duties during the summer of 1879, and was replaced by Lt. Col. George Gibson, who took up the fight to complete the basic facilities at the fort. Gibson was an outspoken advocate of improving the fort. He reported that of the 14 officers stationed at the fort, eight of them were married. "Surely under the circumstances could it be represented to Congress the peculiarly isolated life this little command is compelled to lead among the passes on the western slope of the Rocky Mountains (with little else to look forward to – it being simply their life). I cannot but believe sympathy would be excited to the extent of authorizing the necessary expenditures."

Fires presented a major threat to the fort buildings, as evidenced by the completed lieutenant's quarters that was destroyed by flames only months after it was constructed in 1878. By 1881 the fort's fire suppression system consisted of a water wagon, which was kept filled when not in use, one chemical engine, 13 Babcock fire extinguishers, and water barrels near every building. Buckets and axes were kept in the quarters.

Fort Missoula in 1886 as seen from the sutler's store.
Christian Barthelmess photo
LC-HABS MONT,32-MISS,3--3

For the first few years of the fort's existence the soldiers got their drinking water from a spring near the gravel banks of the river. When the spring proved inadequate, water was hauled by wagon from the Bitterroot River, which General Sherman had called a, "bold stream of pure water." Although the water from the Bitterroot was muddy for a month during spring runoff, it

The Fort's Buildings, 1877-1886

Fort buildings were inventoried and assigned a number by 1886, and again in 1898, when photos were taken. Some buildings that were demolished, as well as laundress buildings and the Chinese laundry were never listed on these inventories. This chart is a compilation of the early inventories plus additional research.

1877 Old officer's quarters, log. Building 20 - cost unknown
Old officer's quarters, log. Building 22 - cost unknown
Old officer's quarters, log. Building 24 - cost unknown
Old officer's quarters, log. Building 26 - cost unknown
Old administration building used as officer's quarters, log. Building 27 - cost unknown
Old school hall, used as band barracks, log. Building 28 - cost unknown
Double NCO quarters, log. Building 34 - cost unknown (now labeled T-201, this building still exists)
Double Officer's Quarters, frame. Building 3 & 4 - cost $3,000

1878 Root Cellar, 20' x 40'

1879 Double Officer's Quarters, frame. Building 1 & 2 - cost $3,000
Double Officer's quarters, frame. Building 5 & 6 - cost $4,188.75
Carpenter's shop, wood. Building 41 - cost unknown
Post hospital, frame. Building 16 - cost $1,967.55, remodeled in 1888 - cost $5,642

1880 Double Officer's quarters, frame. Building 8 & 9 - cost $4,155
Double Officer's quarters, frame, Building 10 & 11 - cost $4,155
NCO staff quarters, frame. Building 15 - cost $316.38
Paint and saddler shop, frame. Building 30 - cost $1,624
Granary, wood. Building 39 - cost unknown
Employees quarters, frame. Building 42 - cost $350
Magazine, stone. Building 46 - cost $485 (still exists)
Sawmill, frame. Building 45 - cost $3,000 (not including pumps and machinery)
Hospital dead house, frame. Building 17 - cost unknown, date of construction approximate
Ice House, frame. Building 18 - cost unknown, date of construction approximate
Guardhouse, first story log, 2nd story frame added in 1887. Building 29 - cost $327.96
Carriage House, Building T-202. Moved from site in 1958, returned to original location in 1974 (still exists)

1881* Commissary storehouse, frame. Building 32 - cost $2,800
Quartermasters storehouse, frame. Building 33 - cost $2,800
Officer's quarters double, frame. Building 12 & 13 - cost $4,155
Infantry barracks, frame. Building 29 - cost $2,738
Infantry barracks, frame. Building 23 - cost $2,738
Post bakery, frame. Building 35 - cost $39
Coal shed, frame, Building 40 - unknown cost
Post hall and chapel, frame. Building 14 - cost $711.45, improved in 1885

1882 Infantry barracks, frame. Building 21 - cost $3,000

1883 Teamster's quarters, frame. Building 36 - cost $150
Quartermaster's corral, frame. Building 37 - cost $1,240.75

1884 Infantry barracks, frame. Building 25 - cost $3,000

1886 Engineer's quarters, frame. Building 43 - cost $170

*By 1881 the fort also had an office of the commanding officer, adjutant's office, count room, library, school, bath house, and engine room.

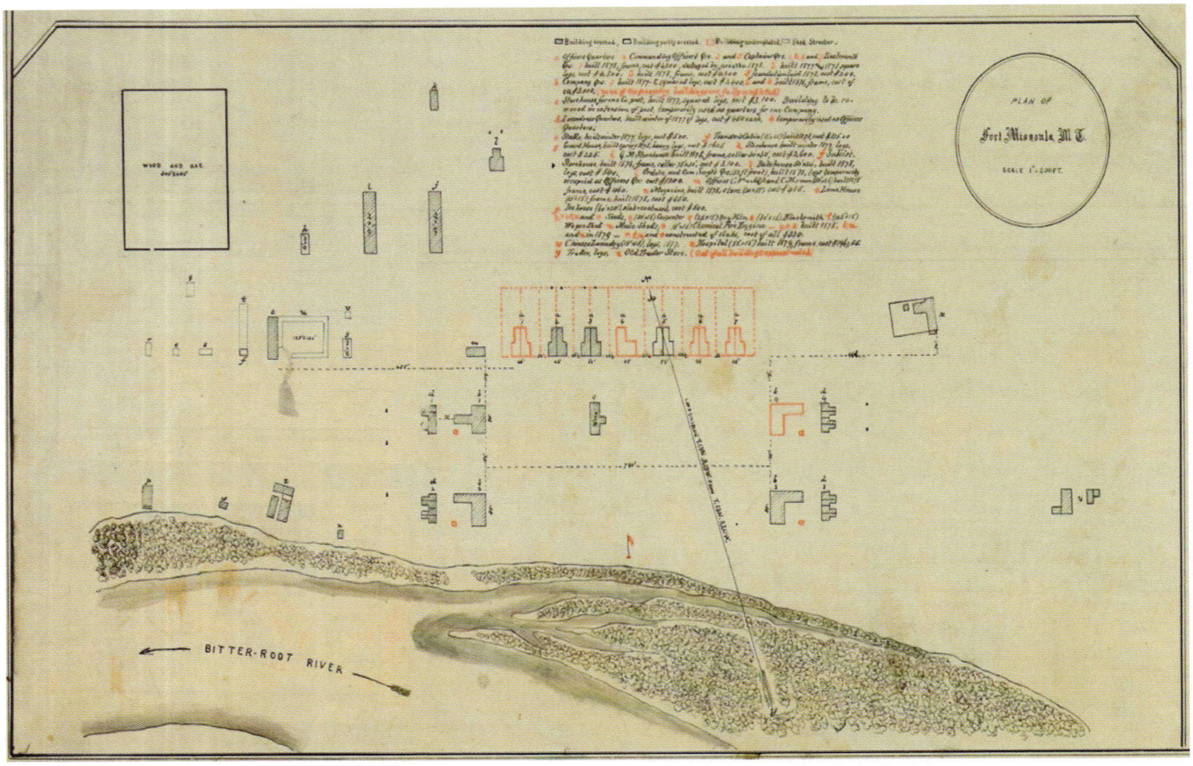

This 1879 map shows the buildings completed at Fort Missoula in gray. Buildings planned but not yet begun are outlined in red. Buildings under construction were outlined in black.
HMFM

provided an excellent source of drinking water. The post relied on a single water wagon which was filled with buckets half a mile above the post, with water deposited in barrels located near the entrance to most buildings. The barrels were equipped with siphon hoses.

Lt. Col. Gibson repeatedly lobbied his superiors for a windmill, development of an artesian well, or a steam-powered sawmill with a water pump to provide a steady supply of water to the fort. The War Department turned down Gibson's original plan for a sawmill, but eventually approved $3,200 to build a steam-powered sawmill equipped with a water pump and tank. The pump could supply 300 to 400 gallons per minute. A wrought iron pipe was installed in the center of the river just below the sawmill and west of the powder magazine. The water tank was built near the sawmill, and held 29,000 gallons. This water was distributed by wagon until 1883, when a water system with a 14 x 20 foot water tank, three-inch water mains and 18 fire hydrants was installed.

Originally the soldiers at the fort relied on pit latrines, but in 1885 a system of drainage pipes was installed behind the barracks, chapel, officers row, and a portion of the shop area. The network of pipes drained untreated wastewater into the Bitterroot River west of the sawmill. The War Department Quartermaster General decided in 1886 to contract for a dry earth privy system at Fort Missoula, and $2,389 was authorized for such a purpose three years later. Solid waste was deposited in metal cans, and once a day was covered with dirt. Officer's quarters probably had a form of indoor "earth closets." The fort did not have a true sewer system until 1903.

Reconstruction of the Mullan Road

The Military Road from Walla Walla to Fort Benton had originally been constructed in 1859 (at a cost of $230,000), but the road had not had any maintenance since it was completed in 1862. Miners using the road to access Montana from the west often burned the bridges to slow down any competitors following behind.

The St. Regis portion of the road alone had 40 bridges (substantial structures built by Mullan) which needed to be repaired or replaced. The road had washed out in numerous places, was covered with fallen timber, and long stretches of the road needed to be corduroyed with logs.

After General Sherman passed over the road in 1877, he ordered the commands at Fort Missoula and Fort Coeur d'Alene to work together to repair the route. Captain William H. Penrose led 51 men of Company C and Company I out of Fort Missoula on August 1, 1879. They proceeded west along the Mullan Road on a mission to conduct major repairs on the Military Road. Penrose took four six-mule wagons, an ambulance, two pack mules and six saddle horse. Each wagon carried 4,000 pounds of rations and equipment, which included axes, shovels, picks, crosscut saws, rock drills, two kegs of blasting powder, log chains, as well as carpenter, blacksmith, and saddler's tools. Captain Penrose also requested that Assistant Surgeon S.Q. Robinson accompany his detachment, and the officers remaining at Fort Missoula received permission to contract for medical care in Missoula (at no more than $4 per day).

Penrose and his men found the road nearly impassable for wagons when they were just two days west of Missoula. Landslides had covered the grade, stream erosion destroyed crossings, and hundreds of rocks and trees had fallen across the road. After two weeks working on repairs, Penrose rode ahead to meet with a Lieutenant from Coeur d'Alene at Crow's Nest on August 15. The two officers compared notes, then returned to their respective commands to continue work. Penrose and his men started the return trip on August 27, knowing there was major work to be accomplished on the way down. Trees that looked like they would fall were cut 200 feet on either side of the road. The soldiers from Fort Missoula graded 115 miles, constructed 26 bridges, and installed innumerable culverts during 1879. After his return, Lieutenant Penrose wrote a detailed report suggesting further improvements to the road, and suggested that work begin early in the spring. Lieutenant Penrose in his report of the summer's work invited, "the attention of 'The General' [Sherman] to the immense quantity of work done by the command; no one can appreciate it who was not with us to see for themselves." He asked for extra duty pay for his men, which was granted.[8]

Captain Charles Hobart and 30 men left the fort on September 10, 1879, with a mission to build a telegraph line to Helena. Local contractor Alfred Cave won a bid to provide 1,500 telegraph poles at $1.20 per pole, to be delivered from Fort Missoula to points as far away as 60 miles east of town. During this assignment 1st Lieutenant Edward A. Belger died of acute dysentery and diarrhea on October 8, 1879, and was buried in the Fort Missoula cemetery. Two weeks after the lieutenant's death, Assistant Surgeon Robinson escorted Belger's destitute wife and three children to the Utah Northern Railroad. Six years after Belger's death, the officers at the fort donated 50 dollars to purchase a headstone.

General of the Army Sherman recommended that $30,000 be set aside to continue work upon the road in 1880, but General Philip Sheridan decided that sum was excessive and allocated only $12,000 to do the work. Maintenance continued on the road in 1880, with an emphasis on building a telegraph line to Coeur d'Alene along the route. Captain George Head and B Company left the fort in June 1880 to construct 112 miles of telegraph line to the summit of the Coeur d'Alene mountains. Much of this line was strung from tree to tree, but by 1881 tie cutters for the railroad often dropped trees over the line. During the late summer of 1880 Captain Penrose once again took two companies to improve the Mullan Road, and work continued on the road until 1883, when the Northern Pacific Railroad completed their Northern Route, and the Mullan Road lost its strategic importance. Future Copper King W.A. Clark founded a mail route from Fort Missoula to Fort Walla Walla using horse couriers that followed the Flathead River through Perma and Plains. Clark sold this mail route to the Northern Pacific in 1883.

The Survey Error That Threatened Fort Missoula

After many of the buildings were already under construction in 1877, Captain Rawn ordered surveying instruments from the Chief Quartermaster's office in Washington DC, but the post was not adequately surveyed until the summer of 1878, when a shocking error was discovered. An Executive order on August 5, 1878 added 560 acres to the Fort Missoula Military Reservation. The land in the new addition was north of what is now South Avenue, south of Spurgin Road, and bounded by Reserve Street on the east and 37th Street on the west. Alfred Cave's wheat farm sat squarely in the middle of this parcel, and was surrounded on three sides by the Military Reservation.

The Military Reservation was now almost two square miles in size (1,200 acres) but when Lt. Williams of the 3rd Infantry began to survey this addition, it quickly became clear that due to an error in the original survey, many of the buildings constructed during the past year were located not inside the Military Reservation as supposed, but instead on land set aside for public schools. The War Department was notified on August 27, 1878 that much of the fort had been built in Section 36 rather than Section 31. Once aware of the error, Secretary of War George W. McCrary requested that Congress purchase the eastern half of Section 36 (360 acres) from the state to be added to the Military Reservation. Congress failed to act on this request, despite the fact that it was repeated annually until 1889, without result. Nevertheless, General Sherman issued an order on December 15, 1878 directing the soldiers at Fort Missoula to keep intruders off the fort grounds, including the school land.

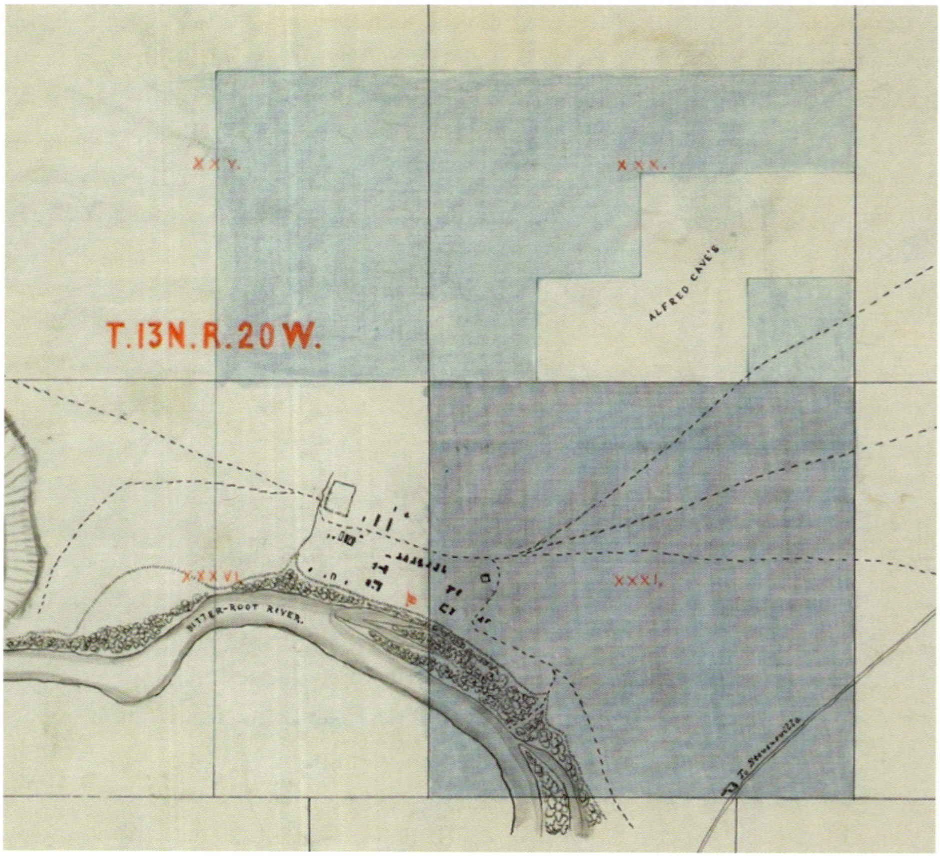

This 1879 map of Fort Missoula shows the original military reservation (Section 31) in dark blue. Land added to the reservation by executive order in 1878 is shown in light blue. Unfortunately, much of the fort had been mistakenly constructed in Section 36, land deeded to Montana Territory for the support of schools.
HMFM

The questions about ownership of the land greatly concerned successive commanders of the fort, and resulted in a whole flurry of correspondence that passed between Fort Missoula, the Department of Dakota, and the War Department. For instance, on February 20, 1879 Lt. Col. Chipman wrote for clarification of his right to expel intruders from school lands, citing conflicting opinions he had received from the Secretary of War and the US Attorney General. Chipman wrote that, "As parties have already intruded upon the School section and others are preparing to locate in the West half of the section with a view (it is supposed) to carrying on an illegal liquor traffic with the soldiers of this garrison." Colonel Chipman asked whether he was allowed to eject the settlers or if he should call the US Marshall instead. A Private Malmstrom was mugged by two Indians who demanded tobacco, but the case had to be turned over to civil authorities since it occurred in Section 36.

Despite the uncertainty about ownership of some of the Fort Missoula land, President Rutherford B. Hayes signed an Executive order on June 10, 1879 that set aside a Timber Reserve of 1577.41 acres in Pattee Canyon, six miles southwest of the fort. The fort now consisted of 2,777.41 acres, 1,200 acres in the fort proper.

More than ten years after the survey error came to light, the Army learned that the Northern Pacific Railroad also had a claim on land used by the Army's Target Range in Sections 25 and 35. Secretary of War Redfield Proctor asked US Attorney General William H.H. Miller for another legal opinion on the status of the disputed land at Fort Missoula on April 22, 1889. Miller ruled that the Army had only limited occupancy rights to the land unless the state and the railroad would agree to relinquish claim to the land.

Life of the Soldier

The entire US Army had only 25,000 enlisted men and 2,000 officers by 1874, and these numbers would not increase until the Spanish-American War in 1898. Once the men assigned to the engineers, quartermasters, commissary detachment, medical detachment, West Point detachment, and Fort Leavenworth prison guards were subtracted, the Army's fighting force was only 19,000 men at best, consisting of 25 infantry regiments, 10 cavalry regiments, and five artillery regiments. New enlistments were curtailed and many officers, considered surplus because of their age or lack of advancement, were forced to resign. The remaining officers were typically veterans of the Civil War who had endured a severe rank reduction in order to remain in the Army. The road to advancement depended on an officer's accomplishments in battle, leading officers like Lt. Col George Custer to commit rash acts in hopes of attracting the attention of superior officers.

By the fall of 1877, in the wake of the Nez Percé war and Custer's defeat the year before, the Army had 3,300 soldiers in Montana. A typical infantry company was supposed to have a complement of 41 men, including 29 privates. However, men were often detached for other duty, on leave, sick call, or otherwise absent, so that many units often had only half or three-quarters of their complement available at any one time. At least 20 percent of the soldiers were foreign-born, and many could neither speak nor understand English. Desertion rates in the wide open West were a major problem as well. Many enlistees saw a hitch in the army as a free ticket to the gold fields of the west.

An infantry regiment in 1876 had ten companies, compared to 12 for the cavalry. After the Battle of the Little Big Horn Congress authorized a strengthening in the size of cavalry companies, but did not increase the size of the Army, resulting in a further reduction in the size of infantry companies. These factors resulted in very weak garrisons at many frontier posts, and when trouble arose the Army would have to ship in additional troops. To make matters worse, many officers often spent years away from their post on recruiting or other special duties. As an example, Captain James H. Gageby arrived at Fort Missoula with the 3rd Infantry in 1877, but left on a recruiting trip the following year and did not return until 1881. Two years later he left on sick leave, and did not return until 1885.

Life at Fort Missoula was highly regimented, with bugle calls directing the soldiers from dawn until dusk (reveille was usually at 5:00 a.m. and retreat around 8:30 p.m.) Beginning in 1883 and continuing until 1942, Fort Missoula had an 1861 Civil War cannon converted to a salute gun that fired over the banks of the Bitterroot River to announce reveille and retreat each day. The salute cannon could be heard throughout much of the Missoula Valley.

Infantrymen were issued knapsacks but most preferred to stow their gear in a blanket roll slung over a shoulder. The regulation bayonet was often left behind when the men were in the field because most soldiers preferred a sheath knife. An exception was made for the trowel bayonet issued to the 7th Infantry, which proved its worth at Fort Fizzle and the Battle of the Big Hole. The men usually carried little more than a rifle and canteen in the field. For the first twenty years of its existence, troops at the fort carried Model 1873 "trapdoor" Springfield rifles, which fired a .45-70 cartridge. Officers were issued with a single-action 1872 Colt Army revolver firing a .45 caliber cartridge. Up until 1880 infantrymen carried Civil War era cartridge boxes designed for paper cartridges, which were gradually replaced by cartridge belts with canvas loops.

The soldiers of the 1870s were issued equipment from warehouses bulging with Civil War era equipment. The Army did not improve its gear until it began running out of certain sizes of uniforms in the 1870s, and most soldiers received no modern equipment until the 1880s. The infantrymen were issued blue-striped pants and blouses of a darker blue, but most frontier units wore a variety of uniforms, civilian clothes, and home-made or adapted equipment. Many of the clothes were ill-fitting, and the wool uniforms often proved too hot for a Montana summer and too thin for a Montana winter. Beginning in 1881 the soldiers were outfitted with buffalo hide coats and pants, fur-lined mittens and ear muffs. The standard-issue campaign hats disintegrated when they got wet, and the Civil War-era forage caps were not much better. As a result the early soldiers adopted a wide variety of headgear. The Fort Missoula garrison complained for several months in 1879 that they were out of forage caps and stockings. In 1880 infantrymen were issued white pith helmets, with ornate spiked versions issued to officers and musicians. Infantrymen were also issued canvas gauntlets in the mid-1880s, and received canvas leggings a few years later.

Each company had several laundresses, who had been authorized to receive room and board from the army since 1802. The army provided daily rations, plus tents, hatchets and knives, cooking gear, and straw bedding. The soldiers paid to have their clothes cleaned at a rate set by the post administration in accordance with local labor rates. Soldiers at Fort Missoula probably paid their laundress about one dollar each per month, while officers would pay twice that. The money was subtracted from each soldier's wage on pay day, and before any other creditors such as the post sutler. The laundresses also helped the officer's wives with cooking, nursing, and cleaning. The women were required to be of good moral character, although a few practiced prostitution on the

The Officer's Club

Building T-3 was one of the first buildings completed at Fort Missoula, and was constructed with 10 to 12-inch diameter western larch logs. The building was intended for laundress quarters but was used originally to house officer's families until their quarters could be completed. It was also used to house non-commissioned officers (NCOs). Originally it was divided into four units, but in the mid-1920s the interior walls were removed and it was converted into an officer's club and post hall. During the remodeling an old Springfield rifle and several rounds of ammunition were found under the floorboards. The rifle was hung on the wall of the officers club. Also found under the floor was a memo that had been distributed to all post commanders at the time. It read, "The practice of shooting buffalo from barracks windows will be discontinued, for sanitary reasons." A swimming pool and tennis courts were built near the officer's club. Although it was known to be the oldest building on the post, it received little maintenance, and the sill logs were rotting away by the late 1960s. The building burned in late 1972. The post chapel, which was remodeled into the post headquarters (T-1) in 1940, can be seen in the background of this 1910 photo.

LC-HABS MONT,32-MISS,3-4

side. Many laundresses wound up marrying non-commissioned officers, (four married NCOs were allowed in each company) and as a result the NCO quarters on some posts were known as "Suds Row." Enlisted men's wives were usually not allowed to live on the post unless they were a laundress. The army eventually decided that the cost of providing for laundresses was too expensive, and the program was officially phased out in the early 1880s. Funding authority for their rations expired, however the practice continued unofficially at many posts for years to come.

Soldiers were responsible for their own cooking and cleaning. Each company would appoint men for a period to cook for the rest. Their rations consisted of salt pork, salt beef, flour, coffee, hardtack, beans, dried peas, sugar, molasses and salt. Quality of the food depended on the availability of rations, and the skill of the cooks. Scurvy was common due to the lack of fresh fruit. Hunting, fishing, and vegetable gardens provided what little fresh food and variety the soldiers enjoyed. Other foods like eggs, milk, fresh meat, and vegetables were bought from local farmers. Canned fruit, sardines, and oysters were often available from the sutler's store. Food supplies in 1879 were described as "ample and generally good," and by 1890 soldiers were receiving better food and equipment issued to them.

Poor food, poor hygiene, and a lack of knowledge about the cause of many diseases led to frequent outbreaks of typhoid fever, diphtheria, cholera, measles, and influenza. The post was quarantined in 1882 due to an outbreak of smallpox. Soldiers also suffered from scurvy, venereal disease, lice infestations, frostbite, hypothermia, and heatstroke. The Surgeon reported in 1883 there had been two deaths from disease, one man froze to death, and a fourth was shot. There were only two deaths in 1885, one killed in a saloon and one man died after falling off a mule. The regimental surgeon had few tools to combat disease and injury. Mercury chloride was used as an emetic and to treat venereal disease. Chloroform, ether, laudanum and whiskey were used as anesthetics and painkillers. Surgeons also relied on a collection of herbal treatments.

Beginning in 1879, the post surgeons at the fort began keeping daily weather measurements. Initially they had a standard thermometer, a set of maximum and minimum thermometers, an instrument shelter, and a rain gauge. Eventually they added wet and dry bulb thermometers to determine the dew point, as well as a Fortin barometer. When the fort was closed at the outbreak of the Spanish-American War in 1898, these instruments were transferred to the care of Professor Morton J. Elrod at the nearby Montana State University, who continued the daily observations.

Boredom at the isolated posts was endemic, and soldiers sought out recreational opportunities. Soldiers often bathed, swam, fished and boated in the nearby Bitterroot River. Card-playing, minstrel shows, baseball, foot races, and horseshoes were popular diversions. Will Cave attended a minstrel performance put on at the Missoula court house by men of the 7th Infantry shortly before they left town. He reported that while it was not strictly professional, it "bordered on the excellent."

Gardening was also popular, and helped supplement the drab rations. Eventually the post chaplain was responsible for overseeing the gardens. Hunting and fishing also helped augment the Army-issue rations. Lieutenant F.P. Avery of the 3rd Infantry declared Fort Missoula had "everything that a hunter could desire, from grizzly bear to prairie chicken. I had

The fort's salute gun, an 1861 Civil War cannon converted to fire blank charges, announced reveille and retreat each day from 1883 until the 1940s. It was fired towards the Bitterroot River, and the blast could be heard throughout the valley. The gun was donated to the Historical Museum at Fort Missoula by Hayes and Amalia Otoupalik in honor of Josef Otoupalik. It now sits in front of the main entrance of the museum.

great sport last winter hunting deer after a heavy fall of snow on snowshoes, with tolerable success. This spring I gave my attention to ducks and geese, with good results. I received a fine trout rod from the East, and have declared war on the finny tribe."[9] Lieutenant Thomas S. Wallace died of exposure a few miles from Fort Missoula while hunting on December 8, 1878. After separating from his companion, he attempted to cross the "Hellgate" River in the dark, but his horse balked and he was thrown into the water. He managed to pull himself out of the river but soon died of hypothermia. His saddled horse and hunting dog both returned to the fort safely. "He was a brave and promising young officer, and his loss is keenly felt by all."[10]

The Post also had an "overseer of schools" who was in charge of a 40-pupil school plus the reading room. Enlisted men and children both learned English and US History at the post school, which opened in 1882. Col. Chipman requested half a dozen newspapers and at least a dozen periodicals be furnished to the post library, including the *New York Daily Graphic* and *New York Herald*, *the Army-Navy Journal*, and *Harpers Weekly*. *Forest and Stream* made the list the following year. The fort had its own newspaper in the 1880s called the *Rally*. By 1882 a wagon ran into Missoula each morning for the benefit of the officer's families at Fort Missoula.

Boredom and isolation often led to drinking, and frontier soldiers were plagued by very high rates of alcoholism, especially among the officers. When Col. Chipman traveled to St. Paul to participate in the Court-martial of another officer in 1879, he left Captain William H. Penrose in charge of Fort Missoula. Penrose had served with the regiment since the opening battles of the Civil War, and reached the rank of brevet Brigadier General during that conflict, then spent more than a decade as a frustrated lieutenant before his next promotion. Penrose often served as acting commander of the fort when superior officers were absent, and headed up efforts to repair the Mullan Road. Nevertheless, Penrose was charged with two counts of drunkenness in 1879, and reduced in rank to lieutenant. Penrose was again arrested in 1880 for breaking his pledge to remain sober, and was sentenced to one-half pay for one year. (Penrose would eventually retire as a full colonel in 1896.)

President Rutherford B. Hayes banned the sale of alcohol on military posts in 1881, but that didn't solve the problem. Lt. Colonel George Gibson, who succeeded Chipman, requested the discharge of one soldier in 1885 due to his chronic drunkenness. He, "is simply one of these wretched bargains with which the United States Government is unfortunately afflicted very often in its military arm of service. Lost to all sense of decency and propriety, as far as drinking is concerned, he swills until he falls by the wayside, a helpless mass of humanity challenging the sympathy of passers by to get him into the post to prevent his being laid up with pneumonia or possibly being frozen to death." Gibson wrote that court martial had had no effect on his behavior, and "the greatest punishment that be possibly inflicted on him would be to throw him once more on the tender mercies of the world."[1] Post sutler McCormick was accused of selling whiskey on the post in 1883. (Three years earlier McCormick had been "thrashed" with a whip by Lt. Cooke, the fort's Quartermaster because of "official difficulties.")

This structure was typical of the early log buildings constructed at Fort Missoula in 1877 and 1878. These buildings were originally designed as laundress quarters, but during the first few years served as company barracks or housed the families of officers until frame buildings could be erected.
UM - 94.1603

Discipline was always a problem at frontier posts. Orders issued at Fort Missoula included forbidding the discharging of firearms towards the post commander's quarters, and another that ordered, "The practice of shooting buffalo from barracks windows will be discontinued, for sanitary reasons." Post records indicate that an average of two to four soldiers were in confinement at all times, necessitating a round-the-clock guard, which strained the already understrength garrison. One prisoner at Fort Missoula was chained to his bed in the hospital except during mealtimes or calls of nature, when he was to be watched by hospital orderlies, yet he still managed to escape during the summer of 1879. At one point Colonel Chipman requested permission to transfer his four military prisoners to a larger post, as he had a hard time keeping them under guard and at hard labor, and he thought if they escaped their recapture was exceedingly remote. Escapes in fact were frequent. One convict escaped from the fort on May 12, 1879, and several weeks later, on July 5th, 1879, two prisoners in the stockade convinced their sentry to desert with them and all three disappeared. On May 22, 1879 the garrison at Fort Benton captured and sent back a man who had deserted from Fort Missoula the previous November.

Many deserters had enlisted just to be transported to the West, where they hoped to find work in the mines. They often waited for an opportunity to vanish, with a horse and a rifle if possible. The fort's Annual Report in 1884 listed 46 desertions out of a total complement of 178 enlisted men.

Most recruits arrived at the post with little or no training, and generally arrived at Fort Missoula in October. The fort had only 137 men present and accounted for on October 8, 1879, but received 55 recruits three weeks later. The garrison declined again in December, when 11 men were discharged. The fort received 39 recruits a year later in October 1879, but in 1880 received only 20 recruits. Until the railroad reached Missoula, these green recruits were marched overland from Fort Benton, and many apparently had trouble adjusting to the Montana climate in October. Captain Head wrote in the fort's 1880 annual report that "Recruits intended for this post should be sent early in the spring or fall, so as to become accustomed to the climate and avoid the hardships otherwise entailed in reaching their destination from the terminal point of river navigation."

Relationships with the Local Tribes

During the first few years the soldiers at Fort Missoula spent most of their time constructing buildings at the fort, but they were also frequently called upon by both Native Americans and settlers to mitigate problems and settle disputes.

Early in 1878 officers at Fort Missoula heard rumors that scattered bands of the Nez Percé tribe who had escaped to Canada were trying to return to their traditional homeland. Detachments of soldiers were sent to outlying communities and to scout mountain passes and trails.

The most serious Indian engagement by Fort Missoula soldiers after the Battle of the Big Hole occurred after Lt. Thomas S. Wallace led a mounted party out of Fort Missoula on July 14, 1878 on the trail of 40 Nez Percé rumored to be returning from Canada. Wallace had 13 soldiers from Companies B, H, and I, plus a guide known as "Shirt Collar Bill," and two citizens who soon dropped out. The Indians had stolen horses and it was rumored they had previously committed a murder. Wallace located the band on July 21, 1878 near the Clearwater River in Idaho. A week after leaving Fort Missoula, Wallace's small command attacked the Indian camp by surprise, killing six and wounding three. Many of the Indian horses were killed as well, and 31 Nez Percé warriors were captured. (Montana pi-

A Salish camp on the Jocko River.
Edward Curtis Photo - LC-USZ62-89991

oneer Frank "Sandbar" Brown would later claim that Lieutenant Wallace had wiped out another party of Indians shortly before this encounter.) Another company left the fort two days after Wallace, headed for Cadotte's Pass northwest of Helena, where they were to block the movement of hostile Indians towards Missoula.

For the most part, relationships between the local tribes and the soldiers at Fort Missoula were cordial, and according to Colonel Chipman, "Many pow-wows with the chiefs and agents were held." Chipman was in especially close contact with local Indian Agent Peter Ronan, whose "name, tact, and character are still reverenced"[12]. Chipman also communicated regularly with a number of Jesuit priests, including Fathers Ravalli, Minitree, and Catholdo at the missions at St. Ignatius and St. Mary's (Stevensville). Local scout Delaware Jim, had arrived in the area many years before with Captain John Mullan and was often employed (for the princely sum of five dollars a day) to negotiate with the Native Americans.

One of the primary duties of the soldiers at Fort Missoula was to escort bands of local Indians to and from the Judith Basin and Musselshell Valley of Montana for the annual buffalo hunt. Typically these detachments consisted of one officer, one non-commissioned officer, and four privates, each from a different company. This was considered just enough of a force to discourage trouble between their charges, local settlers, and bands of roving Blackfeet. Typically Agent Ronan or the chiefs themselves would request permission from the commander of Fort Missoula to travel to the buffalo country. The request would be passed along to regimental headquarters at Fort Shaw, which usually approved the hunts without conditions. Chipman asked for clarification from the Department of Dakota on his responsibility to oversee non-treaty Indians like Chief Charlo's band of Salish, living just a few miles south of the fort. On April 2, 1879 Colonel Chipman received a telegram from Fort Ellis instructing him to send a mounted detachment of 10 men to escort Chief Charlo's band to Missoula from the Deer Lodge Valley. By the time the telegram arrived and the detachment hit the road, Chief Charlo's band was only three miles from Missoula. Just days later Chipman wrote Fort Shaw seeking routine permission to allow 20 to 30 lodges of Flathead Indians under Chiefs Arlee and Aeneas to travel east to the buffalo country, as they had done the year before.

The commander at Fort Missoula also found himself at the center of many disputes between settlers and Indians. Lt. Col. Chipman wrote letters giving Indian individuals the right to travel in pursuit of horse thieves and tried to get payment for an Indian horse sold to General Howard in 1878. Chief Arlee visited Chipman on his way to a buffalo hunt in 1879 to complain that a white man married to a Flathead woman was trying to sell the reservation land that he lived on.

Despite the efforts of the authorities to keep the peace, there were occasional problems. On August 14, 1879 Chipman wrote to Indian Agent Peter Ronan at the Jocko Agency, telling him that, "a number of Indians attached to your reservation are in the vicinity of the town of Missoula, are drinking and while intoxicated commit depredations upon citizens, stoning and otherwise molesting them." He asked Ronan to make sure the Indians were returned to the reservation. A year later another complaint was lodged about Indians looting gardens and orchards in the Missoula area.

The soldiers at Fort Missoula not only dealt with the local Salish, Kootenai, and Pend d'Oreille (collectively known to the whites as Flatheads) but many visiting Native Americans as well. Col. Chipman wrote, "this locality has been for many years a favorite bartering place among the Indians, and during the spring and summer is visited by numerous small parties of British Kootenais, Spokanes, Kalispels, Colville, and other tribes..." The soldiers also encountered many reservation Indians traveling without the proper passes, and occasionally escorted them back to their respective reservations.

The 3rd Infantry troops left Fort Missoula in 1888, and were replaced by the "Buffalo Soldiers" of the 25th Infantry, who would have their own interactions with local and visiting tribes of Indians.

Tensions between Neighbors, 1878-1888

- **1878**, July 21 - Lieutenant Wallace and 13 soldiers attacked a band of Nez Percé warriors near Clearwater, Idaho, killing six, wounding three, and capturing 31.
- **1879**, July 6 - One Indian and one white settler were killed in an incident at Lincoln Gulch on the Blackfoot River.
- **1880** - Col. Gibson asked that the post be reinforced during the summer of 1880 due to rumors that the Nez Percé, Umatillas, and Spokanes to the west planned to band together and move through Missoula to the buffalo country.
- **1880**, September 25 - Col. Gibson was ordered to receive the surrender of a group of Nez Percé at the Jocko Agency. They were brought to the post since there were not enough soldiers to supervise them on the reservation.
- **1881**, October 20 - Company H of the 3rd Infantry was dispatched from Fort Missoula to Stevensville after two Salish men were killed by a white man named Morris in a dispute over a horse. "Much excitement" ensued over fears the Salish might revolt, but most tribal members were hundreds of miles away on a buffalo hunt. The soldiers had only proceeded about five miles when they received word that further violence was unlikely, and they turned back.
- **1882**, August 29 - Companies B and D were sent to St. Ignatius to help prevent violence on the reservation.
- **1883**, May - Military units across Montana were ordered to round up and deport the many Cree Indians who had left Canada in search of better conditions in the United States. Small numbers of Cree were arrested on the Jocko Reservation and held temporarily at Fort Missoula.
- **1883**, August 8 - Major William H. Jordan received word from the telegrapher at Evaro that a group of white settlers had been surrounded by Indians and that shots had been fired. He was also informed that other Indians were converging on the scene. Indian Agent Peter Ronan felt further trouble was likely, and requested help from the Army. Major Jordan and Companies B, D, and I left Fort Missoula and caught a train heading north. At nearby Evaro they found that a band of young Nez Percé, Umatillas, and Spokanes had been drinking and causing trouble in the area. One white man had been robbed of his horse and $210. The victim's father had wounded one of the thieves when he attempted to recover the stolen goods. Tensions escalated and some of the Indians tried to take a gun from a railroad employee at Evaro while others threatened a haying crew at Camas Prairie. Major Jordan and the local sheriff first arrested a saloon keeper who had been selling whiskey to the Indians, and on the following day they detained 40 Indians at Arlee. One with a history of violence was sent to Fort Missoula. On August 10 Lieutenant Avery led his company to arrest three of the robbers, but they had fled. Agent Ronan ordered the rest of the troublemakers to leave the reservation at once, and their arms and horses were returned. Jordan and his detachment returned to the fort on August 10, 1883.
- **1883**, October - Agent Ronan requested further help, and Lieutenant Avery and 15 men arrested 10 Indians who had been causing trouble on the reservation.
- **1884**, September - Lieutenant J.P. Thompson led a detachment to the Jocko Reservation at Agent Ronan's request to arrest more "lawless Indians."
- **1885**, December - Ninety Fort Missoula soldiers were again called to action after a storekeeper in Arlee shot two Indians who tried to rob him. Indian Agent Peter Ronan managed to calm the crisis and the troops were recalled before they could board the train in Missoula.
- **1887** - Companies B and F of the 3rd Infantry Regiment were transferred from Fort Missoula to Fort Custer during the short-lived Crow Incident, instigated by a young warrior known as Sword-Bearer who led a group of hotheaded young men of the tribe. The men from Company B were present at the Battle of Crow Agency on November 5, when Sword Bearer and his followers charged a skirmish line of soldiers, killing one and wounding two (none from Fort Missoula). Seven of the Crow were killed and nine were wounded, including Sword Bearer. Many of the young men fled into the mountains, but the wounded Sword Bearer returned to the Crow camp, where he was killed by a tribal policeman, putting an end to the violence. The infantrymen returned to Fort Missoula on November 13.

Target Range

The Target Range neighborhood west of Fort Missoula was named after the Army's shooting range in the area. The Army took an increased interest in target practice after the Battle of Little Big Horn, and troops were supposed to practice their marksmanship twice a week. Due to ammunition shortages and other duties this was often ignored, but target practice was enthusiastically endorsed at certain times during the fort's history when there were no more pressing duties. Throughout 1882 target practice was held every Monday and Friday.

Beginning in 1878 the soldiers used an area at the base of McCauley Butte and half a mile northwest of the center of the fort for target practice. The shooting range had several firing lanes once it was fully developed, with a maximum distance of 1,000 yards. The targets were set up at the base of the butte, and could be raised and lowered for scoring. Most soldiers practiced at ranges of 200, 500 and 600 yards, and the best marksmen often represented Fort Missoula in regional competitions against shooters from other other posts. During very cold weather troops practiced drilling and aiming their rifles inside the buildings.

In 1879 Lt. Col. Chipman wrote that he had 14,350 rounds of .50 caliber rifle ammunition on hand, (probably indicating that part of his unit was still armed with the obsolete Springfield Model 1866 Trapdoor Rifle) and called that amount inadequate. He also ordered 40,000 rounds of .45-70 ammunition to be sent from Fort Shaw, and requested this shipment be expedited. Captain W.C. Wilkinson was the highest scoring marksman in the Army in 1884, and Fort Missoula had the highest marksmanship scores in the entire Army in 1885, perhaps because the soldiers at Fort Missoula were chosen to test several new repeating bolt-action rifles. One company of soldiers retained their standard-issue Springfield rifles, while the remaining companies were equipped with the Chaffee Reece Rifle, the Hotchkiss Rifle or the Remington-Lee Rifle. The new rifles were tested throughout 1885, but the Army ultimately rejected all of the new rifles.

During the 1890s, operation of the rifle range became more complicated when Target Range school was built nearby. Early teacher Minnie Spurgin recalled, "In 1894 Father helped organize the Target Range District for the McCauleys, Kelleys, Maclays and Jane Slack at the Fort; [They] needed a school. The school house stood in the corner of McCauley's field farther east than it is now located. One year I had the house full, for all the officer's children from the fort came. The soldiers hauled our drinking water."[13] Frieda Klapwyck, another early teacher described the school. "Selecting a name for the school could not have been very difficult with the Army target range almost in it's back yard. Children attending classes received extra education. They remember the thrill of hearing bugles sound reveille, the beat of the drum corps, and guns firing into the hill. They watched maneuvers as the Army trained men in fields near by. The Target Range was a favorite place to explore, dig for spent bullets and collect arrow heads left behind by Indians."[14]

Antonio Bertapelle remembered, "There was a lane, closed off by a gate, which led around the east base of the Butte. When the soldiers from the fort were having their rifle training, a soldier was posted at that gate to keep anyone from going through and finding themselves right behind the targets."[15] The range had been located so that any stray bullets would hit the butte, but Clyde Maclay, who irrigated a potato field for Charlie McCauley on the far side of the butte from the range, remembers stray bullets splashing in the water. "The soldiers must have shot wildly to fire over the butte. Bill [Maclay] was told that once a bullet landed at their house!" (at the corner of Blue Mountain & O'Brien Creek Road).[16] During the 1920s one local youngster collected lead from the firing range and sold it to a junk dealer in town; he reported he made as much as eight dollars per day, but he didn't find all of the lead. Ray Rademacher recalled, "the south side of the McCauley Butte had been the back stop for the rifle range and, during the 1940's, yielded precious pounds of lead which we dug up and patriotically gave to the war effort."[17]

The McCauley Butte range was closed in March 1929, and was replaced by a new range in Pattee Canyon. A metal detector sweep in 1985 found shell casings for .45-70, .30-40 Krag, .30-06, and pistol cartridges in .38 and.45 auto calibers. The land once covered by the Target Range is now occupied by the agriculture program of the Missoula County Public School district and the Industrial Technology division of Missoula College.

Rogues and Heroes at Fort Missoula

Lieutenant Francis Fremont of the 3rd Infantry Regiment was the son of General John Fremont, the controversial explorer, presidential candidate and US Senator. An 1879 graduate of West Point, Francis helped conduct a census on the Jocko Reservation in 1881, and served as the acting commander of Fort Missoula in March 1888. Fremont would eventually rise to the rank of major, but after leaving Missoula he became notorious for his misbehavior during three widely publicized courts-martial. He was found guilty of striking a soldier in the Philippines in 1901. Bad debts resulted in a second court-martial in 1907, which he blamed on excessive alimony payments and a bitter divorce from his wife Caroline. Fremont's notoriety was insured when he was convicted an unprecedented third time for disrespecting a superior officer in 1909, effectively ending his career. A small headstone labeled Fremont Child, no date of birth or death given, marks the final resting place of one of Fremont's children in the Fort Missoula cemetery.

Major Gaines Lawson served with the Union Army in Tennessee during the Civil War. Thirty years after the war he was awarded the Congressional Medal of Honor for an incident that occurred in 1865. His citation read, "Went to the aid of a wounded comrade between the lines and carried him to a place of safety." Captain Gaines Lawson led three companies of the 25th Infantry to the Jocko Reservation in 1889 to keep the peace. He served as acting commander of Fort Missoula from July 16 to 25, 1891 and April through July 1892.

Charles L. Hodges was fourteen-years-old when he enlisted as a private with the 65th New York Volunteers in 1861. He fought in many of the worst battles of the Civil War, including Fair Oaks, Seven Pines, Malvern Hill, Antietam, Fredericksburg, Marye's Heights, Gettysburg, the Wilderness, and Spottsylvania Courthouse. He was wounded twice in 1864, but rejoined his unit in 1865. After four years of service Lieutenant Hodges was mustered out at the end of the war, age 18 years and four months. He joined the Regular Army in 1869, and served with the 25th Infantry from 1875 to 1900. He was promoted to captain in 1891, and served as commander of Company H and as the regimental quartermaster at Fort Missoula. According to Colonel Alexander Burt, "Captain Hodges' company would be a special character of men, and an especially good company. The company reflects the character of the captain."[17] Hodges served as the Army's Acting chief of staff in the Philippines in 1907, and later served as head of the Department of the Lakes and temporary head of the Department of Dakota. He was promoted to major general in 1910, and retired the following year after nearly 50 years of service.

Ulysses Grant McAlexander was 25-years-old when he arrived at Fort Missoula in 1889, two years after graduating from West Point. His career with the 25th Infantry at Fort Missoula was relatively undistinguished, but Colonel McAlexander became a military hero in 1918 when he led the badly outnumbered 38th Infantry Regiment of the Third Infantry Division at the second Battle of the Marne in France. McAlexander refused to retreat in the face of a ferocious German offensive, even as other regiments pulled back on his flanks. With his ammunition supply dwindling and with Germans all around, McAlexander picked up a rifle and ordered his men to stand their ground. For his actions holding fast under the German onslaught, McAlexander was called the "Rock of the Marne" and was promoted to brigadier general. The 38th Regiment and the Third Infantry both adopted "Rock of the Marne" as their unit nickname. McAlexander retired in 1924 as a major general and is buried in Arlington National Cemetery. His tombstone reads simply, "Rock of the Marne."

General Ulysses G. Mc Alexander
Oregon State University

The Fort Missoula Timber Reserve

The soldiers at Fort Missoula needed timber for building, and soon identified the Pattee Canyon area southeast of Missoula as an excellent source for the straight, uniform western larch trees preferred for log buildings. The Army asked that the area be set aside as a timber reserve, and it was originally surveyed in extremely cold weather during the winter of 1877-78, in order that logging could begin in the spring. Since the grid surveying system was not yet laid out in the mountains, the timber reserve was defined by metes and bounds using bearing trees, and the irregular shape of the reserve incorporated the draws where the largest timber grew. The land was reserved by the military in 1878, and President Rutherford B. Hayes established the Fort Missoula Timber Reservation of 1,577 acres by executive order on June 10, 1879.

John McCormick and T.J. Demers, the post traders at Fort Missoula, bought a steam sawmill in 1878 and set it up at the mouth of Pattee Canyon. It burned down in 1881, but after much lobbying by Lt. Col. Gibson, the Army authorized construction of a government sawmill at Fort Missoula later that year. The sawmill employed 20 soldiers full-time, and was improved over the years of its operation. Congress appropriated $1,000 to build a road into the timber reserve in 1884. A logging camp was also established in the Bitterroot Valley in the 1880s.

The timber reserve was horse-logged throughout the 1880s and 90s. Cabins were built just outside the timber reserve as local people used the logging slash to sell as firewood in town.

In 1901 the timber reserve was resurveyed. By this time there were established logging roads and skid trails (some of which are still evident today). Most of the land was transferred to the US Forest Service in 1926, except for 240 acres reserved as a military rifle range near the present-day picnic area. The target range had earth backstops and concrete foundations. There were firing lines at 100, 200, 300, 500, 600, and 800 yards. The Pattee Canyon picnic area and other improvements were built by the Civilian Conservation Corps in the 1930s. During the late 1930s the CCC also established a ski area for the Forest Service in the area of the former timber reserve. They built three ski runs, a lift and warming hut in 1939. The firing range in Pattee Canyon was closed in 1945, and President Dwight Eisenhower issued an executive order on November 5, 1952 mandating that the firing range acreage be incorporated into the Missoula Ranger District, Lolo National Forest. The odd-shaped boundary of the Fort Missoula timber reserve that was established in 1879 now defines the Pattee Canyon Recreation Area.

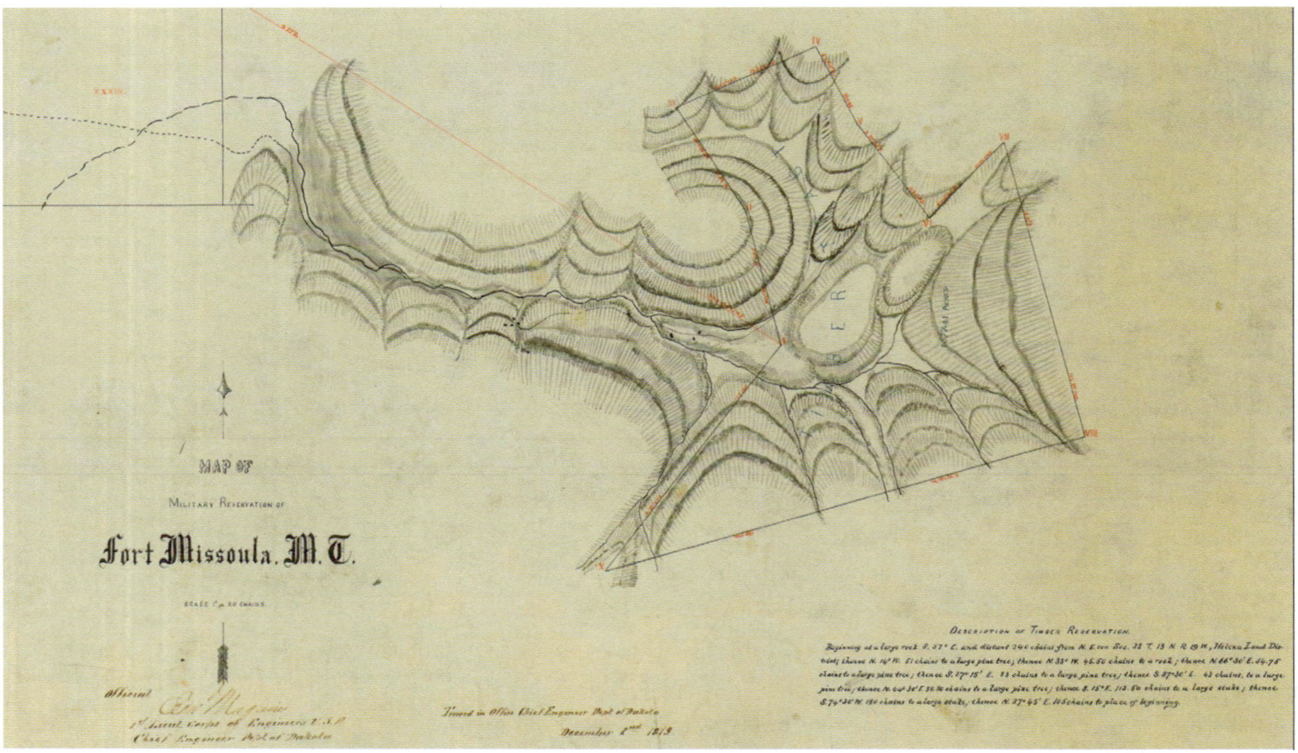

4

The Buffalo Soldiers

"It is a splendid regiment and worthy of unstinted praise."

Anaconda Standard - August 6, 1894

During the spring of 1888, after more than ten years at Fort Missoula, the 3rd Infantry Regiment received orders to trade posts with the 25th Infantry Regiment stationed in the Dakotas and Minnesota. Colonel George Andrews, the commander of the 25th Infantry arrived on May 26, 1888, and his unit formally replaced the 3rd Infantry Regiment in early June.

Although the officers were white, the 25th Infantry was a "crack black regiment." The 25th Infantry Regiment had been formed by the Army Reorganization Act of 1866, which called for the establishment of two regiments of black cavalry (the 9th and 10th), and four of black infantry (which were soon consolidated two, the 24th and 25th Regiments). Few people realize that during the Indian Wars, fully twenty percent of the cavalrymen were black.

White officers often noted the black soldier's loyalty, dependability, good humor and perseverance in the face of adversity. The 24th and 25th Infantry Regiments had the lowest desertion rates in the Army, and much lower alcoholism rates than white soldiers. They also had a much higher rate of reenlistment. Unlike many white soldiers, the black soldiers viewed the army as their career. Most black soldiers were illiterate and were leery of showing individual initiative, but they were also well-disciplined, obedient, and had an overall good record in combat. These units spent much of their time marching, drilling, target practice, and practicing ceremonies. As early as 1880 General William T. Sherman supported abolishing segregated units and allowing blacks to serve alongside white soldiers.

Like other black units in the segregated US army, the men of the 25th were equipped with the poorest of equipment and were often discriminated against by white soldiers. Despite these hardships, the regiment had the lowest desertion rate in the army and one of the highest reenlistment rates by 1896.

Upon their arrival in western Montana, the *Weekly Missoulian* declared, "The colored soldier will add novelty to Fort Missoula, if nothing more." Four companies of the 25th, approximately 220 men, were stationed at the fort initially, including Companies G, H, I, K, plus the Headquarters Company and the Regimental Band. Four other companies of the 25th were sent to Fort Shaw, and two companies went to Fort Custer. The regiment had been commanded by Colonel George Lippett Andrews since 1871.

Officers of the First Battalion of the 25th Infantry. Chaplain T.G. Steward stands on the left of the back row. Colonel Burt is second from the left in the center row.
Nara 111-SC-83633

The new garrison found the barracks in good condition, but the band found itself quartered in one of the fort's first buildings, a crude, over-sized and drafty log cabin. To keep warm they had to block off a portion of the building and patch cracks between the logs. Housing for officers was also in short supply.

The population of Missoula County exploded between 1880, when western Montana had 2,500 white residents, and 1890, when there were more than 14,000. By the mid-1890s the city of Missoula had 4,000 residents, compared to the 250 living there when the fort was founded in 1877. Montana became a state in 1889, and the Missoula and Bitterroot Valley Railway built the Missoula-Skalkaho portion of the Bitterroot Branch that same year. The new railway line, which would eventually be acquired by the Northern Pacific Railroad, ran through the southeast corner of the Fort Missoula Military Reservation, and Post Siding was put in to facilitate unloading cargo and men bound for the fort. The new railroad siding plus installation of a telephone line to the fort in 1889 gave the Army the ability to respond quickly to trouble.

When not assigned to other duties, the soldiers spent a considerable amount of time in target practice and drills. They routinely marched long-distances up the Bitterroot, Blackfoot and Clark Fork Valleys. They marched to Deer Lodge, Helena and as far as the Canadian border. Many of these trips were training soldiers for mapping and reconnaissance duties, while others were battalion-sized simulated combat drills.

The Army Reorganization Act of 1866 mandated that black regiments be provided with a chaplain, and that every permanent post establish a school for enlisted men. The chaplain's primary function was to educate the black soldiers, although the Act also stipulated that black soldiers could not become officers. When Chaplain George W. Simpson was assigned to the fort, Colonel Andrews wrote a letter recommending he not come because of the severe housing shortage. Some of the officers and their families lived in town, and Andrews noted that the fort was close enough to Missoula that soldiers could easily attend religious services there.

Chaplain Theophilus G. Steward arrived at Fort Missoula in 1891. Steward was an accomplished writer and speaker, and was considered a leading black intellectual. He had been reluctant to become an Army chaplain due to a perception that most Army officers had little use for chaplains, and particularly black chaplains. Steward was pleasantly surprised when he arrived and was invited to live with Colonel Andrews and his wife until his quarters were finished. Mrs. Andrews introduced Steward to many of the local merchants, and when his family arrived in Missoula she invited them to dinner. In addition, she directed the church choir and played the organ for many of Steward's services.

Colonel Andrew S. Burt left the 25th Infantry in May 1898 and was promoted brigadier general of volunteers. His wife Elizabeth chronicled life at Fort Missoula in her book, *An Army Wife's Forty Years in the Service 1862-1902.*

Robert Snow

After a gracious welcome from the officers at the fort and most citizens of Missoula, Chaplain Steward was shocked when after more than a year in Missoula he met a colleague from Fort Keogh at the new Florence Hotel, the center of Missoula's social life at the time, and was refused admittance to the dining room. Steward demanded a written apology from the hotel management, and wrote the newspapers in Missoula and Helena. The *Daily Missoulian* declared that "Rev. Steward is a gentleman of education, refinement and unquestioned honor, and his remarks upon the somewhat ticklish question, 'the color line,' will be read with the deepest interest." Missoula ministers mounted a letter writing campaign that overturned the rule. Steward would later write, "My commanding officer, Col. Andrew S. Burt, backed me squarely in my protest and went with me to consult the most prominent lawyer of the place." According to Steward, the public pressure had the desired effect. "The next day the proprietor came out to the post to see me, apologized and begged and requested that no action be taken against his house."

Colonel Andrews retired after 22 years at the command of the regiment, and Colonel Andrew S. Burt, who had enlisted as a private during the Civil War, was appointed to command the 25th Infantry on July 4, 1892. He had fought throughout the Civil War, had served at Fort Laramie and the ill-fated Fort C.F. Smith and had participated at the Battle of Rosebud, but was new to the 25th Infantry.

His wife Elizabeth wrote with some trepidation, "What about going to a colored regiment? We had always been with white soldiers and knew nothing of this regiment, neither officers, nor ladies, nor men. My heart was heavy; but my husband was too good a soldier to utter a word of regret."[2] Mrs. Burt soon lost her misgivings at her husband being assigned to a black regiment. She found, "The officers of the garrison were fine soldiers and agreeable gentlemen. The first impression of the colored men in the ranks was good. They were soldierly, clean, obedient, and respectful. Upon closer acquaintance they improved, and I soon began to like them."

An unidentified sergeant of the 25th Infantry Regiment and his wife posed for this photo in 1888.
UM

"Of the officer's wives, I would say that I found them true Army women... I can truly say that there are no more ideal women in any walk of life; educated and refined, they are good wives and devoted mothers." Mrs. Burt also liked her accommodations in the commanding officer's quarters at Fort Missoula. "A lovely house it was, by far the most palatial of any we had ever had in our army life." She was fond of the two, "glowing crackling fires" in the downstairs rooms, and the wood stoves in the other rooms that provided "delightful warmth." She noted "A large porch across the front covered with Virginia creeper, made the house very attractive. The front windows looked over the parade grounds to the Commanding Officer's office, with trees in the background. The Bitterroot River flowed back of them and the eye followed to the Bitterroot mountain range beyond; a charming landscape, always delightful in its varying moods. What could we ask better."[3]

Raising a Little Hell

Although the soldiers of the 25th Infantry were highly disciplined, they were not immune to the lure of whiskey and women, and local newspapers found rich material in some of their antics. The *Weekly Missoulian* (November 6 1889) reported the fate of one soldier. "Colored Sam Griswold Donates $40 to the County Court" for "indiscriminate use of a six-shooter" on a Sunday afternoon while he admitted to being "pretty drunk."

A little more than a month later Private Jacob Jones was fined $25 and court costs for assaulting Lizzie Maroney at the "notorious Four-Mile House." The paper made light of what was obviously a serious situation. "It seems that Jones became rather much filled with whiskey and tried to improve Lizzie's looks by using a razor."[4]

The sutler or post trader was a private contractor, sanctioned by the Army, who could sell all sorts of goods, including liquor. The sutler often provided card tables, billiard tables, and a separate bar for officers and enlisted men. It was generally the center of the post's social life. When the idea to abolish the post trader and instead run an army-operated post exchange was put forth in 1889, Col. Andrews was opposed, arguing that the sutlers kept the men from going to town and getting into trouble there. He also noted that few of his officers were interested in being the manager of a coffee house, billiard parlor, or beer garden. Despite his misgivings, the sutler system was abolished in 1890, and replaced by the post canteen, which eventually became known as the post exchange, or PX. The post canteen only sold beer and wine along with other goods. Hard liquor and gambling were outlawed. The soldiers could still find plenty of liquor just outside the fort boundaries however.

Private Edward D. Bolton, Company H of the 25th, visited Allen's Club, located on the Bitterroot River near the fort on the evening of October, 18th, 1897. Allen's Club enticed the soldiers with whiskey and card games, with beans used instead of poker chips. According to the account in the *Daily Missoulian*, "The game had proceeded along until a late hour. Drinks were downed with regulation regularity and when it got along toward four o'clock this morning the players were feeling just full enough to dispute over minor things." Fellow soldier Elias King accused Bolton of anteing only 19 beans when he should have anted 20. Bolton exploded in anger, "calling King all the vile names he could lay his tongue to." King tried to calm Bolton, who instead drew a razor, grabbed a chunk of firewood, and went after King, who in turn pulled out a .38 revolver and fired several shots. Shot in the thigh and head, Bolton fell mortally wounded. King traveled to Missoula and voluntarily surrendered to the city's night policeman, who turned him over to Sheriff McLaughlin. Bolton was buried in Section A, plot 21 of the Fort Missoula cemetery on the day after his death. At some point Bolton's marble headstone was stolen from the cemetery by vandals. It was unearthed at the base of a spruce tree at the Rattlesnake Nursery gardens in 1988, 91 years after the shooting.

Indian Troubles

The Missoula County sheriff requested assistance from the troops at Fort Missoula on June 11, 1889. The sheriff wanted to arrest some troublesome Indians at Ravalli who were wanted for murder. Two Spokanes, Pierre Paul and La La See, plus two Kootenais named Antley and Pascal, embittered by past injustices, had killed several white men since 1887. The murderers were protected by friends and relatives on the Reservation, plus a band of armed followers who guarded the roads. Colonel Andrews replied to the sheriff that he could not send troops unless he received a formal request from the Indian Agent, and the sheriff decided to wait on the arrests. On June 24 an excited deputy sheriff arrived at the fort and again requested soldiers and arms, but Andrews gave the same reply. The sheriff attempted the arrests on his own, resulting in the shooting of an Indian. Fearing an uprising on the reservation, Indian Agent Peter Ronan sent a telegram to Andrews on June 25, asking for the immediate dispatch of troops. Andrews sent Captain Gaines Lawson and three companies to the Reservation by train, and Ronan had them camp at the Agency until an Indian council was completed. Presence of 130 soldiers calmed the situation, but the troops remained until July 9, when two companies returned home. The third company remained an additional three days at the request of the governor.

The buffalo soldiers endured subzero temperatures at Fort Keogh. This photo was taken December 14, 1890 by Christian Barthelmess. A hand-written note on the back reflects the routine prejudice the soldiers encountered. The photo is described as, "Some of the coons that are in camp at Keogh."
LC-DIG-ppmsca-11406

Two of the companies stationed at the fort, K & I, were skeletonized in 1890 due to orders from the War Department, with their men and officers transferred to other companies. That same year Captain D.B. Wilson took one of the 25th Infantry company's to Demersville (south of Kalispell) after complaints from settlers of local and Canadian Indians causing trouble. Wilson's men arrived on April 7, 1890.

After surveying the situation, Wilson decided most of the problems could be alleviated if the settlers would stop selling whiskey to the Indians. Nevertheless, his company remained in the area until July 19th, when it was replaced by another company, that stayed until September. In August Chief Aneas Paul delivered three of the wanted men to the Sheriff, and the fourth was captured a few days later. Pierre Paul, La La See, Antley, and Pascal were found guilty of murder, and despite Agent Ronan's objection, received the death penalty. The four Indians were hung together in Missoula on December 19, 1890.

Lieutenant Colonel Van Horn led Companies C, E, F & H (the latter two from Fort Missoula) to Fort Keogh on November 29, 1890 in response to the "Ghost Dance" rebellion of the Sioux at the Pine Ridge and Rosebud Reservations in South Dakota. According to the *Yellowstone Journal and Livestock Reporter* of December 6, 1890, "Two companies (colored) from Fort Missoula arrived at Keogh yesterday morning and three of the same darky hues from Fort Shaw are expected today."

The soldiers of the 25th Infantry acted as a reserve force and did not see action during this campaign, although they did endure temperatures of negative 19 degrees while they were camped out in Sibley tents. The chaplain at Fort Keogh, Father E.W.J. Lindesmith, was invited to dine with the soldiers, and on December 5, 1890 he shared their baked beans, rice, bacon, and boiled beef, and engaged the soldiers in a discussion of religion. According to Lindesmith, the soldiers of the 25th Infantry, "were a credit to themselves and their officers." The soldiers stayed at Fort Keogh for another two months, until February 5, 1891.

Chief Charlo and the Bitterroot Salish

One of the justifications for building Fort Missoula was the presence of hundreds of non-treaty Salish living in the Bitterroot Valley. Under pressure from the government, in time most of the Bitterroot Salish had reluctantly moved north to the Jocko Reservation in order to get government assistance, and by the mid-1880s only Chief Charlo and a few hundred stubborn followers still clung to their ancestral land in the Bitterroot. The commanding officer of the fort had requested government aid be given to the Bitterroot Salish in 1880 due to their "splendid conduct" during the Nez Percé war. The Salish had watched helplessly as the Missoula and Bitterroot Valley Railroad was built through their property without permission or compensation in 1887, although Lt. Col. Horace Jewett, the commander at the fort, had tried to stop construction. Charlo's people were destitute by the time General Henry Carrington arrived in 1889 to negotiate a new agreement with the Salish. After years of resistance Charlo, who had simultaneously kept peace with the white settlers in western Montana for decades while resisting every effort to leave his home, reluctantly agreed that his hungry people would move to the Jocko Reservation. The agreement was signed on November 3, 1889, but Congress delayed passing the needed law. Expecting to move, the Salish did not plant any crops in 1890, and were near starvation when they finally received $1,500 from the government to buy rations. Thirty-six years after the Hellgate Treaty included a deceptive clause designed to rid the Bitterroot Valley of Indians, the proud Salish tearfully bid goodbye to their homeland on October 15, 1891. Although some modern accounts claim the Salish were forcibly removed from the Bitterroot by Fort Missoula soldiers, there is no evidence to support that claim. Charlo had asked that there not be a military escort, a request which Colonel Carrington indicated he would respect. "The Fort Missoula correspondence, post orders, and post returns indicate that the Fort Missoula soldiers were not involved with the

Chief Charlo and a few hundred other Salish resisted leaving their traditional home in the Bitterroot Valley for decades.
LC-USZ62-116119

Salish march to Jocko."[5] Charlo and his roughly 200 followers, accompanied by 400 horses and a handful of cows, camped the first night on the Maclay Ranch near Lolo. The next morning the elders of the tribe paraded across the Higgins Bridge in their best clothes, with the young men blocking the cross streets to allow the column to pass. They arrived at the southern end of the Jocko Reservation on October 17, 1891. Many of the Salish walked the entire 75 miles to their new home. "Chief Charlot's countenance retained its habitual expression of stubborn pride and gloom, as he advanced on foot, shaking hands with all who had come to greet him," Mary Ronan wrote to her son.[6] Houses were built for the new arrivals, and they were given rations, but not everything they had been promised. Chief Charlo successfully prevented violence between the Salish and white settlers during his lifetime, but never forgave the whites who had betrayed his people. He died early in 1910, just before the Flathead Reservation was thrown open to white settlement in violation of the Hellgate Treaty which his father Victor had signed.

Police Duty

Many Cree Indians fled to Montana after the Riel Rebellion in Canada during 1885. With no land of their own, they wandered from place to place, dependent on handouts from the military, citizens, and other tribes. They were repeatedly denied their own small reservation and were never far from starvation. Reacting to citizen complaints about the "dirty Cree," in 1896 Congress appropriated $5,000 to round up the bands roaming throughout Montana and deport them to Canada. Military units around the state received orders to detain and deport all of the Cree. Lieutenant John J. Pershing of the 10th Cavalry rounded up the first group near Fort Assiniboine, where many Cree had been employed as woodcutters. Pershing also traveled to Fort Missoula, where the soldiers persuaded a large band of Cree to voluntarily return to Canada. The 25th Infantrymen helped police western Montana and the Flathead Reservation, but the roundup snared Indians from many tribes, complicating the task of the soldiers. At first the Cree were deported to Canada by rail, but when funds ran out 192 men, women, and children were forced to walk from Helena to the Canadian border, a journey in which several of the tribal elders died along the way.

Some Cree were arrested upon reaching Canada, while others were relocated to Canadian reservations. Many of the Cree, however, immediately returned to the United States, and in some cases beat the soldiers who had detained them home. The government finally set aside the Rocky Boy Reservation in 1916 for some of the "landless Indians" of the Cree and Chippewa tribes.

Two small boys keep a close eye on Indian visitors to the fort.
UM 98-0241

Labor troubles erupted during the summer of 1892 in the Coeur d'Arlene mining district in Idaho. Miners went on strike over a pay cut and longer hours, and on the 4th of July of that year union men defaced an American flag. Within the week explosions rocked a number of mines, and several company men were killed and wounded by gunfire and explosions. Hundreds of non-union men brought in as strikebreakers were taken captive by the striking miners, and the governor of Idaho declared martial law. Three companies (F, G, and H) of the 25th Infantry, comprised of seven officers and 148 men, were dispatched from Fort Missoula to Idaho by rail at 8:30 a.m. on July 12. They had orders to report to Colonel William P. Carlin of the 4th Infantry. They arrived at Mullan early the next morning to find the track ahead had been blown up by strikers. The officers telegraphed their situation to Colonel Carlin, and were ordered to proceed by the Coeur d'Alene, Harrison and Union Pacific Railroad to Wardner Junction, which they reached on the evening of the 14th. For the next two weeks they guarded trains, depots, and railroad yards. During the course of their duties they arrested strikers, scouted for trouble, and provided armed escorts for citizens. They returned to Fort Missoula by train on July 28.

The 53 men of Company F returned to Idaho during the early winter of 1893 at the request of Colonel Carlin. The Colonel's son, also named William, was overdue on a hunting trip along the Clearwater River. Company F marched the 90 miles to Clearwater in an unsuccessful attempt to find the lost hunting party. The hunters, minus one ill member who had been left to die in the snow, were eventually rescued by a unit from the 4th Infantry. The men from Fort Missoula marched home in the snow after being in the field from November 10th to the 24th.

The financial panic of 1893 caused numerous banks, railroads, and mines to fail, which resulted in tremendous unrest among ordinary workers. By 1894 unemployed men in the Midwest under the leadership of Jacob Coxey began a protest march on Washington DC. News of this protest march was embraced by unemployed railroad workers and miners in the Pacific Northwest. As trouble looked increasingly likely, the garrison at Fort Missoula was beefed up. On May 6, 1894 Company B of the 25th Infantry arrived from Fort Buford, North Dakota. At the end of the month Lieutenant D.B. Wilson led Companies B and G to Arlee to assist US Marshals, just as the situation deteriorated. "Coxeyites" hijacked a train in Noxon, although it was soon recaptured in Thompson Falls, and several members of "Coxey's Army" from the west coast were arrested. The soldiers remained on alert for the next month.

Almost simultaneously, the American Railway Union went on strike throughout much of the country in supports of striking workers at the Pullman factory in Illinois. Railroads throughout the state were shut down, and vandals attacked railway property. President Grover Cleveland ordered the Army to make sure strikers did not interfere with the railroads, and the Adjutant General authorized "necessary force" to protect property of the Northern Pacific Railroad (NP). During July, August, and September of 1894 nearly the entire 25th Infantry was employed in guarding property and preventing vandalism by strikers... Companies B and H guarded NP property in Missoula during the week of July 8-15. The situation was so dire that local businessmen E.L. Bonner and A.B. Hammond asked that two troops of cavalry be stationed at the fort, and offered to build barracks for them. Reinforcements would have been welcome, as the soldiers were confronted with large numbers of angry strikers. Historian John M. Carroll wrote in *The Black Military Experience in the American*

Men of the 25th Infantry drill with a Gatling gun on the parade ground at Fort Missoula while a small boy (far right) watches them.
UM 84.0332

The soldiers of the 25th Infantry marched all over western Montana. This formal pose may have been taken near Lolo Hot Springs
UM-Elrod Collection B,I j-3

West that, "The troops did not make themselves very popular while serving as policemen during the military control of the Northern Pacific Railroad in Missoula, Montana, either. They executed their responsibilities in the best military manner but won nothing but the dislike and distrust of the civilians - in a situation that was strained to begin with because the troops were black."

Company F traveled to O'Keefe's Canyon near Evaro on July 8 to guard two iron railroad trestles. Lieutenant Caldwell and 26 men guarded O'Keefe's trestle, while Captain Andrews and 26 men guarded Marent's trestle. On July 29 Captain Andrews and 31 men returned to Missoula, leaving Caldwell and 17 men to guard the two trestles. Caldwell's detachment was relieved on August 15.

Companies A and D from Fort Custer were sent to Livingston on July 8, 1894. Company A guarded Northern Pacific bridges, rolling stock, and workshops around Big Timber, while Company D did the same in the Livingston area. These men were in the field until early September.

Captain Charles L. Hodges and Company H spent most of the summer in Anaconda. "There were several instances when blunder might have led to serious results, but at these times the conduct of the men was admirable."[7] The *Anaconda Standard* declared, "...the conduct of the soldiers, during the time that they were on duty here, was exemplary, and demonstrated beyond a doubt the excellence of the Negro as a soldier..." Railroad authorities also praised the soldiers, and even the strikers were quoted as saying "... if the soldiers had to be called out there could have been none better than the companies of the 25th Infantry who were encamped here."[8]

"When asked by a *Standard* reporter the other day as to the disciplinary measures necessary to handle his command, Captain Hodges replied, "There are none. The men are soldiers because they like the life, and during the time that we have been in camp here there has not been an instance of insubordination, and not a man has been punished, simply because it wasn't necessary."[9] Once the Army reopened the rail lines, the strike lost momentum and at the end of the summer the soldiers returned to their post. "The men are orderly and quiet, and all who have visited the post and studied existing conditions involuntarily share the pride which Colonel Burt and his officer feel in the Twenty-fifth Infantry. It is a splendid regiment and worthy of unstinted praise."[10]

The 25th Infantry Regimental Band

The musicians stationed at Fort Missoula soon became very popular with local citizens. Shortly after arriving at the fort, the marching band of the 25th Infantry led the Memorial Day parade through downtown, and "discoursed the sweetest music ever heard in Missoula along the line of march."[1]

The musicians of the 25th Infantry Regimental Band were popular throughout western Montana.
UM-Elrod Collection B,I.j-4

The band began giving regular concerts every Thursday evening, and once the word got out, other communities around the state requested the band for performances, although Colonel Andrews felt it necessary to inform them that the soldiers were "colored."

When leading Missoula citizen C.P. Higgins died in 1889, the funeral procession was led by the Regimental Band, which was given a place of honor just in front of the Masons.

A Celebrity Arrives at the Fort

Noted American writer and humorist Mark Twain found himself deeply in debt by 1895 due to failed publishing and printing ventures. Twain owed $160,000, much of it borrowed from his wife's estate, and in desperation embarked on a world-wide speaking tour in 1895 to pay off his debts. The year-long adventure was billed as "Mark Twain's Tour Around the World." His wife and daughter accompanied him, as did his business manager Major J.B. Pond and his wife.

Two weeks after beginning the tour he appeared in Great Falls, where the ailing 59-year-old Twain gave a lackluster performance. He had a much better reception in Butte, but found disappointing audiences in Anaconda and Helena. He was not originally scheduled to perform in Missoula, so Mrs. Elizabeth Burt, wife of Fort Missoula's commander, was understandably upset when she received a message from her husband at 2:00 pm on August 5 that read, "Mark Twain, his wife and daughter, will dine with us today." This brief notice sent Mrs. Burt into a panic. The garden yielded fresh lettuce and peas, while the "chicken coop supplied fine broilers. Our good black cook did her best and had a soup and salad." By the time the Twain family arrived, the round table was decorated with fresh-cut roses, the silver had been polished, fresh ice cream had been made, and the coffee was brewed. The dinner guests were unaware of the, "most trying occasion" their trip had caused, and after dinner were entertained by a short band concert before Twain headed off to his lecture.

Twain spoke at the Bennett Theatre in Missoula in a two-story brick building, with tickets priced at less than a dollar. The officers of Fort Missoula and their families made up a large percentage of the audience in the small hall. Dressed in a suit and a white shirt, Twain was described as "this justly celebrated genius."

"...He speaks with a twang and a drawl that is in keeping with his humor and would be amusing if he were speaking solemnly, but when it is used in telling funny stories it is more than amusing, it produces spontaneous laughter in every audience he has ever tried it on." [11] "The audience was large, select and fashionable and thoroughly in touch with their intellectual entertainer."

The officers had come up with an elaborate ruse to trick the noted humorist at a reception after the lecture. Every time Twain tried to tell a story, he was interrupted by one of the officers, who begged to tell his own story, followed immediately by a story from another officer, until Twain declared, "I beg you give me just one chance." Realizing the joke was on him, Twain declared "Say boys, I haven't had one put over me as good as that since the old Comstock days."[12] Major Pond reported "The day has been one of delight to all of us."

The next morning Twain and his family returned to Fort Missoula for a parade by the regimental band and the fort's garrison, followed by lunch. Twain attempted to walk to the fort, but lost his way, and was picked up by Major Pond in an Army ambulance. Upon arriving, Pond reported that the practical jokes continued when a black NCO approached Twain and informed him, "I have orders to arrest and take you to the guardhouse." Twain was marched across the parade ground to the guardhouse, where Colonel Burt rescued him.

That afternoon Twain's party caught the train to Spokane, but he would write, "In my preliminary run through the smaller cities on the northern route I have found a reception the cordiality of which has touched my heart and made me feel how small a thing money is in comparison with friendship."[13]

Mark Twain's business manager, Major Pond, took this photo of the famous author and humorist visiting with Colonel Burt at Fort Missoula.

Courtesy of Mark Twain Archive, Gannett-Tripp Library, Elmira College, N.Y.

A rare look inside an unknown Fort Missoula building in the 1890s. The room is highly decorated with several American flags, animal pelts, Chinese lanterns, woven rugs, stacked rifles, and a star-shaped wall-hanging made of cavalry sabers.
UM Elrod Collection B-I_j-06

Lieutenant Moss had his men practice fording rivers and overcoming obstacles to prepare them for the trip to St. Louis. The men of the Bicycle Corps found that weather, poor roads, flat tires and inadequate food were their biggest challenges on the trip.
Photo by Edward Boos. UM 672-239

Lieutenant Moss and the fully-loaded members of the Bicycle Corps practiced for their trip to St. Louis in 1897. Most of their gear was wrapped in a shelter half and strapped to the handlebars, with the rest stored in a case between the frame. The soldiers carried the heavy Krag-Jorgenson rifle over their shoulders the entire trip, resulting in several damaged rifles.
UM 73-31

5

The Bicycle Corps

"A Bicycle Corps pulls out ahead. It is heavy wheeling and pretty bumpy on the grass, where they are compelled to ride, but they managed far better than one would anticipate."

Fredric Remington- 1896

Wheelmen in Blue

A number of officers in the Army, National Guard, and military academies experimented with the military use of bicycles in the early 1890s, but bikes really didn't come to the attention of the US Army until General Nelson Miles became interested in bicycle troops during the early 1890s. Miles ran into resistance from the Army brass, but various posts, particularly in the Department of Dakota, experimented with bicycles.

Fueled by cut-rate prices, vastly improved "safety bike" designs, and the introduction of pneumatic tires, bicycling enjoyed a tremendous popularity during the 1890s. Bicycle racing and long distance touring became popular, and the regular *New York Times* feature, "News For The Wheelmen," kept readers abreast of other new technological developments like the diamond frame, pneumatic tires, ball bearings, coaster brakes, cushioned saddles, and adjustable handle bars.

Safer and more reliable bicycles resulted in more than two million bikes sold in the US between 1894 and 1897. General Nelson Miles, who would soon become Commanding General of the US Army, started promoting the military use of the bicycle as early as 1891 after he took up bicycling himself in his fifties. European armies had been experimenting with bicycles since the 1870s, and by 1895 General Miles advocated for the establishment of a full regiment of bicycle soldiers. Various National Guard units, citizen militias and military academies formed small-scale bicycle corps, and several authors produced unofficial manuals for military bicycling. Most of the early experiments focused on delivering messages over long distances.

Fresh from West Point, a far-sighted young 2nd Lieutenant named James A. Moss arrived at Fort Missoula. He read military journals to pass the time, and was inspired by several articles describing the military potential of the bicycle, and the experiments of several European armies with bikes. Moss suggested to Colonel Burt that Fort Missoula would be an ideal location to form a bicycle corps. "I am very desirous of organizing at this post a detachment of cycle infantry," he wrote. "I am very anxious to test the practicability of the bicycle in going over some of our mountain trails."[1]

Moss's letter eventually made its way to General Miles, who quickly approved it upon the condition that Moss acquire the needed equipment at no cost to the Army. Lieutenant Moss convinced the A.G. Spalding Co. to donate 10 bicycles to the Army in May 1896. Spalding hoped to secure a lucrative future contract with the Army. These bikes arrived in July, and were soon equipped with lamps, air pumps, spare parts, and cyclometers (a brand new device that measured mileage by counting the rotation of the wheels). They also had wooden rims, which soon rotted.

Moss polled the soldiers at the post and found 46 who had experience riding. Moss chose eight men from companies B, F, and H, including Private John Findley, who had spent four years working as a bicycle mechanic for Imperial Bicycles. The fledgling Bicycle Corps began daily practice rides of 15 miles, and soon worked their way up to 40 miles per day. Moss determined that the cost of the bicycle corps was one-third less than that of a comparable cavalry outfit covering the same territory. Moss sent his uniformed cyclists pedaling through the valleys of western Montana in the summer of 1896. At first the bicycle corps specialized in delivering messages to remote outposts. Moss spent three weeks in late July and August drilling the men, utilizing the several manuals that had been produced, and soon found the prescribed drills were impractical at best. Riding in formation was particularly troublesome, although the men soon mastered crossing fences, and developed techniques to cross streams as well. During this period they rode from 15 to 40 miles per day, carrying their rifles and equipment. Finally Moss received permission to take an overnight trip to Lake McDonald, near St. Ignatius. Moss kept meticulous records of every item of equipment carried by each of the seven men on the trip. The average weight of each bicycle loaded with gear was 76.2 pounds, while the riders averaged 155.7 pounds. Hampered by mud, they covered 51 miles in 13 hours, and camped at Mission Creek. Food on the trip consisted mainly of fresh biscuits, bacon, and beans. They also carried smaller amounts of deviled ham, Armour's beef extract, rice, prunes, canned corn, syrup, coffee, sugar, baking powder, salt, pepper, and lard. Their rations were supplemented by fresh trout caught in Lake McDonald. They also carried a change of clothes, a blanket, shelter half (half of a two man tent), personal gear, cooking equipment, hatchets, and spare parts and tools for the bicycles. Half of the soldiers carried a nine-pound regulation 1892 .30-40 Krag-Jorgensen rifle and 30 rounds of ammunition, while the other half carried .38 caliber revolvers and 30 rounds of ammunition.

The bicycle soldiers returned to Fort Missoula on August 9th after two days of rain storms and slogging through mud. Despite the mud and hardships, Moss considered the first ride to be a success, and almost immediately asked permission to take his Bicycle Corps on a ride to Yellowstone National Park, a much more ambitious trip. For this ride the Corps consisted of nine men, plus extra bike parts, a rudimentary medical kit, and a 4x5 Kodak camera. They left for Yellowstone at just after 6:00 in the morning, on August 15, only six days after returning from the previous ride. On the second day, one man fell out with intestinal cramps, and Moss gave him money to return to Missoula by train. It took the remaining riders three days to ride over the Continental Divide to Helena. They spent a night at Fort Harrison, where they replenished their supplies, then pushed on to Townsend the following morning. After the usual flat tires and mechanical breakdowns, they crossed the Missouri River in the dark, and reached camp at 9:30 that evening. Their route took them to Three Forks, and then on to Bozeman. Proceeding on, they rode past the remains of Fort Ellis, abandoned ten years before, and soon encountered a detachment of infantry, as well as a company of the 10th Cavalry from Fort Assiniboine, accompanied by famous western artist Frederic Remington. Although Remington failed to produce a painting of the Bicycle Corps, he did record his perception of the men. "A Bicycle Corps pulls out ahead. It is heavy wheeling and pretty bumpy on the grass, where they are compelled to ride, but they managed far better than one would anticipate."

On the day before they reached Fort Yellowstone the corps recorded that all of the tires were rotting, the tires of two bicycles were completely shot, and seven hours were spent repairing tires so the Corps could ride the last six hours. They spent 36 hours at Fort Yellowstone, where they restocked their rations before heading into Yellowstone National Park on August 25. The soldiers especially enjoyed shaking hands with each other while standing on opposite sides of the Continental Divide. When a tourist asked a soldier where they were going, the soldier famously replied, "we just following the lieutenant." The Bicycle Corps left Yellowstone Park on September 1, and the riders were again plagued by rain and equipment breakdowns. One of the wooden rims fell apart near Bozeman, but later that they day they encountered a "bicycle tramp," who had been riding over several western states. For $3 he offered to ride the six miles into Bozeman, purchase a new rim, and return before 6:00 a.m. the following morning, a feat he successfully accomplished. With all of their bicycles back in action, the Corps returned to the fort on September 8, after traveling 790 miles in 16 days.

Moss seemed determined to squeeze in as much training as possible before winter set in. Shortly after returning home from Yellowstone, the soldiers of the Bicycle Corps conducted exercises with other units of the 25th on September 13th. They scouted ahead of the main column, served as couriers, and identified potential campsites. When inclement weather shut down the activities of the Bicycle Corps, the soldiers returned to their regular duties, and the bicycles, somewhat the worse for wear, were returned to the Spalding Company.

Lieutenant Moss filed numerous reports on the successes and failures of the Bicycle Corps, and General Nelson Miles soon recommended to a Congressional committee in December that every infantry regiment establish a bicycle corps of 10 men or more. He even suggested that the Army manufacture its own bicycles. Neither idea went anywhere.

Despite the hardships, the trip to Yellowstone National Park had proved successful enough that Lieutenant Moss decided to push his Bicycle Corps to the limit, and during the winter of 1896 he planned an ambitious new trip. On January 22, 1897, he requested permission to lead 20 riders on a trip from Fort Missoula to St. Louis, Missouri. Although it seemed an arbitrary destination, Moss had thought about this carefully. "By selecting St. Louis as our objective, we had a long route with high and low altitudes; moist and dry climates; up grades and down grades; the mountainous and stony roads of Montana; the hummock earth roads of South Dakota; the sandy roads of Nebraska and the clay roads of Missouri." Since many of the roads in the West were little more than unimproved horse trails, Moss planned to follow the route of the new Northern Pacific railroad to Billings, then along the route of the Burlington railroad to St. Louis.

Both Colonel Burt and General Miles supported Moss's proposal, and the Secretary of War approved a round trip to St. Louis of 3,800 miles, with the condition that the trip could be accomplished without any additional costs to the War Department. Moss was sent on detached duty from Fort Missoula to prepare for this trip. Moss traveled to the East Coast, where he made a "profound study" of bicycles, tactics, tires, and equipment. He also wrote several articles and pamphlets describing the experiences of his Bicycle Corps the previous summer, and visited a number of bicycle manufacturers, seeking an improved machine for his proposed trip. The publicity also brought a number of suggestions from inventors for improved gear, although many of these suggestions were of little practical use.

Blowouts and flat tires had plagued the Corps the year before, and Moss ordered tires from several different manufacturers. The Spalding Company once again manufactured the bicycles used for the trip, with several modifications suggested by Moss. Most importantly, the new bicycles would have experimental metal rims on the wheels, rather than the problematic wooden rims used the year before, along with improved spokes. The new Spalding "Army Bicycle" arrived on June 4, 1897. They were based on the regular 1897 models, a medium-quality bike which sold new for fifty dollars. The "Army Bicycle" had a strengthened frame, a cover over the gears, luggage racks, and a specially designed metal pan to hold mess gear and provisions. The soldiers added such innovations as toe clips, cyclometers and custom-made gear cases designed to protect the chain from mud. Fully outfitted, the bikes weighed 59 pounds.

Moss returned to Fort Missoula in June 1897 and began recruiting a new Bicycle Corps. Five of the soldiers from the previous year signed up as did 35 rookies, most likely because the Bicycle Corps provided an opportunity to break the monotonous routine of life at the post. The soldiers came from Companies B, F, G, and H. Moss chose 20 men for the ride. The rudimentary Army regulations on bicycling required a medical officer along on the trip, and the duty fell to the regiment's Assistant Surgeon, J.M. Kennedy. Unlike the other members of the Bicycle Corps, Kennedy was a reluctant recruit, although he was technically Moss's second in com-

The Bicycle Corps pushed their bicycles to the top of Minerva Terrace at Mammoth Hot Springs in Yellowstone National Park in 1896.
MHS Haynes Foundation Collection 36-16

mand. Bicycle enthusiast Edward H. Boos, a reporter from the *Daily Missoulian*, also accompanied the expedition. A new but important addition to the Corps was Sergeant Mingo Sanders, respected by the men and relied on by Moss. A lance corporal headed up each of the two squads. Moss immediately began training rides, extending the distance and difficulty day by day.

Moss was nothing if not a meticulous planner, and he laid out a detailed route to St. Louis that predicted an eight-day journey through Montana, six days to cross a corner of Wyoming and a sliver of South Dakota, then 21 days across Nebraska, and finally six days through Missouri. Moss chose his route carefully, shipping rations, supplies and spare bicycle parts to 19 railroad stations along the route, no more than two days apart. (The necessity of stockpiling rations all along the way raised questions about the viability of long distance use of bicycles in actual warfare.) Moss also took along a wide variety and large quantity of spare parts for the bicycles, including spare rims, a selection of tools, and patch kits. Every other soldier carried either a wrench or oil can. To fix flat tires, there were 10 repair kits, an air pump for every three soldiers, and five pounds of tire cement. Each man was expected to carry about 50 pounds worth of gear on his bicycle. Moss carried a revolver, one soldier had a shotgun, and the rest carried the standard 9-pound Krag-Jorgensen rifle on their backs, as well as 50 rounds of ammunition in a canvas belt around their waists. The men also carried a canteen on their bodies, while the rest of the gear was strapped to the bicycle itself. Moss meticulously worked out where each piece of gear would be carried. A leather strap secured each man's coffee cup under the seat of the bicycle, while every other man carried a coffee pot, stuffed with a blanket, on his handle bars. A canvas bag was hung inside the diamond frame, and a tin case with cooking utensils and all of the rations rested on the frame and was strapped to the handlebars. The handlebars also held a knapsack, with blanket roll, shelter half, and tent poles strapped above it. Every two men shared a towel and bar of soap, while the squad leaders each had a comb, brush, and box of matches.

The Epic Trip to St. Louis

A local newspaper described the US Army's first extensive test of the bicycle as, "Bad roads, Hard Winds, Alkali Water, Rattlesnakes and many other pleasures." Armed with the grandiose title of the Fort Missoula Bicycle Corps, twenty-three soldiers pedaled their heavy, balloon-tired bicycles past the front gate on a cloudy gray day in 1897. The "wheelmen" faced 1,900 miles of unpaved roads. Along the way they would encounter blizzards, hailstorms, rattlesnakes, intense heat, and roads that were never intended for bicycling.

Less than two weeks after the new bicycles arrived from the factory, the morning cannon salute at 5:40 in the morning on June 14, 1897 announced the departure of the twenty-three cyclists from Fort Missoula. Besides Lt. Moss, the expedition included Army surgeon Jason M. Kennedy, reporter Edward H. Boos of the *Daily Missoulian*, Sergeant Mingo Sanders, two corporals and 17 privates. Boos, the only civilian on the trip, wore captain's insignia and signed his correspondence "Official reporter 25th US Infantry Bicycle Corps." He rode a 25-pound Sterling bicycle, and his articles were picked up by newspapers from San Francisco to New York. It was a cloudy gray day when they pedaled their heavy, balloon-tired bicycles past the front gate of Fort Missoula.

Townspeople cheered as the soldiers pedaled through downtown Missoula, but the cheers soon gave way to the sound of falling raindrops. It first rained at Blackfoot, falling in sheets, soaking the soldiers and weighing down their already heavy equipment. Much of the soil around Missoula consisted of a sticky gumbo clay deposited by Glacial Lake Missoula tens of thousands of years earlier. If the bicyclists traveled on the already rutted roads, this clay clung to boots, wheels, spokes, gears and pedals, and had to be regularly scraped off with a knife or stick. According to Boos, "The soil in these woods is a black, clayey composition called 'gumbo' and is the terror of any wheeled vehicle..." The soldiers followed the Blackfoot River to Clearwater Junction, and found it easier to ride on the vegetated ground on the side of the road. They continued through Ovando and halted for the night at Cottonwood Creek near Helmville after an arduous ride of 54 miles. The rain continued throughout the night and the next morning, and they were forced to retreat to the nearby graveled and graded railroad bed of the Northern Pacific Railroad. The mud and rain continued through Avon, and they had to walk nearly to Elliston. Four days after leaving the fort, they reached Mullan Pass, and crossed the Continental Divide in a blinding storm that dumped several inches of fresh snow and limited visibility to twenty feet. Rather than pushing their way uphill through sticky mud, now the challenge was to keep the bicycles from rolling out of control down the mountain. "The ascent was a great test for the machines and for physical endurance, but it was easy compared with the descent." They walked their bikes down the steep grade on the eastern side of the Rocky Mountains late on the afternoon of the 15th. Boos reported that on some sections they were forced to carry their bicycles on their shoulders. They slipped and slid through torrents of water which ran down the pass, cursing all the way, and by nightfall reached Fort Harrison, their first resupply spot that lay just outside of Montana's capital city of Helena. "A wetter, chilled, or more fatigued body never stopped to rest." After a day's rest, they pedaled eastward again, but the roads were so poor that the cyclists rode much of the way along railroad tracks, their heavy bikes jolting over every tie. Punctures, often caused by prickly pear cactus, were a constant problem, but on the following day they made good progress through Townsend and camped that night on the banks of the Gallatin River. On the following day they passed through the small town of Logan, named after Captain Logan of the 7th Infantry who had died at the Battle of the Big Hole.

Pushing on, they found that local farmers in the Gallatin Valley were irrigating their fields and the roads were covered with standing water. Closer to Bozeman they encountered terrific ruts in the road, and several soldiers had accidents that damaged the bicycles. They regrouped when they reached Bozeman late that afternoon, and paraded through town in formation. "The citizens turned out and showed much interest."[2] They pushed on for another two hours that night, climbing up the Bozeman Pass, covering 50 miles for the day. The next morning they passed through Livingston, where much of the town turned out to see them. The Big Timber wheelmen rode to Livingston to accompany them to Big Timber, where they encountered an Army veteran, who insisted they proceed to the nearest bar and have a drink with him. Local bicyclists accompanied them as they left town. They dined that night on rabbit and curlew shot by the side of the road. Fresh game was a luxury. One of the enlisted men told a newspaper reporter in St. Louis that while chickens were plentiful along the route, "the Army regulations are very strict, and we did not have any chance to get 'em. We had to cook our own food on the way, and officers would have soon detected the odor, and an inquiry would have resulted."[3] Moss wanted to make a good impression, and even though the soldiers tended to get strung out for miles along the road, he insisted they assemble to ride together through each town as they passed through the small towns of the Yellowstone Valley. The cyclists routinely encountered massive potholes, vicious dogs, and the resentment of many. Although people in almost every town turned out to see the column of blue-coated soldiers on bicycles, many people viewed all "wheelmen" with suspicion. It was not uncommon for horsemen and wagon drivers to deliberately block roads or try and drive the cyclists from the roads. Young boys often threw rocks or thrust sticks into their

Due to the muddy and often impassable roads encountered during the arduous trip to St. Louis, the "wheelmen" often found it easier to ride along the steady and firm railroad bed, despite rough going over the ties.
Photo by Edward Boos. UM 672-240

spokes. Boos reported "The country people in this part of Montana have little regard for wheelmen."

Near Laurel, they encountered "three old country women" whose team took up the whole road. "We asked for half the road and were laughed at-but we had a chance to pass and took advantage of it. The women were so surprised and astonished that they forgot about their horses, which took fright and ran off in the rough ground."[4]

The 25th Infantry cyclists had covered an estimated 421 miles by the time they reached Billings mid-morning on June 23. They stopped long enough to restock their supplies, and have new coffee pots made. Their tin coffee pots had not held together, so the replacements were made of more durable galvanized steel. The departure of several of the soldiers from Billings was delayed while a local mechanic repaired their bicycles.

After leaving the mountains behind, the soldiers assumed the trip ahead would be easier. They were wrong. Leaving Billings that evening, they pedaled up a steep grade in the face of a headwind. More rain turned the clay soil of the Crow Indian Reservation into a quagmire, and the men struggled on as best they could through the mud. "We looked at our bicycles but hardly recognized them, the mud covered every part of the machine, not a spoke was to be seen, the wheels were simply disks of gumbo." Cold and soaked, they found shelter that night in an old Indian cabin, and soon had a roaring fire going. Despite picking up two days of rations in Billings, they consumed huge amounts of calories each day, and were out of food by the next day, when the still-wet soldiers faced more hours of pushing through more mud. One unidentified enlisted man would later be quoted as saying, "one day we rode five hours on one egg and a piece of bread."[5] The mud and rain made the journey, "simply awful." Finally, and with much relief, they encountered a dry road leading downhill, and "some of the soldier's wheels ran away and one of them was badly damaged."

Fortunately, Lieutenant Moss had a spare frame and other bike parts waiting at Fort Custer when they arrived, but the bicycles were holding out better than their weary riders. Only six tire punctures, a bent wheel and a broken axle were reported during the first 500 miles. Boos reported that "After four hours of mud, hard work, and torture, machines were inspected and not a loose bolt or nut was found, proving the machines able to handle the rough usage." Boos wrote that, "At Fort Custer we had good board but too dainty for our appetites."[6] They left half their blankets at Fort Custer.

The men arrived at the Little Big Horn Battlefield on the evening of June 25, twenty-one years to the day after Lieutenant Colonel Custer and five companies of the Seventh Cavalry had ridden to their death. The Corpsmen camped that night below the battlefield, and Boos traced Custer's route on his bicycle while the others made camp and searched for relics among the piles of horse bones which still littered the battlefield. Regarding the death of Custer and his men, one of the soldiers was heard to remark, "Reckon them other boys was chawed tuh def by skeeters."[7] They rested for a full day at the battlefield, where Boos calculated they had averaged 41 miles per day, including the two rest days. They covered an average of 60 miles per day when they were riding full-time.

The Bicycle Corps stands at attention before their sergeant. The bicycles and stacked rifles can be seen in the background. Each soldier carried a canvas shelter half which could be connected to form a two-man pup tent.
UM 73-30

They crossed the flooded Little Big Horn river at least six times, carrying the bicycles across three of those crossings, but Boos found enough energy to remark on the colorful wildflowers he found in eastern Montana. The Corps endured a severe lightning storm on the road to Wyoming, and witnessed a cattle stampede. They crossed the Wyoming border under a scorching summer sun, and sheltered that night in a barn near Parkman, Wyoming. "We were glad to get out of Montana, where rain was our continual annoyance, and especially glad to get out of the Crow Reservation over which we had traveled since leaving Billings." The roads were better for cycling in Wyoming but the weather continued to plague them. After a night at the Sheridan Inn, "Buffalo Bill's Hotel" in Wyoming, where Boos, Moss, and Kennedy ate dinner. "The first square meal we have had for some time," Boos remarked.[8] "Moss had three pieces of pie."

Too little water was as much a problem in Wyoming as too much water had been in Montana, and the soldiers suffered from throat parching dust as they pedaled across the cactus-infested northeast corner of Wyoming. The only drinking water was found in stagnant railroad tanks. By the time they reached Gillette the soldiers were muddy and exhausted. They ate a midday meal in welcome shade, but once back on the road they encountered drifts of hail, "fully eight feet high" from a previous storm. The roads were blocked and they reluctantly returned to the railroad bed.

Moss decided to push on as fast as possible to get out of the Badlands. Told by locals that the road to Moorcroft was good, Moss determined to cover the intervening 30 miles as swiftly as possible. They were halfway there when the front axle of one bicycle snapped in half. With no spares to be found, Private Elwood Forman was forced to walk his bicycle the remaining 14 miles into Moorcroft. Leaving Sergeant Sanders in charge of the column, Moss and three men, including the cook, hurried on to set up camp and prepare a meal. By midnight Moss and his men had reached the railroad bed of the Burlington and Missouri. The soldiers were cold, tired and hungry, but there was no wood for a fire. Three other soldiers eventually caught up with Moss after being guided into camp by rifle shots. Exhausted, they continued riding, but one soldier soon collapsed from exhaustion and dehydration. Leaving him behind, Moss and the others pressed ahead, but an hour later Lieutenant Moss experienced hallucinations and fell to the ground in an exhausted sleep at two in the morning. The soldiers halted until morning, and it took them another hour of riding to reach Moorcroft, where they waited for the others to straggle in. After a few hours rest they started out again by mid-afternoon, and crossed into the southwest corner of South Dakota. The men hadn't had a bath in two weeks, and took advantage of a much needed swimming hole at Newcastle, Wyoming. On July 3rd they were met at Crawford, Nebraska by the band of the 9th Cavalry from Fort Robinson, who entertained them for a few hours while a local mechanic helped repair their bicycles. The cheering residents of Crawford welcomed the soldiers to the town's Fourth of July celebration, and as they rode out of town accompanied by the music of the band, "thousands of spectators who lined the sidewalks on either side of the street rent the air with the wildest cheers to speed them on their journey."

Conditions improved on the following day and the Corps covered twenty miles in an hour and a half on good roads. Their progress slowed again when they entered the Sand Hills of Nebraska and found the roads covered with eight to ten inches of fine dust. They returned once more to the railroad bed, but by this time many of the soldiers were feeling the effects of bad water, 110 degree heat, and bicycling through thick sand. Some miles past Alliance Lt. Moss and several of the other men began feeling ill from the stagnant alkali water they had been drinking. Moss, fell off his bicycle, and was so ill that the others flagged down a passing train and sent him back to Alliance. The soldiers, who had by now pedaled 1,000 miles, left Alliance on the morning of the 6th without Moss. Surgeon Kennedy was now in charge, and he had the men follow the railroad tracks to avoid the thick sand on the roads. The extreme heat began to take a toll on the men, who were still dressed in their wool uniforms. Once the doctor came down sick, it fell to reporter Boos to diagnose those who were really sick from the slackers. Near the end of the trip Private Eugene Jones declared that he was too ill and weak to continue on. Moss was convinced that Jones was a malingerer who was faking his symptoms to get a free ride to St. Louis on the train, and instead sent him back to Fort Missoula.

After recuperating, Moss caught a train from Alliance and soon rejoined his command, but he found that over half the men were sick, and several were too sick to travel in the heat. Some of these men were designated the, "sick brigade," and sent ahead by train to give them time to recuperate. The riders stayed in the Nebraska National Guard barracks that night as a huge storm raged outside, and Moss decided to spend the next day making repairs and waiting for the roads to dry. On the following day they met a family of German immigrants who plied the hungry soldiers with milk, bread, cookies, and cake. Boos reported, "when the corps left the place I dare say that not a crust remained in the bread box of the dear woman."

The stories cabled by reporter Boos created much interest in "Uncle Sam's Riders." Newspapers across the country, including the *New York Times*, closely followed the progress of the Bicycle Corps, and the uniformed "wheelmen" were such a curiosity that by the time they reached Missouri on July 17th the citizens of nearly every town turned out to see the strange sight. The cyclists were forced to camp on the statehouse lawn in Lincoln, Nebraska and were mobbed by curious citizens.

Many rural residents were suspicious of the blue-coated soldiers, and their reception was not always so cordial. The wounds of the Civil War still ran deep and Yankee soldiers, especially black Yankees, were not welcome in parts of Missouri. Lieutenant Moss authorized a midnight raid on one farmer's hen house when the man drove them off his property. Moss had earlier warned the men that foraging was a court martial offense, but on this occasion declared, "if I find a mess of chickens here in the morning, I'll consider it an act of Providence." The men dined well the next morning.

Moss felt he could read the character of the local inhabitants by the condition of the roads. "Where the roads were properly graded and well worked, the inhabitants were well informed, used modern farming implements, had fine wind-mills and other conveniences. On the other hand, where the roads were in a bad condition and evidently much neglected, the people were narrow-minded, devoid of any knowledge of the topography of the country and behind the times in everything."

Five soldiers in the "sick brigade" arrived at the fairgrounds in Hamilton, Missouri shortly after their comrades had broken camp, and pedaled on hoping to catch up. They were delayed by heavy rain at St. Charles, just 20 miles short of their ultimate destination, and used the delay to make some much needed repairs. Although most of the men were reported to be in good spirits, their bicycles and gear were worn out. The *St. Louis Post-Dispatch* reported their uniforms were dirty, faded, and worn. "Their natty blue coats couldn't be sold for just rags in a second-hand clothing store."

Forty days after leaving Fort Missoula, the soldiers of the Bicycle Corps were escorted into St. Louis by local dignitaries, bicycle clubs, mounted police, and 1,000 fellow bicyclists on July 24. Thousands of curious onlookers lined the streets as they pedaled the last few miles to their campsite at Forest Park. The bicycle clubs rode ahead to form an honor guard as the weary troopers rode to the Cottage in Forest Park. Moss, Kennedy, and Boos led the way, while the soldiers formed into columns of four. The Associated Cycling Clubs hosted a steak dinner for the enlisted men, who regaled local cyclists with their adventures, while Moss, Kennedy and Boos were entertained by the leading citizens of St. Louis. The trip was completed at 6:30 Saturday afternoon on July 24. As they pitched their tents, an estimated 10,000 citizens flocked to a reception, where the soldiers exhibited their bicycle drills.

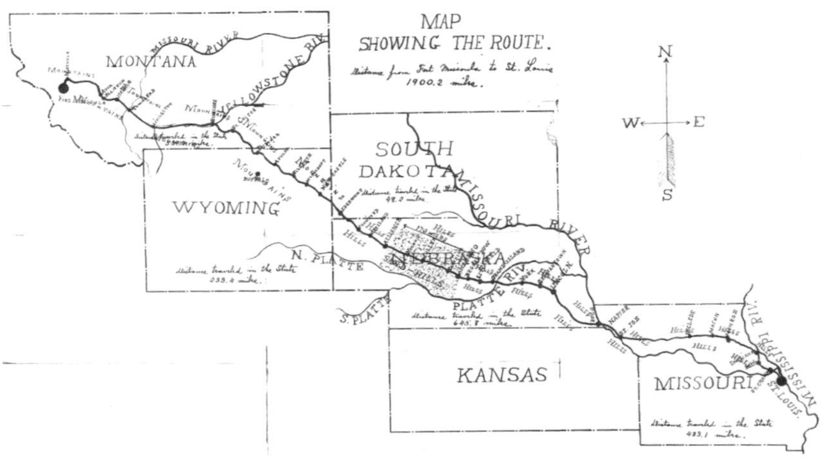

Lieutentant Moss produced this map of the journey from Fort Missoula to St. Louis. The total distance ridden was 1900.2 miles over 41 days.

Moss spent several days compiling a report for General Miles, and reported that over the 1,900-mile journey they had averaged, 6.3 miles per hour of cycling, and had made 55.6 miles per day of actual travel. Five rifles had been damaged during the ride. The meticulous Moss kept detailed records of miles traveled, condition and grade of the road, the wind and weather, and the number of hours delayed due to repairs, lunch, etc. They were on the road for 41 days, with 34 days of actual travel. Moss calculated they were delayed for 13 hours repairing bicycles, 4 hours fixing flat tires, 117 hours for lunch, and over 71 hours for other causes. "Every ounce of food eaten, every day's events, mishaps, and experiences are set down with military exactness, yet in a style that makes the subject entertaining reading for wheelmen."[9] Despite the rain which had plagued them two out of every three days, Lieutenant Moss and his men had conclusively demonstrated that bicycling was an effective means of military transportation. Although one man had been unable to keep up and had returned to Missoula halfway through the trip, the soldiers and their bicycles had stood the trip remarkably well.

They stayed in St. Louis for a week while Moss requested permission to make the return trip lightly equipped and on a route that passed through Chicago, but Miles ordered the Corps to return home on the train, news that was greeted with cheers from the soldiers. Their amazing journey over the Rocky Mountains and across the Great Plains had been chronicled by newspapers nationwide, and several European armies studied the results of Lieutenant Moss's trip. Lieutenant Moss's picture appeared in the *New York Times*, and a long interview with Boos was covered by the German paper *Anzeiger*.

Moss's report made several recommendations, first among them that every member of a bicycle corps, "should be experienced, intelligent men, who thoroughly understand, and can take care of their machines." He also stated he would not contemplate such a trip again unless the men had at least three years of bicycling experience, and recommended that any future bicycle corps have an experienced mechanic with adequate tools. He

Lieutenant James Moss

Born and raised in Louisiana, a very young James Moss graduated at the bottom of his class at West Point in 1894. Due to his low ranking the choice assignments were already taken, and he was sent to the 25th Infantry at Fort Missoula, along with his West Point classmate Lieutenant Samuel Creden. Moss and Creden shared quarters at the Fort until Creden contracted typhoid fever and died in February, 1896. Saddened by the death of his friend, Moss moved his belongings into quarters which he called the Garret, and threw himself into the research that would lead to the birth of the Bicycle Corps. A reporter for the *St. Louis Globe-Democrat* described him as "a bright and intelligent young man, of slim build, but wiry and quick in his movement." After leading the Bicycle Corps to St. Louis, Lieutenant Moss served with the 25th Infantry in Cuba and the Philippines, where he received the Silver Star for bravery. Colonel Moss commanded the 367th Infantry Regiment (also a segregated black regiment) during World War I, and wrote numerous military field manuals as well as popular books on military life and the US flag. His writings reflect his respect for the bravery and dependability of black soldiers, whom he served with for 19 years, but they also reveal a patronizing attitude typical of many white officers of the time. Moss retired from the military in 1919, but late in 1920 he was appointed a colonel in the Quartermaster Corps, and helped reform Army accounting procedures. He retired again in 1922 to write more books, and served as president of the National Flag Association, where he was instrumental in creating Flag Day.

Interviewed by the *Daily Missoulian* in 1925, Brigadier General Moss (retired) wrote, "not many years ago the bicycle was looked upon as a mere toy, a kind of 'Dandy horse' and the riders were considered as fit subjects for pity." Moss went on to say the bicycle, "bids fair to figure conspicuously in the warfare of the future." General Moss died in New York City in 1941, the victim of a car crash between a bus and the cab he was riding in. He is buried at Arlington National Cemetery, as is his old comrade, Sergeant Mingo Sanders.

Lieutentant James Moss graduated at the bottom of his class at West Point in 1894, and as a result was assigned to a black regiment at remote Fort Missoula.

Class Photo Special Collections, U.S. Military Academy Library also recommended that bicycle soldiers carry carbines rather than the longer, heavier rifles, and that all gear be carried on the frame of the bicycle, rather than on the body of the soldier. Moss made a number of recommendations for military bicycles, including tires that would not puncture, improved rims, strengthened forks and frames, shock absorbers on the front forks, and brakes. Moss recommended that bicycle corps be used primarily for courier duty, scouting, reconnaissance, and other areas where speed and stealth were necessary. Moss declared that the bicycle was better than a horse as long as the roads were not muddy and did not rise or fall more than 4.5 percent, but recommended retaining horse cavalry for the transportation of large numbers of men. Moss reported that 17 tires were destroyed and six bicycle frames were damaged, and that five of the inexperienced riders were responsible for most of the breakdowns. Five rifles were also damaged on the trip. Moss noted that during the 1,900 mile ride, the longest continuous ride was seven miles before the soldiers were forced to dismount due to hills or road conditions.[10] Moss told the *St. Louis Post-Dispatch*, "We expected hardships when we started out, but nothing like what we encountered. There was no conditions of weather we did not endure. No topographical obstacle we did not overcome. We wheeled across mountains, through sand hills and over hard and muddy roads… The trip to my thinking, established the bicycle's place in military tactics."[11]

Several European armies studied the results of the Bicycle Corp's epic journey over the Rocky Mountains and across the Great Plains on heavily loaded bicycles, and the US Army seriously considered establishing an entire regiment of bicyclists. According to one correspondent, "...the command of the regiment of bicycle infantry will be vested in Lieutenant J.A. Moss of the 25th US Infantry, who has done more for military cycling and made the matter a deeper study than any man in the Army."

The Bicycle Corp's successful journey to St. Louis proved to be the high-water mark in the US Army's short-lived experiment with bicycles.

Surgeon Kennedy told the *St. Louis Post-Dispatc*h. "Heat and cold bothered us less than hunger and thirst. We passed many sleepless nights shivering around the campfire and days when the sun beat upon the baked earth that had never known shade, but worse than that was the torture of thirst and the sickening feeling of starvation. The men stood the hardship wonderfully. They are peaked and drawn, but I hardly think they have lost weight despite constant diarrhea."

Moss also weighed and measured each of the soldiers. Some increased their muscle mass, while others lost weight. Moss wrote in his final report that, "The regulation ration is not sufficient for a cyclist who does much

After completing a reenactment of the Bicycle Corp's epic ride to St. Louis, students and faculty members from the University of Montana celebrate under the Gateway Arch.
Courtesy of Pferron Doss

The 1974 Reenactment Ride

University of Montana faculty members Pferron Doss and Richard Smith, along with student Dave Watson, decided to reenact the ride to St. Louis after researching the Bicycle Corps. They enlisted seven other students from the Black Studies Department, and left Missoula in mid-June of 1974. They were accompanied by a recreational vehicle driven by Bernestine Smith pulling a trailer with extra bicycles and parts, and kept in touch with two-way radios. Averaging 77 miles per day, they traveled between towns on the same day of the year as the original expedition, and rode from 5:30 or 6:00 a.m. to about noon. At Marysville, Missouri the entire town turned out to see them. Despite riding for the most part on paved roads with modern bicycles, they soon came to appreciate the hardships endured by their predecessors 77 years earlier. "If you really want to see the United States, get a bicycle. You see every pebble, every blade of grass," said Doss.

riding. Two days rations generally lasted us for four meals." He thought that, "The wind is one of the worst and most discouraging things to contend with."

When Moss and the men returned to Missoula, the bicycles were returned to Spalding. That winter Moss spent his time studying the experience of European conservation corps, and in February 1898 asked permission to send a 20-man corps on a ride from Fort Missoula to San Francisco and back. General Miles once again endorsed the plan, as long as it cost nothing, but the War Department refused the request, stating that sufficient experiments with the bicycle had already been made. This decision, combined with deteriorating relations with Spain, spelled the end of the Fort Missoula Bicycle Corps, but not the end of military cycling. Despite the mud that clogged their tires, the rain that soaked them day and night, and the illness, "skeeters", and exhaustion that took their toll, their 40-day journey to St. Louis proved the feasibility of using bicycles in a military context. During World War I Britain, France, Germany, Belgium, Turkey, and China fielded hundreds of thousands of bicycle troops, and bicycle troops were also used effectively by various armies during World War II and the Vietnam War.

The 25th Infantry goes to War

Colonel George H. Barton arrived at Fort Missoula in September 1897 to inspect the command. He reported, "In comparison with other battalions in the district it has no superior." Barton felt that Colonel Burt had trained the men to a high level, and declared, "The discipline of the command is praiseworthy." Despite this glowing recommendation, not all was well at Fort Missoula. Captain R.H.R. Loughborough filed a formal charge of wrongdoing against Colonel Burt on November 2, 1897. No action on his charge was taken, but six weeks later Lt. Col. A.S. Daggett also officially quarreled with Burt, who was sustained by the War Department. The *Daily Democrat Messenger* of Missoula alleged that illegal gambling was common at Fort Missoula, but world events were about to preclude any further investigation into this.

Tension between Cubans and their Spanish rulers had been growing for some time, fueled by the American newspapers owned by Joseph Pulitzer and William Randolph Hearst, which published inflammatory stories of Spanish atrocities in order to boost their readership. Their inaccurate and sensational "Yellow Journalism" helped create an anti-Spanish fervor in America. The USS *Maine* visited Cuba to help defuse tensions and protect American citizens and property, but the *Maine* blew up and sank in Havana Harbor on February 15, 1898. At least 260 American sailors were dead, and two days later the flag at Fort Missoula was lowered to half-staff. A US Court of Inquiry declared the ship had been destroyed by a Spanish naval mine, although no conclusive evidence of that has ever been found. A boiler explosion or spontaneous combustion or an undiscovered fire in the forward coal bunker which ignited the powder magazine are all likely causes of the explosion. Inflammatory coverage of the story by the Hearst and Pulitzer newspapers influenced public opinion even further. As a result, relations between the US and Spain rapidly deteriorated.

With war on the horizon, the Army on March 20, 1898 ordered the closure of Fort Missoula, citing the fact that there was no clear military reason for a fort in western Montana, as well as the fact that much of the fort was built on land the Army did not have title to.

Chaplain T.G. Steward recalled, "It was on a bright day during the latter part of March and near the close of the day as I was looking out of the front window of my quarters that I saw the trumpeter of the guard come out of the Adjutant's office with a dispatch in his hand and start on a brisk run toward the quarters of the Commanding Officer. I immediately divined what was in the wind, but kept quiet. In a few minutes "officers' call" was sounded, and all the officers of the post hastened to the administration building to learn the news." The 25th Infantry had received orders to mobilize for war, and the soldiers began boarding up the buildings at the fort and moving their furniture and other belongings into the gymnasium before their departure. The 25th Infantry was the first regiment mobilized for the war. "What could be more significant, or more fitting, than that these black soldiers, drilled up to the highest standard of modern warfare, cool, brave and confident, themselves a proof of American liberty, should be called first to the front in a war against oppression," wrote Steward.

Reveille sounded at 4:30 a.m. on April 10, 1898, and every soldier was present and accounted for. "What is more not one was found to be under the influence of liquor."[12] With the women and children following in wagons, the soldiers marched to the siding of the Bitterroot Branch and boarded a passenger train, which took them to Third Street, where they disembarked to parade up Higgins Street to the Northern Pacific Depot. Missoula citizens turned out en masse to cheer off the soldiers of the 25th. The *Daily Missoulian* reported "people were standing on every freight car and elevation, some with cameras and some without, to get a good farewell look and shot. The cheering crowd extended as far as the Rattlesnake Bridge." The popular regimental band, which would be sorely missed by the citizens of Missoula, broke into "The Girl I left Behind Me," but the music was drowned out by the cheers of the crowd.

Colonel Andrew S. Burt said of the send off, "In all my 36 years of service I have never seen a more popular turnout to bid troops farewell, with the exception probably of the time of the Civil War, than was accorded us by the people of Missoula this morning." Chaplain Steward also wrote of their departure. "Many were the compliments paid officers and men by the good people of Missoula, none perhaps more pleasing than that furnished by a written testimonial to the regret experienced at the departure of the regiment, signed by all the ministers of the city."[13]

The train took them to Helena, where they were joined by the other four companies of the 25th from Fort Harrison and Fort Assiniboine. After a parade through Helena, Colonel Burt told a reporter, "nothing would please me better than to come back to Missoula some time and spend the rest of my days, and were it not for the impending war that threatens this country, I would that this train and regiment would be ordered back to that beautiful little post on the banks of the Bitter Root."

The 25th Infantry was destined for Cuba, where tropical disease and poor rations would kill more men than Spanish bullets. Companies A and G were sent to Florida for training, while the rest of the regiment went to Georgia. Spain declared war against the US on April 24, 1898, and the US reciprocated the following day. Colonel Burt, who had commanded the 25th Infantry for the past six years, received an appointment as brevet general of volunteers in May, and he was replaced by Lt. Colonel Aaron S. Daggett. The 25th boarded ships in Florida for the short journey to Cuba, where on July 1 they led the charge at the Battle of El Caney, capturing the blockhouse at the summit. The regiment lost one officer and three enlisted men killed, with seven officers and 28 men wounded, including Private Eugene Jones, the "malingerer" who Moss sent home during the ride to St. Louis. Privates J.H. Jones of D Company and T.C. Butler of H Company captured the Spanish flag in the blockhouse, but an officer of the 12th Infantry ordered them to turn the flag over to him, and tried to claim credit, leading to an official protest by Lt. Colonel Daggett. Daggett also singled out Lieutenant Moss and two other lieutenants for gallantry

The First Battalion of the 25 Infantry Regiment marched across the Higgins Bridge for the last time in 1898 as they left Missoula for the Spanish-American War.
UM 76.0200

and "meritorious service" during the battle. Two weeks later the 25th Infantry was advancing on Santiago when the Spanish surrendered the city on July 14. Yellow fever began to decimate the American ranks, and after hostilities formally ended on August 12, 1898, most of the soldiers were sent home.

Rather than returning to Fort Missoula as Colonel Burt had hoped, after the war the 25th was sent to the southern Rockies, then on to the Philippines for a three-year stint fighting nationalists.

After returning to the States, a battalion of the 25th Infantry, including many of the officers and men who had previously served at Fort Missoula, was transferred to Brownsville, Texas in late July 1906. The black infantrymen immediately encountered intense racial prejudice. Men who had served their country for decades encountered signs that read, "no soldiers or dogs allowed." They were banned from the town after a fistfight between a soldier and a resident. Scarcely two weeks after arriving in Brownsville, a prolonged gunfight on the night of August 13, 1906 killed a bartender and wounded a policeman. It was blamed on the soldiers, despite the fact that the non-commissioned officers testified that all of the men were in their barracks at the time, with their rifles accounted for. General Andrew Burt testified before a Senate Committee that Sergeant Mingo Sanders told him. "So far as I know, our men were not in it. I tried to find out. I tried to find out if they were in it, and I am satisfied, sir, that they were not in it. I tried all I knew how." When asked if he believed Sanders, Burt replied, "Oh, he was telling absolutely the truth as he saw it, as he knew it."[14] Burt also stated "I do not mean to say that the Twenty-Fifth Infantry were all angels with wings sprouting, but they were very near it. I mean to say they were a good class of men, as a rule."[15] Nevertheless, this incident grew into a huge scandal, and President Theodore Roosevelt, who had once asked Sergeant Mingo Sanders to share rations with his Rough Riders in Cuba, signed an order to "discharge without honor" 167 soldiers of the 25th Infantry, many of them with years of loyal service, for a "conspiracy of silence." The soldiers had their pensions and back pay revoked, and were ineligible for any civil service jobs. One of the men affected was Sergeant Mingo Sanders, who had nearly 25 years of service and had been invaluable to Lieutenant Moss during the long bicycle trip to St. Louis. This gross injustice was only acknowledged in 1972 when the Army belatedly found the soldiers innocent and recommended they be pardoned. President Richard Nixon granted the pardon (but did not grant back pay or benefits) in 1972, when only two of the 167 wrongfully discharged men were still alive. The last survivor was awarded a small pension in 1973, 67 years after the incident.

Missoula Volunteers bound for the Spanish American War

Immediately after the 25th Infantry left the fort, Will Cave organized a troop of local volunteer cavalry at Fort Missoula. As a teen Cave had watched the first troops arrive in Missoula to construct the fort, and had participated in the campaign against the Nez Percé. After a career with the Missoula Mercantile and a stint as Missoula County Auditor, Cave helped organize what would become known as Troop F of the Third US Volunteer Cavalry. Cave signed up 50 men within a few hours on March 30, 1898, and notified Governor Robert B. Smith that Missoula was prepared to send a company of volunteers in case hostilities with Spain broke out. Cave and his volunteers thus became the first civilian volunteer unit accepted for the Spanish American war.

Troop F eventually became part of the Third US Volunteer Cavalry, known as "Grigsby's Cowboys" and composed of four troops from Montana, four from South Dakota, two from North Dakota, and one from Nebraska. Troop F was inducted into federal service in May 1898, and left the fort by the end of that month. A Minnesota newspaper described them on their way to war. "The boys were a hardy, rugged lot, and if the songs which were distributed among the spectators at the depot are any indication of the fighting qualities of the cowboys, they could lick a whole regiment of Spaniards."[16]

The Third Volunteer Cavalry was sent to Camp Thomas, Georgia, but never left the US during the war. Like so many of the units during that war, the soldiers suffered terribly from heat, disease, and poor rations. Troop F returned to Missoula in September 1898, with the loss of one man dead of illness, and many more suffering from disease.

A company of the 24th Infantry was assigned to the fort in 1902, and a full battalion of the regiment was sent to Missoula in early 1903. The fort's second contingent of buffalo soldiers stayed until 1905.
UM 86-0136

Sergeant Alexander Pillow was originally a squad sergeant with Company G of the 25th Infantry. An excellent marksman, Pillow represented Fort Missoula at rifle competitions at Fort Snelling, Minnesota. As the post's ordnance sergeant, Pillow remained at Fort Missoula when the 25th Infantry left the post. He was the only noncommissioned officer at the fort from 1898 to 1901, and usually had half a dozen enlisted men to help him secure and maintain the fort. Local residents often addressed Sergeant Pillow as Commandant or "colonel."[6] Captain Frederick Perkins, the commander of Company C of the 8th Infantry, arrived to repair and prepare the post for reoccupancy on August 4, 1901. Sergeant Pillow retired from the Army in 1902 and was buried in the Fort Missoula Cemetery after his death in 1928.

The name of **Sergeant Horace Bivins**, a buffalo soldier who served as post ordnance sergeant, is scratched inside the Powder Magazine along with the serial number of his rifle. A famous marksman who had turned down Buffalo Bill Cody's offer to join his Wild West Show, he had previously served with the 10th Cavalry in the Apache wars, as well as at Fort Custer and Fort Assiniboine in Montana. During the Spanish-American war he fought alongside the Rough Riders at San Juan Hill, earning the attention of Teddy Roosevelt and a Silver Star. After a year in the Philippines, he was appointed ordnance sergeant, and was sent to Fort Missoula in 1902. He married Claudia Browning from Billings, and they lived in the existing NCO quarters at the fort until 1906, when he returned to the Philippines. After serving at a number of forts throughout the west, he bought a farm in Billings and retired from the military in 1913. When World War I broke out he abandoned his crops and once again volunteered. He was appointed a captain of infantry, and served at Fort Dix, New Jersey until 1919, then returned to Billings where he raised vegetables and learned taxidermy.

The dog in the photo was named Booth. Trained at Fort Custer, Booth accompanied Bivins to Cuba and the Philippines, where he performed admirably. When Bivins returned from the Philippines, US authorities refused to let Booth back into the country. He was given to some officers, and eventually disappeared.

6

The Early Twentieth Century

"Public safety unquestionably forbids the abandonment of Fort Missoula"

Senator Thomas H. Carter

Although the post had initially been ordered abandoned[1], Senators Thomas H. Carter and Joseph Dixon objected, and the Adjutant General of the Army temporarily revoked the order on April 2, 1898. The Army again stated the fort would not be re-garrisoned in August, to which Senator Carter responded that Fort Missoula was, "One of the best located forts in the West, and I earnestly protest against its abandonment while so many Indians are kept in that vicinity." Citing the need to "restrain" the 2,000 Flatheads on the Jocko Reservation, Carter declared, "Public safety unquestionably forbids the abandonment of Fort Missoula."[2] On the day after Carter's telegram, the Secretary of War directed that no steps be taken to abandon the fort. The Post was to be guarded by a detachment of 20 men, although for a time only a half dozen soldiers from the 6th Cavalry were present. Throughout this period Ordnance Sergeant Alexander Pillow of the 25th Infantry was in charge of the fort, with anywhere from four to nine enlisted men at his disposal.

In 1900 the Department of Dakota declared most of the buildings were in good shape, although some needed to be re-shingled and painted. When the fort was placed on the "abandoned list" in 1900, President Oscar Craig of the University of Montana asked the Army if he could use some of the empty buildings for educational purposes. Craig wanted to move a summer school and the university's biological station (then located at Bigfork on Flathead Lake) to the fort.

The Quartermaster General and a number of other highly placed officers considered Craig's offer but recommended against letting anyone use the facilities unless the Army decided to permanently abandon the fort. The buildings had been constructed for about $60,000, but it was estimated that it would cost the Army $100,000 to replace them. After some deliberation, the Department of Dakota refused Craig's request, stating that the buildings were in generally good condition and were ready for immediate occupancy by troops. The only dissenting vote came from Lieutenant General Nelson A. Miles, Commanding General of the Army, who noted that the construction of Fort Harrison near Helena in the mid-1890s had been intended to replace both Fort Shaw and Fort Missoula. He also stated, "There is no military reason for continuing Fort Missoula as a military post." Indeed, Miles thought the fort would make a fine location for a university, which he recommended.[3] Nevertheless, the Army turned down Craig's request and did nothing to decide the ultimate fate of the fort.

A baseball diamond was one of the first recreational facilities built at Fort Missoula. Many baseball teams were fielded over the years, but Colonel Burt of the 25th Infantry was a particularly enthusiastic supporter of the game. Here a team of Buffalo Soldiers pose for a photo at the fort. These men may have been members of the 24th Infantry.

UM Elrod collection B.I. j-02

Less than a year later, Engineer Major George Pond declared that the fort's rotting water tank needed to be replaced if the post was to be used in the future. Pond also remarked on Sergeant Pillow, the man in charge of the vacant fort. "The Ordnance Sergeant in charge has been very faithful and taken the best care possible of the post with the means at his disposal."[4] In response to Pond's requests about maintaining the post, General Miles seemed to change his mind when he remarked, "Fort Missoula is one of the important and permanent posts and should be put in good condition."[5] A board of officers recommended on February 4, 1902 that the fort be reinstated as a temporary post to be used if needed. Once the decision was made to re-garrison Fort Missoula, several contracts were let late in 1901 for supplies and work to recondition the post infrastructure, and a company of the 8th Infantry arrived to prepare the post for reopening. The Quartermaster General's Report in 1902 recommended either abandoning the fort, or completely rebuilding it if it was to be used in the future. In response, the existing water system was improved and extended between 1902 and 1903 at a cost of $21,000. The sewer system was also improved in 1903 at a cost of $6,605, although raw sewage continued to drain into the Bitterroot River just downstream of the fort.

Due to the original surveying error, much of Fort Missoula was constructed not on Section 31, which had been set aside for a Military Reservation, but instead on state school lands in adjoining Section 36. Concerns about the uncertain title to the land threatened the continuing existence of the fort for more than 25 years.

Authorities at Fort Missoula sent dozens of letters to the War Department, the Department of Interior, the Department of Dakota, and the US House of Representatives between 1879 and 1888. Colonel Andrews had reported in 1888 that "objectionable parties" were erecting buildings in Section 36, and that civil authorities had ejected some of them. Andrews worried that, "unscrupulous speculators" would try to lock up the hay grounds around the fort in order to sell feed to the Army. With the fort effectively abandoned, local businessmen felt the fort might never be reactivated unless title to the land was cleared up.

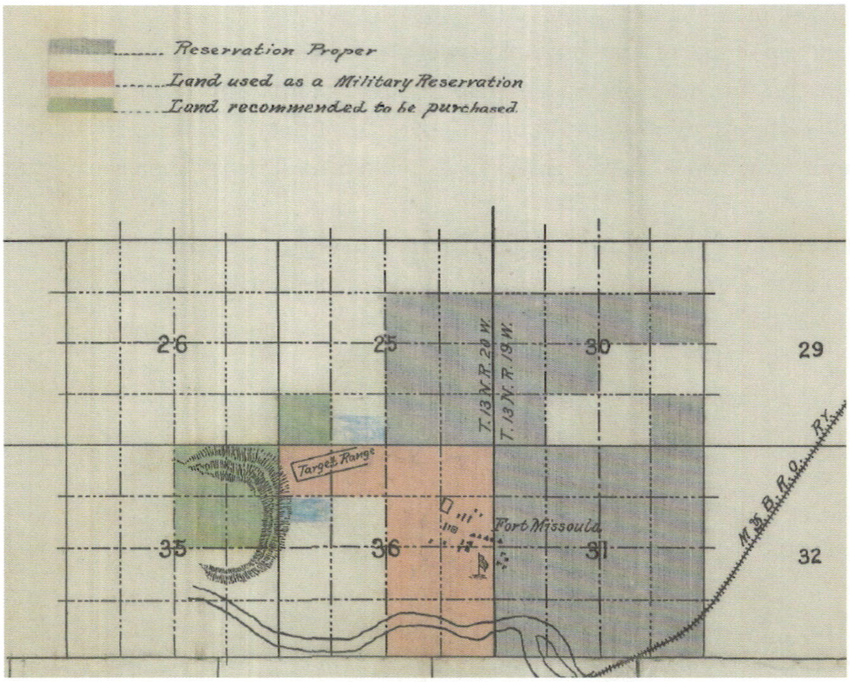

This 1903 map of the fort shows the land the Army wanted to obtain in Sections 36, 35, and 25. The original fort is shown in gray. The land in pink had been actively used by the Army since 1877. Land in green and blue was needed to provide a safe zone around the target range. The boundaries of the land eventually donated to the Army differed slightly from what is shown here. Alfred Cave's wheat farm in Section 30, surrounded by the fort on three sides, was subdivided during this period and is today known as Orchard Homes #3.
HMFM

General William A. Kobbe visited Missoula in March 1903 in order to resolve the land issue. He stated that Fort Missoula ranked first or second in the health of its soldiers, was one of the most popular posts among the Army's officers, and also had low costs due to the proximity of timber, hay, and water. The land question came to the forefront on October 18, 1903 when Private John Tully, Company M of the 24th Infantry, shot and killed Private Thomas Kennedy in the rear of the commissary building with a service rifle. Although the shooting occurred inside a fort building, it was on state land, and Tully was turned over to civil authorities rather than facing the military justice system.

Encouraged by Colonel Kobbe, local

residents began efforts to purchase the disputed 320 acres that constituted the east half of Section 36. The Army also expressed interest in purchasing 80 acres where the target range was located in the northwestern portion of Section 36, as well as 140 acres in adjoining parcels, including parts of McCauley Butte. A group of Missoula businessman raised enough money to purchase from the state the 320 acres in Section 36 by November 29th, 1903. These citizens also convinced the Northern Pacific Railway to donate 240 acres of land (160 acres in Section 35, which included McCauley Butte, plus an additional 80 acres in Section 25). President Mellen of the Northern Pacific Railroad gave a deed in trust for the 240 acres. J.M. Keith, the president of the First National Bank in Missoula, held in trust the land bought by the citizens and donated by the railroad until Congress was ready to take Fort Missoula off of the "abandoned" list.

The purchased land was accepted by an act of Congress on March 9, 1904, and the Secretary of War was directed to accept the gift. During the land transfer John Bonner and E.E. Hershey served as trustees for the citizens of Missoula County. Bonner formally transferred ownership of 160 acres in Section 36 to the Army on February 16, 1906, and Hershey transferred an additional 160 acres on April 23, 1906. The War Department decided to take Fort Missoula off of their "to be abandoned list," but it required an act of Congress to accept the land. With the title cleared up, the challenge was to upgrade the fort's facilities.

The newly acquired land included what is now the western half of the Historical Museum at Fort Missoula, the Rocky Mountain Museum of Military History, the National Guard shops, and much of the Fort Missoula Regional Park. It soon became apparent that the new improvements and clear title to the land did not guarantee the future of the fort. The Army Chief of Staff recommended on March 22, 1906 that the 7th Infantry battalion be transferred elsewhere and the post be abandoned.

The Fort gets a Makeover

Fires took a toll on the fort during the spring of 1903. On January 15, the Company I Barracks (Building 25) burned. Less than two months later fire claimed the bathhouse and sawmill, causing $7,000 damage. Fires were inevitable since nearly all of the fort's buildings were still heated with wood. On April 11, 1903 a contract was let for the annual supply of 2550 cords of firewood at $4.48 per cord.

US Senator Joseph Dixon of Missoula was instrumental in helping transfer title of the land to the Army, and when it appeared the land exchange would be successful, he was instrumental in securing an appropriation of $1,000,000 for the reconstruction of the fort. Dixon convinced Congress to improve Fort Missoula to a modern regimental post. Although no attempt was made to identify a mission for the fort, Congress passed an appropriations bill calling for a major upgrade of Fort Missoula, which President Theodore Roosevelt signed into law in 1904. Due to the size of the appropriation secured by Dixon, the fort was sometimes called "The million dollar post," although the total cost of all of the improvements made to the fort over the next eight years was only $593,941.

The commanding officer's quarters (T-30) was typical of the new buildings constructed on officer's row by 1912.

Construction of a new officer's row, barracks, NCO quarters, hospital, stables, and a post exchange started in 1906, and was mostly complete by 1912. George W. Armitage was the superintendent of construction at Fort Missoula during this era. The bulk of the construction occurred between 1908 and 1911, and most of the new buildings were Spanish-influenced Mission Revival style concrete buildings with red tile roofs. Many of the new buildings were heated with radiators powered by a central boiler system connected by steam tunnels. When completed the fort was large enough to house a regiment, although no full regiment was ever stationed there.

With the buildings came other improvements. By 1903, the fort was equipped with such modern inventions as typewriters and machine-guns. The Missoula Public Service Company brought electricity to the fort in 1910, when they finished a substation nearby. A second parade ground was built in front of the new barracks buildings, and a new 100-foot flagpole was installed in 1911. The new parade ground also had bleachers and a baseball diamond.

Garrison Soldiers

Over the next decade various Army units rotated in and out of the fort, with few staying longer than a year. Soldiers had constructed many of the original buildings, but contractors built the modern buildings, freeing the soldiers for their regular duties, which included a lot of marching, drilling, and target practice. Six officers and 217 men under Maj. Z.W. Torrey left the fort on August 15, 1903 on a five-day march to Morrell's Ranch, 74.5 miles away. They conducted joint field exercises with the First Battalion of the 24th Infantry, which had marched from Fort Harrison, then returned to the fort on September 24. Major Z.W. Torrey, Captain R. J. Maxey and contract surgeon J.N. Merrick led 26 men to the Flathead Reservation on November 26, 1903 at the request of Indian Agent W.H. Smead, who asked them to arrest Joseph Morrigeau and his followers, who had been trespassing and grazing cattle illegally on the reservation. Morrigeau was arrested and evicted from the reservation, and the soldiers returned to their post on November 28th.

Dozens of wildfires swept across Montana and northern Idaho during the summer of 1910, and on August 20 high winds whipped the fires into an inferno. Soldiers stationed at Fort Missoula, Fort Harrison, and Fort Assiniboine, as well as troops from North Dakota, Wisconsin and Washington fought the fires. The soldiers from Fort Missoula at the time consisted of a battalion of 14th Infantry (Companies I, K, L and M, 240 men).

Early on April 11, 1911 former President Theodore Roosevelt arrived in Missoula. Three companies of infantry from Fort Missoula, plus war veterans and warriors from the Flathead tribe escorted the party from the depot to the Florence Hotel. That evening, after a long day of speeches and public events, Roosevelt toured Fort Missoula by automobile.

Fort Missoula, which had once had the lowest desertion rate in the Army when the 25th Infantry was

Heritage Hall

Building T-2 was built as the Post Exchange (PX) in 1906 at a cost of $21,800. Sitting on a rubble stone foundation, the one-and-a-half story brick and wood building contained administrative offices and a 2,000-square-foot gymnasium. Built in a Colonial

Revival style, it was constructed based on the same plans used for a similar building at Fort Lawton, Washington the year before. Soldiers could buy food, beer, wine, jewelry, personal items and gifts at the PX, which also had a lunch counter. On movie night, the soldiers and their families would carry their dining room chairs to the gymnasium. In the early 1960s the PX was used by the US Marine Corp Reserve and the Naval Reserve. Heritage Hall is now owned by the Northern Rockies Heritage Center and is leased for office space, while the gymnasium and grounds are used for numerous weddings and community events. The building has been dedicated to General Walter M. Johnson (see page 79).

The Fort's reconstruction 1905-1911

Building 14 - A 2-story frame duplex built in 1910 for $14,794 was originally a NCO quarters, and was rented to University professors from 1947 to 1957. Ownership was conveyed to the University of Montana on January 17, 1966 and was it used by the Montana Department of Institutions for a Life-Skills Center from 1966 to 1982. (photo on page 121)

Building 16 - Similar to Building 14.

Building T-24 - A 2.5 story concrete company barracks built in a Mission style between 1906 and 1910 for $69,517. It housed up to two companies of soldiers, and was used as a recruiting center beginning in June 1940. Italian detainees were housed there in 1941. The General Services Administration leased the building to the US Forest Service in 1961, and it is now headquarters of the Lolo National Forest and the Missoula Ranger District.

Building T-26 - Same as above. It was used to house Army staff stationed at the Disciplinary Barracks from 1944 to 1947, and served as the Sergeant Ernest Veuve Army Reserve Center from 1957 until 2011.

Building T-27 - A four-plex 2.5 story concrete quarters designed for junior Officers, built between 1906 and 1910 for $30,453. Civilian employees lived there from 1941 to 1943, while military officers or senior enlisted men lived there from 1944 until 1947.

Building T-28 - A single family officer's quarters built between 1906 and 1910, the 2.5 story concrete building cost $30,453, and has been used to house Army Reserve, National Guard and ROTC personnel since 1947.

Building T-29 - Similar to Building T-28.

Building T-30 - The commanding officers quarters was a 2.5 story concrete structure built between 1906 and 1910 for $15,596.

Building T-31 - A 2.5 story single set of concrete junior officer's quarters built between 1906 and 1910.

Building T-32 - Similar to Building T-31

Building T-33 - A 2.5 story duplex officer's quarters built between 1906 and 1910 for $22,587.

Building T-142 - The quartermaster's 1.5 story brick stable was built in 1910 for $19,337. The stable was used as an auto mechanic shop in 1918, and as a vocational shop from 1941 until 1958. The University of Montana acquired the stables in 1966.

Building T-322 - The quartermaster's storehouse was built in 1911 using plans drawn up in 1905. It was used from 1946 to 1952 as a storage warehouse by a local moving company. The building was owned by the city of Missoula for a period, then was deeded to Missoula County in 1973. It is now home to the Historical Museum at Fort Missoula.

Building T-323 - The quartermaster's root cellar was built of concrete with four ventilators in 1908 at a cost of $5,400.

Building T-105 - The post bakery was built by 1915 and cost $8,340. It was later used as storage by the Army Reserve and the US Forest Service.

Top: Residents of the fort take a stroll past officer's row on a sunny winter day. UM 82-0219
Bottom: Officers row as it looks today. The buildings are owned by the Northern Rockies Heritage Center and are rented out as office space to non-profit groups.

stationed there, had by 1912 the third highest desertion rate among military posts. Nearly all of the forts with the highest desertion rates were in the Pacific Northwest, perhaps due to the high prevailing civilian wage in the area at the time. Discipline in general was a problem. The fort averaged 236 men on the post during 1912, and held 162 summary courts and 73 more serious courts martial during the year, one for each man on the post.[8]

Despite the fact that most of the fort's facilities were brand new, in 1912 the Army once again looked at abandoning the fort. Fort Missoula was included in a list of Army posts located for a reason that was now totally obsolete, and the Army stated there was no longer need for, "a restraint upon the Flathead Indians living in the area." Fort Missoula was also deemed to be in a location that was not conducive to "securing economy of administration and supply or a full measure of military effectiveness." The Army recommended that for the posts on this list, "Their garrisons should not be increased and should ultimately be withdrawn to such concentration centers as Congress may authorize."[9]

Fort Missoula sat mostly idle from 1913 until the end of World War I, and was cared for by civilian workers during this time. When the state legislature refused to appropriate money for a Journalism Building at the University of Montana, Dean Arthur Stone asked the caretakers of the fort to loan him three tents and a few stoves in 1914. He pitched the tents on the north side of Main Hall, and established what is now the University of Montana Journalism School.

During World War I the government once again ordered Fort Missoula abandoned in November 1917. Captain H.H. Moore supervised the packing and shipping of the fort's equipment, with priority given to all engineering, hospital, quartermaster, and Signal Corps supplies. The university, with the backing of many Missoula residents, immediately requested that the fort be transferred to the school, but the Army declared the fort was needed for national defense, and hinted at plans to convert both Fort Harrison and Fort Missoula into hospitals.

The Student's Army Training Corps

The Missoula County sheriff received permission from the Secretary of War in 1918 to use the guardhouse at the fort to house prisoners when the county jail was full, marking the first time any of the buildings at Fort Missoula were used by civil authorities. More changes were to come.

There had been rumors that the fort would be turned into a government hospital, but on May 17, 1918 it was announced that Montana State University (Missoula) would host two units of the Student's Army Training Corps (SATC). This program was available to men 18 to 21, and men between the ages of 31 and 45 who could pass the Army physical requirements. It eventually operated at 157 colleges across the country. The university asked for permission to use the Fort Missoula facilities as a training camp for mechanics and truck drivers, and on May 22 the Army's Adjutant General Office gave Montana's Chancellor of Higher Education permission to use Fort Missoula buildings, plus lockers, ice boxes, certain furniture and the sawmill, and to make minor improvements to the grounds. Washington J. McCormick Jr. (a state legislator and future US Representative) was appointed Commandant of Cadets. His father, a Missoula pioneer, had helped Martin Maginnis lobby for construction of the fort in 1876.

Company B of the SATC was stationed at Fort Missoula. These men trained to become vehicle mechanics and drivers.
UM - Sentinel Yearbook 1919

The first group of 200 SATC trainees arrived at the fort on August 15, 1918. President Edward O. Sisson of the University welcomed them, and told the assembled audience, "These young men have gathered from all parts of the state at the call of President Wilson and the army. They are to train and perfect brain and action first to do their special duty as officers and specialists in the vast war machine."[10]

Two courses of study were offered, and were taught by instructors from the university. Company A of the SATC had 302 men living in a tent city at the University until two barracks were constructed for them. Section B had 206 men at Fort Missoula, overseen by six commissioned officers.

The students at the university were expected to meet college entrance requirements exams and take academic courses along with military training. The 206 students of Company B at Fort Missoula could choose between "Emergency War Training for Truck Drivers and Chauffeurs," or "Emergency War Training for Vehicle Repairmen." Equipment was brought in and the students were taught driving skills, blacksmithing, general mechanics, auto repair, and how to use a wireless set (radio).

The SATC men were paid $30 per month, ate in a mess hall, wore uniforms, and were subject to military discipline.

Just two months after arriving, the soldier trainees in Missoula were struck by the Spanish-flu epidemic raging throughout the country. While Missoula fared better than many other cities in Montana (Butte had more than 600 deaths), there were at least 110 local deaths, including 15 of the SATC men and five of their nurses. Another trainee died of scarlet fever.

Fort Missoula was expecting the arrival of an additional 450 trainees when war ended with the Armistice on November 11, 1918. None of the men who trained at Fort Missoula would see action during World War I, but some served with the 9,000 American troops sent to Siberia to protect the Trans-Siberian Railroad during the aftermath of the Russian Revolution.

Immediately after the end of World War I the US Forest Service applied to use the fort as an aviation base to train forest patrols. The War Department acknowledged that the fort was technically listed as a first class aviation base, but declared it was only for emergency use, and the fort would primarily be used as an infantry base in the future.

At the same time, Congress passed a law in 1918 allowing for the lease or sale of portions of the fort. The post commander was given permission to lease 1,040 acres during the summer of 1919 for agriculture use, with one-fifth of the crop to be delivered to the Army. The lessee had to pay a $500 performance bond. Most of this land was north of South Avenue. Harry D. Maclay leased part of this land in 1921, and soon had 135 acres under irrigation. Alfred Cave's former wheat farm, which was surrounded by the fort on three sides, was subdivided into Orchard Homes Number 3, and civilian homes began to appear in the midst of the Military Reservation.

After World War I, the Army reorganized itself for the second time in four years. On August 20, 1920 Fort Missoula became part of the 9th Corps Area, headquartered in San Francisco. This department also encompassed Washington, Idaho, Oregon, Utah, Wyoming, Nevada, and California. A year later a decision was made to re-garrison Fort Missoula. A battalion of the 58th Infantry Regiment, commanded by Lt. Colonel P.H. Mullay and Major F.B. Kobes arrived at the fort in September 1921. This unit became the first battalion of

Soldiers of the 14th Infantry Regiment march across the Higgins Bridge during Missoula's Fourth of July parade in 1912.
J.C. Whitham, Museum of the Rockies 72.20.369

the 4th Infantry (260 men) when the army was reorganized the following year. The SATC program that had brought a truck mechanics school to the fort was replaced by a new program, the Civilian Military Training Camps, or CMTC, in 1921. From 1922 to 1940 month-long Civilian Military Training Camps were held at the fort, usually attended by 200 young men each summer, often held in conjunction with the summer camp of the Montana National Guard. Officers of the 416th Infantry, 104th Division of the Army Reserve also received 15 days of summer training at the fort each year. The summer camps were designed as a month-long training course for warrant officers, enlisted men and civilians to qualify for appointments as either reserve officers or non-commissioned officers. Students who attended the camps for four successive years were eligible to be granted a commission as a 2nd lieutenant in the Army Reserves. Nationwide, approximately 400,000 young men participated in these camps over a 20-year period, including future presidents Harry Truman and Ronald Reagan.

During the 1920s life was routine for the soldiers stationed at Fort Missoula. Long marches were common, including annual 120-mile marches to Idaho and back. Three hundred enlisted men and 10 officers walked to Helena by way of Avon beginning on May 28, 1924, and they returned through the Blackfoot Valley. Mules pulled the machine gun carts, while Major Bradley and his adjutant led their horses the entire way. They marched through four inches of snow on the pass on June 6. They turned their machine guns over to the National Guard for 15 days of training. The battalion's baseball team played at Helena, and some men entered the rodeo in Ovando. That same year company D built the rifle range in Pattee Canyon. They were supposed to be spelled in three weeks, but liked the duty, and requested to stay until November. During the 1920s and 1930s life was fairly idyllic for the soldiers of the 4th Infantry. Post commander Colonel P.H. Mullay wrote, "The schools are excellent, with free tuition for soldier's children."[11] During the 1930s a covered Army truck carried the 20 school children to Missoula. Captain Joel D. Pomerene wrote a three page article for the *Infantry Journal* in 1933 entitled "Fort Missoula - A Happy Hunting Grounds." He declared, "this station is a hunter's and fisherman's paradise."

During Prohibition soldiers frequented an illegal speakeasy which operated in the nearby Pepperpot house. Soldiers supposedly used to bootleg liquor into the fort hidden under crates of produce.

The presence of nearby Target Range School led to one post order that read, "Soldiers stopping at the halfway school house and annoying the good looking teacher must cease immediately or the fort commander would have the school teacher come to the fort, pick out the culprits and he would take action accordingly."[12]

Alice Della Vecchia, a schoolgirl who lived at the fort from 1932 to 1938, remembered "happy times there." She described life at the fort in a letter to the Historical Museum at Fort Missoula. "Watching the parade was fun. Mostly because you could count on "Angel" (misnamed) the mule who regularly rebelled and carried the cannon (flying) back to the barn...When the time came for raising or lowering the flag you would see everyone scurrying to get under cover (so you wouldn't have to stand at attention). It looked like an anthill."[1]3

Children at the fort also found opportunity for mischief, delighting in the noise they could make on the wooden sidewalks and being cited for reckless bicycle riding. Vecchia remembered the time her father, the post's plumber, was called to the commanding officer's quarters to explain why her brother had run an officer's "long johns" up the flagpole.

The War Department once again began studying which Army and Navy bases were surplus and could be closed in 1929, including Fort Missoula. This idea was debated for the next several years. When it seemed likely the fort might be abandoned in 1932, the Department of Interior considered establishing a tuberculosis sanitarium there, but eventually dropped the idea. The Army still intended to abandon the fort in 1933, when the Civilian Conservation Corps was established.

Units stationed at Fort Missoula 1901 - 1940

1901- August Captain Frederick Perkins of the 8th Infantry brought a company (80 men) to Missoula to repair and reopen the fort in August. They stayed until May 1902.

1902 - Company L of the 24th Infantry (70 men) replaced the 8th Infantry in May, and stayed until August, when the Third Battalion of the 24th Infantry arrived at the fort, fresh from the fighting in the Philippines.

1903 - Major Z.W. Torrey and Captain Hoover brought Companies I, K, L, M (200 men) of the 24th Infantry to the fort on January 1. Other battalions of the 24th served at Fort Harrison and Fort Assiniboine. Lieutenant Colonel Danial Comman took command February 15, 1903. They stayed until December 22, 1905, when they were ordered back to the Philippines.

1905 - Twenty-eight years after Captain Rawn and the 7th Infantry left the fort, 202 men of the 7th Infantry (Companies E, F, G, and H) arrived in Missoula on December 23.

1906 - Lieutenant Colonel Charles A. Booth of the 7th Infantry served as commander of Fort Missoula from December 1905 until October 1906. He had previously served in Montana from 1872 until 1878, and participated in the Little Big Horn Campaign. On March 22, 1906 the Army Chief of Staff recommended the transfer of the battalion to another post so that Fort Missoula could be abandoned. Nevertheless a battalion (Companies I, K, L and M, 223 men) of the 6th Infantry Regiment replaced the 7th Infantry in November 1906, and remained at the fort until December 1909.

1909 - Company K of the 2nd Infantry (31 men) occupied the fort from December 28, 1909 until March 20, 1910.

1910 - A battalion of the 14th Infantry (Companies I, K, L and M, 240 men) occupied the fort from March 20, 1910 until February 25, 1913.

1913 - The 18th Infantry arrived to replace the 14th Infantry in February 15, 1913, but remained for less than two weeks before being sent to training in the east. They left much of their baggage at the fort thinking they would soon return, but then were ordered to the Mexican border. Their baggage remained at Fort Missoula until the end of World War I. A caretaker detachment of 15 men maintained the fort from February 25, 1913 until October 1914.

1914 - A battalion of the 14th Infantry, Companies I, K, L and M (225 men), arrived on October 12, 1914, and stayed until April 10, 1915. By 1915 Fort Missoula was part of the Central Command, headquartered in Chicago.

1915 - **1918** - Caretaker detachments of five to 100 men looked after the fort after April 10, 1915.

1917- With US entry into World War I imminent, Company K of the First North Dakota Infantry was sent to Fort Missoula to guard the post on March 25. This unit was withdrawn around June 1.

1918 - Company B of the Student Army Training Corps trained as vehicle mechanics at Fort Missoula.

1921 - A battalion of the 58th Infantry regarrisoned the fort on September 11, 1921.

1922 - The 58th Infantry was renamed the 4th Infantry, and a battalion of the regiment occupied the fort until 1940.

Missoula's First Airshow

Three thousand western Montana residents flocked to the fort as pioneer aviator Eugene Ely gave an exhibition of his airplane, a device few people had seen. Special trains brought spectators from the Bitterroot, streetcars offered a special round-trip ticket and admittance to the event for seventy cents. Flying a Curtiss Pusher biplane, Ely (the first person to land an aircraft on a ship) took off from the baseball field on the new parade ground on June 28, 1911, and made three trips over the fort. A band of Cree Indians camped nearby watched the whole affair without comment. Four months after his flight in Missoula, Eugene Ely crashed his plane and was killed at an airshow in Georgia.

Eugene Levy prepares for takeoff at the parade ground in front of Officer's Row.
UM 92.0244

The Fort's Water System

Army Engineer George Pond inspected the fort late in 1900, and found the water tank and trestle, "worn out and in a dilapidated condition, wholly beyond repair."[7] A contract for a new water and sewer system was alloted to the Allen Black Company on June 20, 1903, and by mid-September the Fort was forced to rely on bottled water while major repairs were made. The Missoula Mercantile was eventually awarded the contract to construct a metal water tower and trestle. A Missoula landmark, the 300,000 gallon water tower was built near the river in 1912, with a pump house at the base. It rises 166 feet over the valley, and can be seen from much of Missoula. During the 1940s the tower was painted in a red and white checkered pattern. Two deep wells were also drilled north of South Avenue in 1936, making the fort's water supply adequate for 715 people. The tower is no longer used to store water. It is now owned by the Northern Rockies Heritage Center, which leases it to a telecommunications company.

The Stable

The fort's original stables and corral were located northwest of the historic buildings. A corral was built near the Bitterroot river, about ten feet above water level and surrounded by a low abrupt gravel bluff. The trees and willow provided shelter for the horses. An early history of the fort reported, "some strange experiences while on guard duty. The officers of the day could tell strange stories of the adventure while making their after-midnight inspection of that corral." A new Mission-style stable (T-42) was built on the east side of the fort in 1910. The building was used to train truck mechanics during World War I, and for vocational training from 1941 to 1947. The historic stable was slated for demolition after Divot Development bought the land for a housing development in 1994. Divot eventually offered to give the building to the Historical Museum at Fort Missoula if the museum could raise the money to move it. The building is now the University of Montana's Biological Sciences Field Research Station. It was remodeled in 1998 for avian research, and in 2009 offices and meeting space were added on the second floor. Besides offices and a conference room, the research station features four aviaries, 10 laboratories, a surgical room, and greenhouses. The stable is surrounded by 150 acres of open fields and is adjacent to 100 acres of ponderosa pine forest.

General Walter M. Johnson

Colonel Walter M. Johnson, a graduate of West Point, was stationed at Fort Missoula during the 1930s, and married a Missoula girl. He helped oversee many improvements at the fort. During World War II Colonel Johnson commanded the 117th Regiment of the 30th Division. His unit landed at Normandy six days after D-Day, and was in the forefront of the fighting from Normandy through France, Belgium and Germany. He was eventually promoted to brigadier general. After his retirement from the Army in 1957, Johnson moved back to Missoula where he became an important supporter of preserving Fort Missoula. Heritage Hall (Building T-2) is dedicated to General Johnson (see page 72).

Chaplain Leslie Fauver Zimmerman

Leslie Fauver Zimmerman served as post chaplain at Fort Missoula during the 1930s, ministering to Army soldiers and CCC men alike. He was transferred to the Philippines in the spring of 1941, and was captured by the Japanese at Bataan. He survived prison camp only to be taken by "hell ship" to Japan as a slave laborer. Before leaving the Philippines he gave his diary to another officer. The other officer buried the diary, which was found after the war and returned to Zimmerman, who was liberated by American troops at the end of the war.

General Frank Milburn

Frank Milburn was a 1914 graduate of West Point, and was appointed professor of military science at the university. Milburn served as head football coach for the Montana Grizzlies from 1926 to 1930. Major-General Milburn commanded several divisions and corps during World War II, and again during the Korean War. Lieutenant General Milburn died in 1962 and is buried in the Fort Missoula cemetery.

This 1931 panorama of Fort Missoula was taken from the water tower.
UM McKay Collection 87-0058 and 87-0057

The Fort Missoula Military Reservation

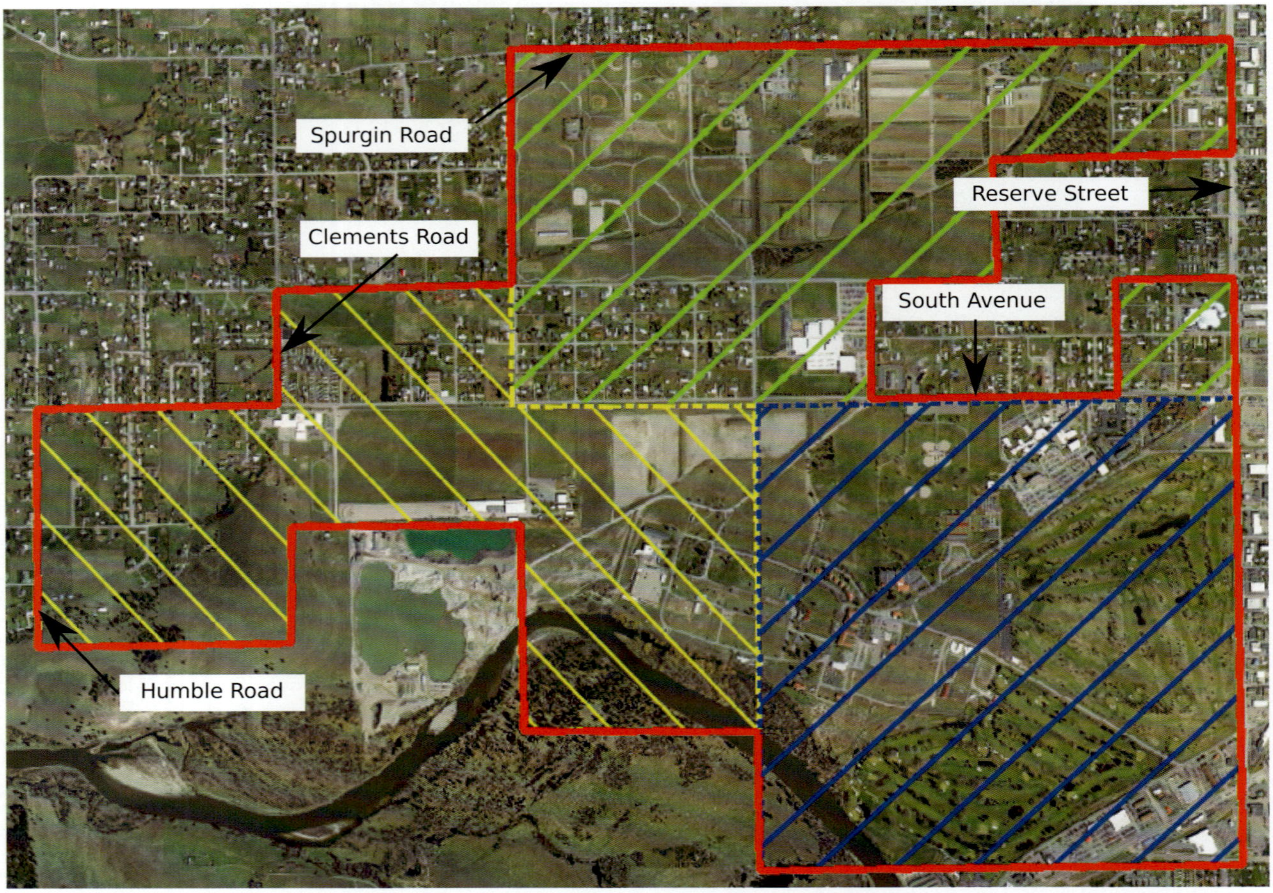

The original Fort Missoula Military Reservation was 640 acres in size (shown in blue crosshatching). President U.S. Grant added 760 acres to the reservation by executive order in 1878 (green crosshatching). Missoula citizens donated 320 additional acres and the Northern Pacific Railroad donated 240 acres to the Army in 1904 (yellow crosshatching). Much of the land on the western and northern edges of the fort was soon leased or sold to local farmers.

Base map courtesy of USGS

Below: A 1946 map of the Army Disciplinary Barracks.

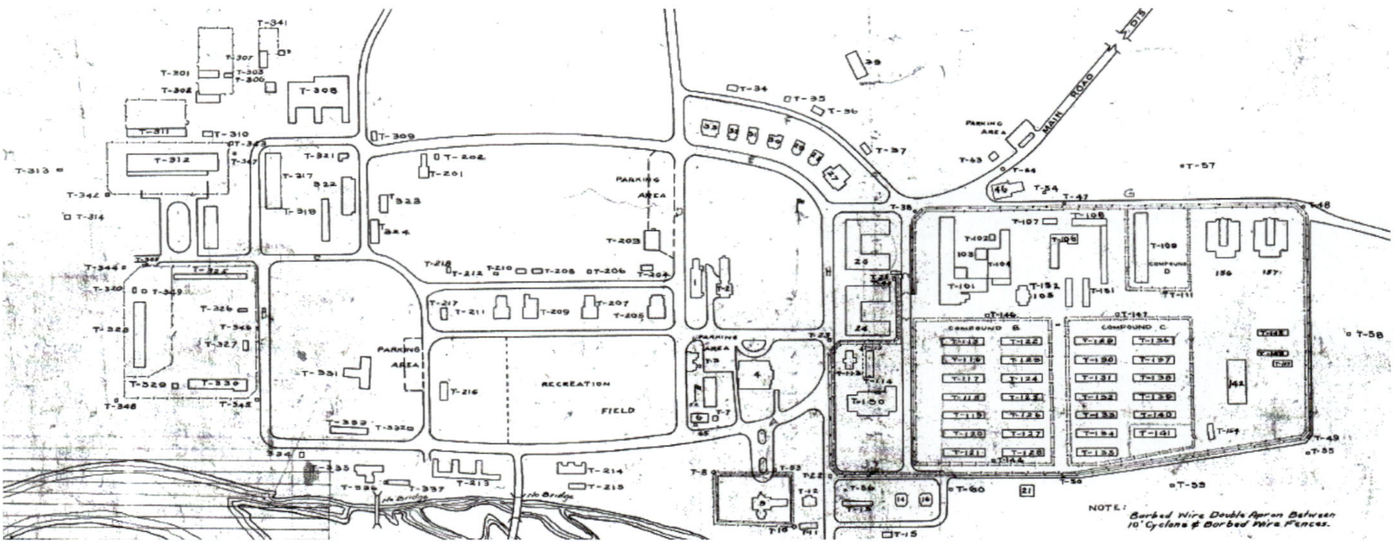

Today's Historic Fort

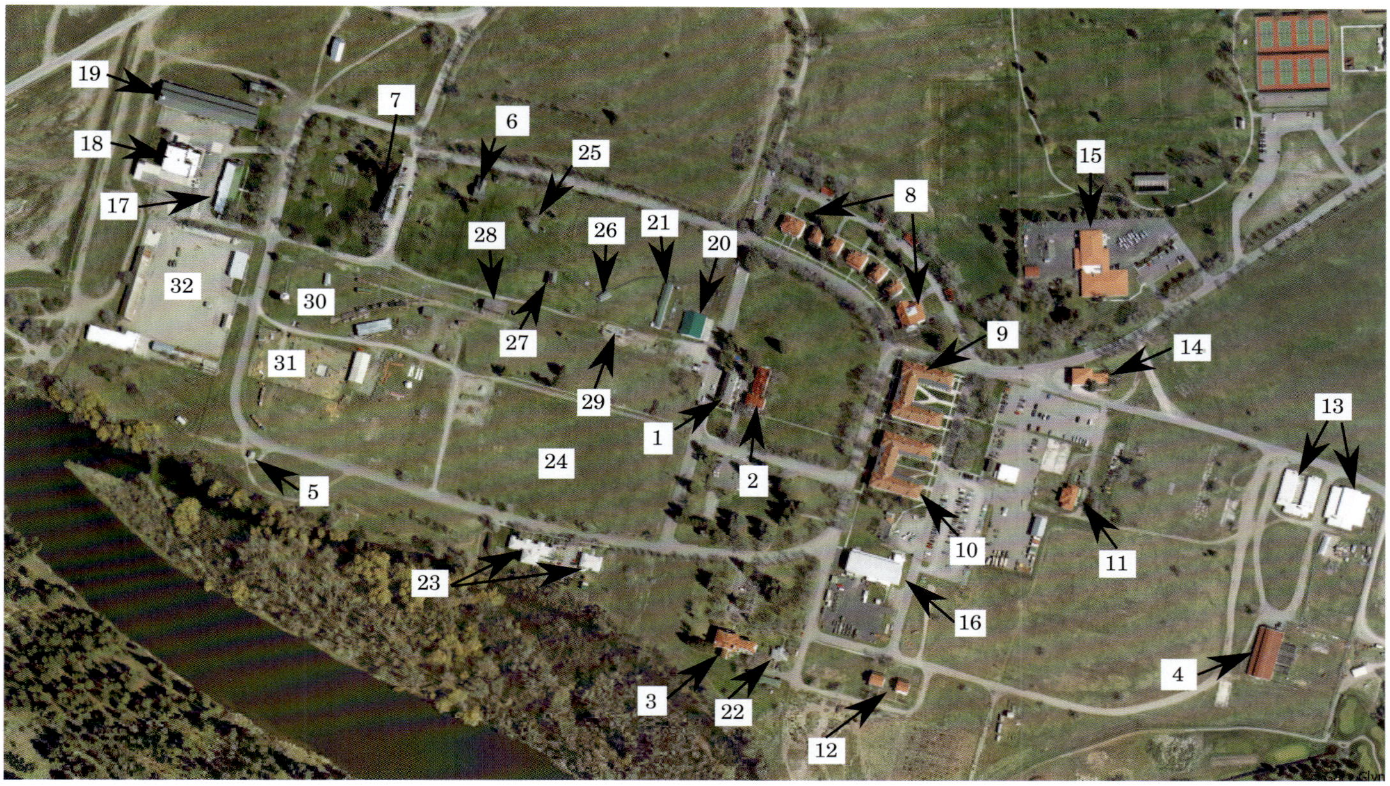

1. The former chapel and post headquarters, T-1 is now owned by the Historical Museum at Fort Missoula (HMFM).
2. The fort's post exchange, T-2 is now known at Heritage Hall and is owned by the Northern Rockies Heritage Center (NHRC).
3. The post hospital is now owned by the Western Montana Mental Health Center (WMMHC).
4. The historic stable is owned by the University of Montana (UM).
5. The powder magazine is owned by the NHRC.
6. The log NCO Quarters (T-201) is owned by the HMFM.
7. The quartermaster warehouse (T-322) is the main museum building of the HMFM.
8. Officer's row is owned by the NHRC.
9. Company barracks T-26 is the Army Reserve's Veuve Hall.
10. Company Barracks T-24 is the headquarters of the Lolo National Forest.
11. The post bakery is owned by the Forest Service.
12. NCO quarters 14 and 16 are owned by UM.
13. The disciplinary barracks cellblocks are owned by UM.
14. The firehouse/guardhouse is owned by the Forest Service.
15. Regional office of the Bureau of Land Management.
16. The disciplinary barracks recreation center is owned by the Forest Service.
17. The CCC administration building (T-316) is home to the Rocky Mountain Museum of Military History.
18. The National Guard maintenance facility.
19. The CCC warehouse (T-312) is owned by the National Guard.
20. The Army garage (T-203) is owned by the HMFM.
21. The restored Alien Detention Center barracks was moved to HMFM.
22. The nurses quarters are owned by the WMMHC.
23. The CCC quarters are owned by the Child Development Center.
24. The fort's original parade ground is part of the HMFM.
25. The homestead cabin and barn was moved to the HMFM.
26. St. Michael's Church was moved to the HMFM.
27. The Grant Creek School was moved to the HMFM.
28. The Drummond Depot was moved to the HMFM.
29. The trolley barn was built at the HMFM.
30. The Forestry Interpretive Area of the HMFM.
31. The UM Woodsmen team competition area at the HMFM.
32. The National Guard vehicle storage area.

"Get Your Nickel Ready"

Horse-drawn trolleys operated in Missoula by 1890, and in 1901 several companies looked into starting an electric trolley company in the city. Citizens began planning electric streetcar routes as early as 1903. Two years later William A. Clark sent an engineer and an attorney from his Butte Electric Railway Co. to plan specific routes and gain right of way. At the same time Clark was planning to build the Milltown dam (completed 1908), which would provide electricity for a streetcar line through the Missoula Light and Water Co. Clark also formed the Missoula Street Railway Company, which agreed to pay the city one percent of the revenue once the population of Missoula reached 18,000. Construction was underway by November 1909 on what would ultimately be 18.5 miles of track. A car barn was built at the foot of Arthur Street, and new bridges were built over Rattlesnake Creek and near Bonner.

The company ordered ten 40-passenger cars, a larger interurban car (#50) as well as freight cars, locomotives and electrical equipment. The *Daily Missoulian* heralded the beginning of electric car service with an announcement stating: "Get your nickel ready." A streetcar fare of five cents was standard across the country, but wages were 30 percent higher in Montana than in other states, so the company decided to eliminate the conductor position to save money. Missoula is considered the first city in the US to successfully operate a one-man trolley operation. The company counted on fast schedules and short layovers to increase efficiency. The faster interurban car traveled between Fort Missoula and Bonner each day, and turnarounds were built at each location. The interurban car was heavier and faster than the ones used in the city, and was involved in the one fatal accident on the line when it collided with another streetcar. On another occasion the air brake system of the Bonner car froze on a cold winter day, and it smashed into a work car in East Missoula, breaking an axle and derailing. The car had to be jacked up and laboriously manhandled back into position.

Top: A Missoula streetcar displaying the "F" of the Fort Missoula route.
UM 74-0296

Bottom: The restored interior of streetcar #50, on display at the Historical Museum at Fort Missoula.

The Missoula Street Railway Company never turned a profit, and the rapid spread of personal automobiles spelled the end of streetcar systems around the state. Motorman Ralph Starr drove Missoula's last streetcar into the car barn just after midnight on Jan. 25, 1932. The 10 city cars and the interurban car were placed on foundations and used as cabins in Sam Mercer's Trolley Cabin Camp near north Russell Street. Gerry Diettert eventually acquired the interurban car (#50), which he donated to the fledgling museum at Fort Missoula in 1974. Archie Roemers sandblasted the trolley, a Girl Scout troop received a $500 grant from *Reader's Digest* to paint it, and a shed was built to house it. Unfortunately, lack of resources led to 20 years of neglect as the streetcar sat outside and rotted in place. In 1993 the museum wanted to sell the trolley to a local business, but a public outcry arose after the *Missoulian* published an article on the proposed sale. County Surveyor Horace Brown then applied for a federal transportation grant, which brought in $80,000 to restore and preserve the historic streetcar, provided the Friends of the Historical Museum come up with $20,000 in matching funds. On April 19, 1996 Car #50, was hoisted onto a flatbed trailer, destined for Big Sandy, where specialist Randy Beaudette began a years-long restoration. The restored trolley returned to Fort Missoula in 2012, and is housed in an expansive barn constructed by Bill Weikel, Carson Vehrs and a host of volunteers.

7

The Civilian Conservation Corps

"Fort Peck and the CCC camp was a lifesaver for an awful lot of young boys like me."
Herbert Jacobson

The American economy went into free-fall after the stock market crash of 1929, and the Army began looking at ways to save money. Plans included closing Fort Missoula or turning it into a tuberculosis hospital for Native Americans, however it was the poor economy that ultimately saved Fort Missoula. Unemployment became so severe that President Franklin Roosevelt established the Civilian Conservation Corps (CCC) designed to put young unemployed men from poor families to work. The CCC came into existence on March 31, 1933 when Roosevelt signed the Emergency Conservation Work Act.

The Army was put in charge of administering the new program as it was the only agency large enough for the task. Fort Missoula was immediately designated as the Northwest Regional Headquarters for the Civilian Conservation Corps, and it became the headquarters and supply center for an area that included all of Montana, Yellowstone and Glacier National Parks, and portions of northern Idaho. Army officers suddenly found themselves responsible for organizing, training, and housing the CCC enrollees, plus administration of the work camps. On August 3, 1933 Army Reserve officers were called up to replace Regular Army men in camp leadership. Administrators at Fort Missoula kept the financial and personnel records, supplied the camps, and oversaw the education programs. The fort also held regular training sessions for district employees and administrators, company commanders, and education advisers. Staff at each district included a commanding officer, adjutant, chaplain, and medical officer. Montana was approved for 25 camps at first, and another was approved later. The first camp was in operation just weeks after the program was authorized. For the next several years the Fort Missoula District administered from 24 to 32 camps during the summer months, with an average of 200 to 225 men per camp. During the first 18 months in operation the Fort Missoula District spent $3.147 million, an enormous boost to the local community during the Depression. One beneficiary was the Miller Creek rancher who had a contract to supply 1,000 cords of firewood to the fort.

CCC trucks from the Fort Missoula District soon became a common sight throughout the state. This 1938 photo shows a truck in front of Barracks 26.
HMFM Walter H. Saxton Collection 1997.023.002b

The enrollees had to pass through Fort Missoula for training and camp assignments. Tents and latrines for 250 men were erected on the original parade grounds at Fort Missoula on April 23, 1933. The Labor Department opened a recruitment office for the Civilian Conservation Corps in Helena, charged with enrolling 5,800 local men, who began arriving within the week. The program was soon expanded to include veterans and Native Americans.

During the first months it was not unusual for 400 to 500 men to arrive at Fort Missoula in a single day. The Army soon ran out of tents, blankets, and mess gear as the first summer saw 6,500 men outfitted at the fort. New recruits were issued clothes, underwent a physical exam, were vaccinated, evaluated for their response to military discipline, and underwent a conditioning regimen. Enrollees were at first between the ages of 17 and 23. They were paid at least $30 per month, with most of their wages sent home to their families. The original enlistment period was for six months. Camp leaders were paid $45 per month, while assistant leaders received $36 per month. Those who passed muster at Fort Missoula were sworn in and sent to a work camp.

The quota for each state was set as a percentage of population rather than land area. Local men were given preference for hiring, but enlistment rates in Montana did not meet the demand, so enrollees from eastern states were brought in. The first trainload of 189 boys from Harlem, the Bronx, Manhattan, and Brooklyn arrived at Fort Missoula on June 1, 1933. Some of the easterners were considered juvenile delinquents who had been dumped into the CCC program, and many had problems adapting to Montana's mountains and climate. These men were dismissed by the dozens, while Montanans complained that the sorely needed jobs should be reserved for locals. On the other hand, the children at Fort Missoula seemed to enjoy having the New Yorkers around. Alice Della Vecchia recalled, "Summer was fun because the CCCs would camp on the parade ground. This was fun because, as a child, you could tell these "gullible easterners" wild tales about the Indians, like they would be coming to scalp. The poor kids didn't know the Indians came regularly to get "Bitterroots" for their medicine, and whole groups marched in then."[1]

The enlistees were organized into sections of 25 men, each with a senior leader and an assistant leader. They wore blue denim work clothes and had a surplus olive drab uniform for dress. A forest green uniform was adopted in 1938 at the request of President Roosevelt. Reveille was at 6:00 a.m., with physical training at 6:30, followed by breakfast. Food was described as, "wholesome, palatable and of the variety that sticks to the ribs."[2] After breakfast they lined up for roll call, then left for work at 7:45. They took an hour break for lunch and worked until 4 p.m., then returned to camp. Lights out was 10 p.m. Each camp was commanded by a captain or first lieutenant, and the military men were often frustrated by the Cs, as they were called. An officer at the Coram camp once told a group of enrollees that, "I know you guys are not in the Army - but I wish to God you were"[3]

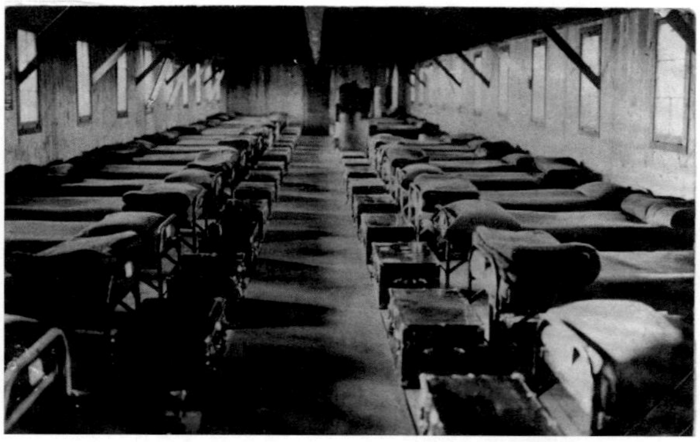

This is a look inside a typical CCC barracks. Once the program got off the ground the CCC adopted standard prefabricated buildings that could easily be disassembled and moved to a new location. These barracks were also used in the construction of the Alien Detention Center at the fort in 1941.
Oregon State University Library

An ice-skating rink on the old parade ground was a welcome diversion for the families of the CCC employees and the soldiers of the 4th Infantry.
HMFM Mildred Siperly Collection 1985.069.002

Fort Missoula oversaw the establishment of 26 camps the first summer. Enlistees lived in tents until wooden barracks could be built. Camps eventually were standardized and built of prefabricated and portable buildings. By 1937, a standard CCC camp contained four barracks, a mess hall and kitchen, forestry agent's quarters, officer's quarters, headquarters, storehouse, welfare building, dispensary, school, lavatory, bathhouse, and latrine.[4]

The Army was in charge of the camps but most of the actual work projects in Montana were overseen by the US Forest Service, the National Park Service, the Bureau of Reclamation, and the Soil Conservation Service. Glacier and Yellowstone National Parks each had six to eight companies working in the summer months. A company was sent to Moiese to help improve the National Bison Range in 1934, and by the end of the summer the CCC men reported they had killed 400 rattlesnakes during their work. Camps were widely dispersed so as to spread the benefits throughout the state. The camps were racially segregated, and camps on the Kootenai National Forest and in Glacier National Park were reserved for black enlistees. Congress expanded the scope of the CCC program when $50 million was authorized for drought control work in June 1933. Drought relief companies were established at Ashland and Forsyth. These men built fences, roads, spring developments, reservoirs, put in cattle guards, culverts, telephone lines, and worked on rodent and insect control.

Forest Service rangers oversaw the majority of the work projects. At first the rangers gave priority to eradication of white pine blister rust, a plant disease with serious economic impacts. Eradication of blister rust involved men crawling up mountains while pulling currant and gooseberry bushes by hand to prevent them from harboring the disease. These men treated almost 750 square miles of rugged country in Montana and northern Idaho. CCC men also tried to eradicate bark beetles. Other enlistees were put to work pulling white bed sheets through the woods to catch ticks. During the spring of 1934 the CCC men captured 54,000 wood ticks destined for the Rocky Mountain Laboratory in Hamilton. The Forest Service employed 45 enlistees at a shop in the old trolley barn in Missoula, where they repaired trucks and heavy equipment. Each camp also had a "flying squad" of 40 firefighters, who had received two days of training in fighting wildfire. There were also 25 firefighters stationed at Fort Missoula who were available to help out anywhere in the district.

Other enlistees constructed or improved 2,500 miles of forest roads and strung hundreds of miles of telephone lines. They also built bridges, trails, fences, administrative buildings, water projects, campgrounds, and 93 forest lookouts. CCC men in the Fort Missoula District planted trees on 27,000 acres of forest land and helped expand the Savenac tree nursery at St. Regis by 50 acres. They logged numerous burned over areas and salvaged huge amounts of saw-logs and posts. Some of the earliest work accomplished by CCC crews in Montana was to improve the access into Missoula's Rattlesnake Canyon and Pattee Canyon, work that would continue over several years. They also helped improve and construct ski areas. From 1938 until 1940 CCC men constructed a 3.5 mile road into Pattee Canyon at a seven percent grade. At the same time 25 men worked on building the Pattee Canyon ski area and campground. During the fall of 1940 a reservoir was built and 1,400 feet of water pipe was laid to supply the the ski area.

Nineteen companies (3,600 men) were transferred south in September 1933 in anticipation of cold weather and only six companies, some 1,195 men, remained in the Fort Missoula District when winter came. Three were stationed at the Ninemile Ranger Station and Remount Station and three were drought relief companies. Two

Many CCC men worked at the district sign shop at Fort Missoula. The shop, which was moved to Nine Mile in 1937, created 44,184 signs, markers, and monuments for historic sites, campgrounds, forest roads and trails. The sign shop produced several versions of this logo, which was used on everything from trucks to uniform patches. RMMMH were stationed near Forsyth while another was near the Gallatin National Forest. The enlistees received Christmas leave, although some stayed in camp. The three Ninemile companies got to come into Missoula for Christmas. Many of the men refused to work in extremely cold weather, and at one Montana camp 55 men from New York were discharged en masse in 1941 when they refused to work in the cold.

While most jobs were outdoors, Fort Missoula enrollees also worked as draftsmen, photographers, and auditors. Others worked at Forest Service headquarters in downtown Missoula, or as clerks, orderlies, statisticians, and pharmacists at local hospitals. Although enlistment was restricted to men, many women found employment with the CCC administration at Fort Missoula. The fort had four movie operators, nine truck drivers, five cooks, three radio operators, 23 typists, 13 office clerks, 16 warehousemen, draftsmen, plus four mail clerks. The CCC administration also employed a surgeon and dentist, three hospital orderlies, and a pharmacist. The first death in the Fort Missoula District occurred from "Mesenteric thrombosis" or a blood clot, on June 14, 1933. At least 77 men died while serving with the Fort Missoula District, from drownings, falls, auto accidents, fights, bad liquor, hypothermia, medical conditions, falling snags and work accidents. Six CCC workers died in forest fires. One of the more spectacular accidents occurred June 26, 1938 when the Milwaukee Road Olympian and a CCC train collided, knocking the CCC train off the rails, and killing a cook.

Many of the enrollees were illiterate and there were complaints the program didn't provide enough educational opportunities. In response, the CCC educational program began in December 1933, with an education advisor eventually assigned to each camp. The educational advisers met at Fort Missoula for a week each winter to plan curriculum. Some men learned to read and write in the camps, and by the spring of 1934 the Fort Missoula District had educational advisers at 14 out of 38 camps. Eventually each camp had a schoolhouse. In addition to typical school classes for those who needed them, instruction was provided in a variety of occupational and artistic courses. Meat cutting classes were held at Daly Meats in 1935, and a craftsmanship class was offered as well. At first classes were held at night, on weekends, or in the winter so as to not interfere with the work. The slogan of one camp at Glacier National Park was to, "Broaden their minds, not their asses." Certificates were awarded upon completion of the coursework. The administration at Fort Missoula also awarded a District Education Trophy, which was won one year by the Birch Creek Camp on the Beaverhead National Forest. The camp near Dillon was considered something of a show-piece for the CCC as the camp offered 32 different classes, and was dubbed the University of Birch Creek.

The administrators of the Fort Missoula CCC District posed for this photo in 1938.
Ray Hanson Collection HMFM 1988.047.001

Carl L. Foss was the District Chaplain at Fort Missoula, and made sure that religious services were available to all CCC enlistees. This service was held at the Flint Creek Camp.
NARA RG 35GE-3G

On weekends the enlistees were free to enjoy sports, hunting, fishing, gold panning, music, theater, gardening and leisure time. Most camps held dances several times a year. Religious services were held at all camps on Sunday, often conducted by local chaplains. Every CCC company had a small library, and the books were periodically rotated between camps. The Montana State University (Missoula) Journalism School gave an award to the best camp newspaper in the 9th Corps. Fourteen camps in Montana had their own paper, but the award was won by a camp in California whose newspaper was called, "The Goldbricker."

The men were regularly lectured on the dangers of alcohol and warned to be on their best behavior, but with thousands of young men away from home for the first time, problems were inevitable. Some deserted their camps, and several were arrested for stealing cars, including two enrollees who not only stole a car, but ran off with two married women as well. The camp at Coram was faced with a near riot on May 3, 1934 when a group of Butte men fought over who got to use the camp's trucks.

One of the largest work camps in the country was Camp Nine Mile, near Alberton, which eventually grew to 44 buildings and a capacity of 500 men. At least three buildings were constructed at the Remount station with CCC labor. One company at Nine Mile spent the winter months making pack saddles for the Forest Service. Camp Menard was built near the Ninemile Remount Depot for the CCC in 1940 and by April of the following year most functions at Ninemile were transferred to Camp Menard. Within 24 months 7,700 CCC men passed through Menard, including Edward Saylor, who would soon gain fame as one of the "Doolittle Raiders."

Missoula's South Avenue was extended west to Reserve Street in 1930, connecting with the original entrance to the fort. CCC men built stone pylons at the entrance in 1935 and also planted most of the Chinese-elm trees lining the roadways at Fort Missoula. The CCC facilities generated considerable traffic, and administrators proposed building a new road due to congestion at the fort's main entrance. What is now called Guardsman Lane was built by a local contractor with CCC help in 1941.

Enrollment in the CCC program began to decline once the economy improved in the mid-1930s, and the Missoula County relief director ordered that all eligible boys in families on relief were required to join the CCC. however by December of 1938 CCC enrollees were no longer required to be a member of a relief family, but did have to be a US citizen, unmarried and out of school, and between the ages of 19 and 23. Men were discharged from the program on their 24th birthday or after a maximum of two years in CCC (although one early enlistee managed to stay in the program for 65 months.)

The census listed 882 people living on the Fort Missoula Military Reservation in 1940, compared to 426 residents in 1930. The Fort Missoula District oversaw 28 CCC camps in 1940, the most since 1936, but the number of men assigned to each company had declined from 185 to 165 due to low enlistment. An auto mechanics school opened at Fort Missoula in 1941, and training of the CCC men changed to emphasize skills needed for national defense, including short-wave radio operation and typing.

The CCC Radio Program

Theron Roth, (right) a CCC enrollee at Yellowstone National Park, receives a radio message from district headquarters at Fort Missoula. Tom Mills of Lolo started the Fort Missoula radio station, which had a 250-watt short-wave transmitter to keep in touch with the 9th Corps headquarters in San Francisco, plus smaller 20-watt sets to keep in contact with the work camps. There were three radio operators at Fort Missoula who owned their own sets, although the government paid for maintenance and battery costs. The radio system reduced costs by eliminating much of the need for telephone and telegraph messages. The fort's radio operators relayed many emergency messages over this network, and were connected to the Army Amateur Radio System, which allowed enrollees to send messages home over the network. By 1940 there was a radio operator at each camp in the district, all trained at Fort Missoula. NARA photo

Departure of the 4th Infantry

On July 1, 1939 a reception and dance was held at the fort as a welcome to the fort's new commander, Lieutenant Colonel Earl Landreth and his wife and two daughters. They weren't destined to stay long. German troops invaded France and routed the British and French armies in May 1940, and the US Army began to prepare for a possible war against the Nazis and the increasingly aggressive Japanese. The First Battalion of the 4th Infantry, which had garrisoned Fort Missoula longer than any other unit, received orders to proceed to a new duty station in May 1940. The fort records from 1877 to 1916 were stored in boxes in the Powder Magazine. In early June the soldiers were transferred to Fort Richardson, Alaska, where the 4th Infantry formed the core of the Alaskan Defense Command. Colonel Landreth commanded 456 officers and enlisted men when they arrived at Anchorage in late June 1940, charged with defending 660,000 square miles of Alaska Territory. The 4th Infantry acted as a reserve force during the invasion of the Japanese-held Aleutian island of Attu in May 1943, and the First Battalion won a Presidential Unit Citation for the battle of Chichagof Valley during the latter stages of that battle. The 4th Infantry remained in Alaska until the end of the war, then served as occupation troops in postwar Japan.

After the 4th Infantry left Missoula, a small detachment of Army Reserve soldiers remained at the fort to oversee the CCC administration and look after the post while the regular Army prepared for a possible war in Europe. The idea of establishing an enlarged government hospital at Fort Missoula was once again resurrected just before World War II, but never materialized. The fort often provided housing for military units that were changing duty stations, and on July 8, 1941 a company of the Third Army Air Corps stopped at the fort with 65 trucks, 175 officers and men. The remaining Army officers, responsible for overseeing the CCC and the summer Civilian Military Training Corps (CMTC), threw a Halloween-themed Army Farewell Party at the end of November in 1941 at the old log officers club. Days later America was at war.

The end of the Civilian Conservation Corps

Major M.E. Sorley was appointed the new commander of the Fort Missoula CCC District on January 15, 1942. An engineer, Sorley had gone to grade school in Missoula 30 years before while his father Lewis Stone Sorley served as a captain of Company K of the 14th Infantry. Major Sorley made plans to put 6,400 CCC enrollees to work at 32 camps, however enrollment had fallen sharply, and many of the planned camps never opened. After the US entry into World War II, the demise of the CCC program became inevitable. There were 14 CCC companies still active in Montana on February 8, 1942, but the Forest Service reported that it had 15 vacant CCC camps available for the immediate relocation of Japanese-Americans from the west coast. The Civilian

Master Sergeant Bozo

Soldiers at the fort took in a starving three-week-old puppy in 1928. Nicknamed Bozo, the small dog soon became the fort's unofficial mascot, a role that was formalized when he was promoted to honorary master sergeant in 1932. Bozo was adopted by Corporal G.T. Hesford, Company B of the 4th Infantry and had the run off the fort for more than a decade. He would respond to bugle calls but was particularly fond of mess call. The paw prints in the concrete step poured at the front of the Powder Magazine in 1934 are believed to be his. Sergeant Bozo's military career came to an end when he was struck and killed by a CCC truck near the front entrance of the fort. Bozo was buried with full military honors on October 24, 1940, and was laid to rest in a place of honor, either in the cemetery or near the flagpole on the parade ground. Some accounts indicate that a small unlabeled stone in the cemetery marks his grave.[5]

Conservation Corps had always depended on an annual appropriation from Congress, but a Senate Committee voted to kill the CCC appropriations on June 25, 1942, and the measure passed on July 1. Roosevelt administration officials met the next day to prepare to disband the CCC. Buildings were to be given to the Army, or to the local community if the Army didn't want them. The organization ceased to exist as quickly as it had been formed, with 550 CCC camps transferred to the Army for housing. All camps in Montana were closed by July 24, 1942.

As if to cap off the end of the CCC era, one of the warehouses on the west end of the fort caught fire late one night in June 1942. The remaining CCC men and local fire departments responded immediately, but the fire was fueled by stacks of mattresses that burned all night. The fire was so bright that it attracted carloads of Missoula residents who showed up to watch the 5,000 square foot structure burn. An ambulance and several trucks were burned, although firemen managed to save 200 precious tires needed for the war effort.

The CCC was the most popular New Deal program in Montana, and more than 40,000 men served in the Fort Missoula District, with 25,600 of them from Montana. The Fort Missoula District was the largest regional headquarters in the nation by 1940, and more than $19 million was spent in the state in support of 61 different camps. Many buildings, recreation areas, roads and trails built by the CCC are still being used to this day. Herbert Jacobson of Sidney enrolled in the CCC when he was 19, and later took a job with a construction crew at Fort Peck. "Fort Peck and the CCC camp was a lifesaver for an awful lot of young boys like me," he recalled.

Scoundrels

Mess Sergeant **Guenther Gustav Rumrich** was born in America to Austrian parents, and educated in Germany. He enlisted in the US Army in 1930, but was thrown into the stockade for desertion. He reenlisted and was sent to Fort Missoula, where he waited for an opportunity to steal the mess fund before deserting a second time in January 1936, leaving his pregnant wife behind in Missoula. Unable to find a job, Rumrich applied (by mail) to become a German spy. Using the code name Crown, he joined a group of spies seeking industrial and military secrets from May 1936 to February 1938. He was described as, "a tall, sharp-eyed individual, with a stiff military bearing and a bristly Teutonic haircut."[6] His downfall came after he impersonated a US diplomat and asked the New York Passport Division to deliver 50 passport blanks to his hotel room. He was arrested by the FBI in February 1938, and charged with being a deserter from Fort Missoula. His testimony resulted in the conviction of three other spies, including a female hairdresser on a German cruise ship who served as a courier. Fourteen other spies fled the country upon learning of his arrest. Rumrich pleaded guilty to espionage and was sentenced to two years in prison.

Arthur Osborne Phillips had served several prison terms for fraud, narcotics possession, and impersonating a doctor by the early 1930s. Phillips had been interested in medicine since he was a teen, and spent his time studying medical textbooks in the prison library. Upon his release in the early 1930s he fraudulently obtained a copy of a medical degree earned by another doctor with the same last name, and used it to obtain employment with the Civilian Conservation Corps. He worked as a doctor for the Fort Missoula District at several CCC camps including Mammoth, Rimini, and Elk Park. By 1942 he was assistant chief surgeon at a hospital in Chico, California, where he performed at least 32 successful appendectomies and other operations. He was arrested when his background came to light, and received a six-month sentence and a $600 fine for practicing medicine without a license, as well as a nine-month sentence for illegal possession of a firearm. Late in 1942 he was also sentenced to five years in federal prison for fraud and falsifying government documents to obtain employment with the Fort Missoula CCC District.

Fort Buildings constructed from 1920 to 1940

- T-1 - Post headquarters (see page 91)
- Building 4 - Log recreation building built in 1940 by the WPA (see page 91). The building had a basketball court, boxing ring, bowling alley, dance floor, and restaurant.
- T-12 - The hospital staff quarters is a 1-story frame residence built in 1938, and now owned by the Western Montana Mental Health Center.
- T-46 - Firehouse/guardhouse (see page 89)
- Building 105 - A 1.5 story concrete post bakery built prior to 1915. It replaced a bakery built in the 1880s.
- T-203 - A warehouse built for the Army in 1940. It is now owned by the Historical Museum at Fort Missoula.
- T-214 - The CCC staff quarters, a 1-story frame building built in 1938, is now home to the Child Development Center
- T-308 - Warehouse and shops built in 1936.
- T-310 - The boiler plant office was built in 1937. After the National Guard took took possession of the building in 1947 it became the caretaker's cottage. It is now used by the Rocky Mountain Museum of Military History.
- T-312 - A 2-story, 29,280 square foot warehouse was built in 1936 and cost $14,000. It was used by the Regular Army and the CCC until 1941, then was used for clothing salvage and repair from 1941 to 1947. It is now part of the National Guard's maintenance facility.
- T-316 - This 1.5 story frame building was built in 1936 at a cost of $8,500. It was used as the CCC administration building and headquarters from 1936 until 1942, then was used as a storage facility by the post engineer and the Montana National Guard from 1942 to 1957, when it became a National Guard Group Headquarters as well as home to the 443rd Field Artillery Battalion. Beginning in 1979 the National Center for Career Education used the building for storage. The Rocky Mountain Museum of Military History began renovating the building in 2000 under an agreement with the National Guard, and it now serves as the main museum building.
- T-327 - Oil storage building, now owned by the Montana National Guard.
- T-328 - Motor pool shop, now owned by the Montana National Guard.

Seen here in the late 1930s, the CCC Administration Building (T-316) is now home to the Rocky Mountain Museum of Military History. The CCC warehouse in the background (T-312) is owned by the Montana National Guard.

The WPA Recreation Building

In 1938 the Fort received $75,000 from the Works Progress Administration to "reconstruct, rehabilitate and improve buildings and grounds at Fort Missoula..." The WPA employed at least 288 construction workers and paid for several projects at Fort Missoula during the late 1930s, including construction of a firehouse/guardhouse and conversion of the 1880s chapel into the post headquarters (Building T-1). The most ambitious project undertaken with WPA funds involved construction of a new recreation center, which was air-conditioned and had a basketball court on the first floor, a basement bowling alley, plus a kitchen, bar, and stage. When completed it was the largest log structure in the state. The formal opening of the WPA recreation hall (Building 4) on

March 16, 1940 featured a nine-course dinner prepared and served by WPA and Fort Missoula employees, followed by a cabaret party at the nearby officer's club. The building hosted many boxing matches and basketball tourneys. The Fort Missoula CCC boxing team won a Golden Gloves championship by winning seven straight title bouts at a tournament held in the recreation center in March 1940. The detainees of the Alien Detention Center used the building for numerous musical and theatrical productions. The building was destroyed by fire on December 7, 1946. (Photo courtesy of Stan Cohen)

The Post Chapel and Headquarters (T-1)

The Fort's chapel was completed in 1885 with a rectory and classrooms built on the north end. During the late 1930's the Works Progress Administration allocated $15,300 to renovate the deteriorating chapel into a new post headquarters building. A concrete foundation was poured adjacent to the chapel and the building was jacked up during the summer of 1938 and moved over the foundation. The high-ceilinged chapel was converted into a two-story administration building, and new windows were added. A courtroom was built to handle disciplinary cases, a heating plant was installed in the basement, and electricity and phone lines were installed. The courtroom was used by the US Department of Justice to conduct Alien Hearings Boards for Japanese and Italian citizens, and later for Army disciplinary hearings. It was leased to the Air Force between 1962 and 1965 and then to the US Forest Service's Equipment and Development center. The Historical Museum at Fort Missoula purchased the building from the Forest Service in 2009 and has since restored the historic courtroom, which was revealed during renovations. Dr. Robert M. Brown said "We didn't know the courtroom was there. We didn't know it was the church. We just loved the basement."[7]

Above: The church jacked up and ready to move in 1938.

The Fire Station and Guard House

Building T-46 was built by the Halloway and George Construction Company in 1940. It was designed to be similar to buildings constructed 25 years before, and cost $59,838. The first floor held a fire station and guard offices, with cell blocks on the second floor. After World War II it continued to be used as a fire station until 1962, when it was converted into the Post Exchange (PX). In 1971 the US Forest Service began using part of the building as office space for an archaeologist and fire dispatchers, while the Army Reserve used the garage as a repair shop. Today it is home to the Forest Service's Fire and Aviation Management division.

This aerial view of the fort taken from the water tower shows two rows of barracks assembled for the Alien Detention Center. Two more rows of barracks were eventually built to the right of this photo. UM 82-0220

A trainload of Italian detainees walks from Post Siding to the front gates of the new Alien Detention Center under the watchful eye of the Border Patrol. UM 84-0297

Many of the civilian employees who had worked for the CCC found employment with the Border Patrol.
HMFM Peter Fortune Collection 2001.048.177

A group of the Border Patrolmen who guarded the detainees at the Alien Detention Center.
HMFM Peter Fortune Collection 2001.048.173

8
The Prisoners of Bella Vista

"Although there were many fences all around, the impressive beauty and landscape made it feel like, 'una Villa,' a village rather than a concentration camp..."

Umberto Benedetti

Missoula's Little Italy

World War II impacted Fort Missoula months before the United States actually entered the war. Italian dictator Benito Mussolini entered into a pact with Nazi Germany in 1940 and subsequently assisted in the invasion of France. In response to the invasion, the United States broke diplomatic relations with the Axis powers and promptly detained 28 Italian ships, 35 Danish ships (Denmark had just been invaded by Germany), and two German ships which happened to be in American ports at the time. At the request of the US, the Cuban government also detained an Italian ship. The largest of the Italian ships was the passenger liner *Il Conte Biancamano*, detained in the Panama Canal Zone after a Central American cruise.

The crews of these ships were allowed to stay aboard their vessels for nine months, from June 1940 until March 1941. The US government provided food and other supplies, as well as tutors from the Works Project Administration for twice-weekly English lessons. The Italians were required to register for the draft, but enjoyed the leisure time. Captain Carlo Fava of the *Dino* reported, "In a way it was pleasant. We were getting our pay from the shipping agent, we could go ashore every night."

When it appeared certain that the US would seize the ships early in the spring of 1941, the Italian government managed to get word to the stranded sailors to sabotage the vessels so that they could not be used by the US Navy. The sailors on the *Il Leme* in Portland, Oregon took these instructions to heart, and smashed all of the gauges, burned out the generators, and ran the main engines after spiking the lubricating oil with abrasives. The windlasses were also destroyed, making it impossible to raise the ship's anchor. Other ships were scuttled in the harbor. Twenty of the 28 ships were ultimately badly damaged, including *Il Conte Biancamano*.

Bill Hallam was one of the Border Patrolman who roamed the outer perimeter of the camp on horseback.
UM 84.0287

All of the ships and their crews were seized by armed US Coast Guardsmen and harbor police on March 30, 1941. Authorities found the crew of the *Il Leme* on deck, their sea bags packed, busily polishing off the remaining stores of wine while "lustily and happily" belting out Italian songs. The sailors were arrested and jailed.

An indignant Captain Giovanni Polonio declared the seizure of the ships and arrest of the crew would lead to war between Italy and the US. He said, "It is really inhuman what they are doing, really improper." He denied that any of his men had committed any crime, and stated, "jail is not the place for us."

Many of the officers and sailors were eventually indicted for damaging the ship's equipment and sent to prison, even though the damage had occurred while the ships were still owned by Italians, and even though some of the sailors claimed they had sabotaged their ships in order to prevent their ship from returning to fascist Italy.

Most of the Italian sailors were then sent to Ellis Island, New York, while

US authorities sought out camps in the interior of the country to house them. Captain Nick D. Collaer of the Immigration and Naturalization Service (INS) was assigned to establish detention camps for the Italian and German sailors at Fort Missoula and Fort Lincoln, North Dakota. Collaer accompanied two detainees, Captain Alessandro de Luca and Captain Francesco La Rosa as they were flown out to Montana in April 1941 to inspect the old frontier military post. The two Italians first saw the fort from the air, and promptly dubbed it "Bella Vista" (beautiful view).

The post was run-down, and in need of serious maintenance, but the US Army agreed to turn much of Fort Missoula over to the INS for a five-year period. The first 125 Italians arrived at Fort Missoula on May 9, 1941 after three days on a train with barred windows. They were met by armed guards. Many of these men were crewmen from the luxury liner *Il Conte Biancamano*, and included entertainers, waiters, and chefs. They brought their musical instruments, their tuxedos, and three dogs with them when they began arriving in force in mid-August of 1941. Besides the sailors, 62 former employees of the Italian Pavilion at the 1939 New York World's Fair were also sent to Missoula for overstaying their visas. One of them was Alfredo Cipolato, a highly trained waiter who had worked at the Italian Village Restaurant at the fair before taking a job at the Fontainebleu Hotel in Miami. "One day I come home, the FBI are there, and they just put me in jail." Picked up in July 1941, he spent a month in the Miami jail before he was sent to Ellis Island with several German detainees, then on to Fort Missoula by train, without so much as a hearing, or even an interrogation.

The detainees were at first quartered in the two large Mission-style barracks built in 1910. The ship's officers requested and were given separate sleeping quarters and dining area. Early arrivals helped complete the chain link fence topped with barbed wire that encircled one of the existing barracks and the land to the east. The fence was 10 feet tall, almost 5,000 feet in length and enclosed 33 acres. Sixteen wood frame barracks shipped from as far away as Alabama were put up by the detainees in May 1941, and another 14 barracks were erected in July and August. These were standard prefabricated buildings previously used in the CCC camps, with sections that bolted together. Supplies of blankets, cots, and kitchen gear were acquired from Army posts and CCC camps. A boiler plant, blacksmith shop, mess-hall, bakery, laundry, print shop, dispensary, and school were also inside the compound. A separate fence was built around the hospital. Forty-foot guard towers were constructed at the four corners of the camp, which were linked by telephone to the main office. The guard towers were equipped with radios, billy clubs, gas masks, and 37mm tear gas guns.

Captain Collaer commanded the camp during the first year, and was also in charge of the camp at Fort Lincoln. Umberto Benedetti remembered that, "The first year in the camp at Fort Missoula was not very good because, although the government sent all kinds of supplies... the officers were bewildered and confused." A dozen Border Patrolmen, including three horsemen, were on duty at all times, with one man roaming inside the camp. John Moe was one of those who worked the interior. "I worked inside, unarmed, alone among 1,300 Italians. I would find some officer that I could talk to, to obtain their history and ensure there were no problems going on in the camp, such as attempts to escape or hostilities between some members. And there were hostilities." For extra security the guards could call on the Missoula Police, Border Patrol guards from the Spokane District, and 75 "crack shots" from the nearby Missoula Rod and Gun Club, (the latter were never needed). There were a total of 62 civilian and Border

Italian detainees unload their baggage upon arrival at Fort Missoula in 1941.
HMFM Peter Fortune Collection 2001.048.218

Patrol guards at the camp, and the chief security officer later recalled that for the most part their jobs could have been done by a Boy Scout. None of the Border Patrolmen spoke Italian, but many of the ship captains spoke English or Spanish, which most of the Patrolmen understood.

The Italians inside the fence were given the authority to create their own organization to deal with US officials, and were soon rewarded with a high degree of autonomy to conduct their own affairs. Captain Fava of the SS *Dino* remembered, "We had our own democracy there. The authorities were very good to us." All visitors entering the camp had to register at the gates, and had to be approved by an Italian official. Even the INS guards requested permission before entering the camp. Nevertheless, the Italians were subject to a certain degree of military discipline. Reveille at the "Campo di Detenzione di Fort Missoula" was at 6:00 a.m., followed by two roll calls at 8:00 a.m. and 8:00 p.m. The Italians elected Captain de Luca as the "mayor" of their new home, and a council was formed consisting of representatives from the different ships and groups represented at the camp. The men divided themselves into various departments to handle the many responsibilities of a self-governing camp, including administration, purchasing, cooking, cleaning, and recreation. Discipline for minor offenses was handled by the Italians themselves. The Italian consul from Seattle visited Fort Missoula and told the men to be on their best behavior. "Very rarely did we have to handle any problems among the detainees," recalled Moe.

The Geneva Convention of 1929 mandated that the detainees were to be provided food and quarters similar to what US soldiers were issued. The detainees were also provided with laundry and cooking facilities, personal items, writing materials, and tobacco. A canteen sold a variety of goods, provided they were not "detrimental to discipline or security of the detention facility."[1] Detainees were allowed at least two hours of recreation per day, were supplied with books and magazines, and were guaranteed access to religious services. Their mail was censored but they were allowed visitors. The detainees had their own carpenters, shoemakers, barbers, a priest, and several world-class chefs, including Orlando Figini, chef at the Italian Village at the World's Fair. They organized a fire department, postal delivery, religious services, formed a library, and produced choir, band and symphony concerts.

Armando Tosi, the manager of the Italian Village Restaurant was repatriated from Ellis Island to Italy, where he was interviewed by a newspaper in Rome. Tosi reported that Ellis Island and Fort Missoula were concentration camps, and the Italian detainees suffered, "bestial treatment."[2] Tosi, who maintained his information came from one of his former employees interned at Fort Missoula, also claimed the Italians were, "watched by policemen, the majority of whom are Jews."

Responding to the charges by Tosi, two prominent Italian-American newspapers, *Corriere D' America* and *Il Progresso*, both based in New York City, investigated the charges. Reporter Gene Rea of *Corriere D' America* paid an unannounced visit to Fort Missoula in August 1941, where he found 993 Italian detainees. "The first sight that I saw of the detention camp was that of a beautiful summer resort." Rea reported that he was allowed unfettered access to the camp, could speak freely to any of the detainees without interference, and that the authorities in charge of the camp did not hinder his reporting in any

Led by the band from the cruise ship *Il Conte Biancamano,* the Italians parade around the camp on November 24, 1941.
Courtesy of Stan Cohen

way. Rea also reported "Fort Missoula is something unusual, for here, in this picturesque surrounding, a new idea has been born. Unlike Ellis Island, the men at Fort Missoula govern themselves... So beautiful is the setting that the name of Fort Missoula is no longer being used. Instead this community has become the city of 'Bella Vista,' with its own autonomous government, protected by the United States."

Writing 40 years later, Umberto Benedetti echoed those sentiments. "Although there were many fences all around, the impressive beauty and landscape made it feel like, 'una Villa,' a village rather than a concentration camp..." He further explained that, "no one really wanted to escape because they were treated very well by the people of Missoula."

The Italians were usually well-behaved, although Moe reported, "near disorder" during soccer matches. The Italians did not always agree on political matters however, and there were disputes between fascists and anti-fascists. One afternoon in early September 1941 a demonstration that Border Patrolman John Moe referred to as the "olive oil rebellion" broke out. Moe recalled, "a couple of them complained to me that they didn't like the olive oil they were being provided. They wanted olive oil three times a day." Alfredo Cipolato remembered that an indignant Italian chef even slapped an American supplier when presented with beef lard instead of olive oil for cooking. When a demonstration erupted in the camp, Moe suspected it had something to do with olive oil. In reality, the truth was much more complicated. Feelings had been running high in the camp after Dr. Orvall Smiley, the camp's Public Health Service doctor, posted a letter written to him by one of the internees, an anti--fascist named Antonio Visini. A fascist among the prisoners took offense at the letter and assaulted Visini.[3] Moe recalled, "some of the fascists broke the ribs and really worked over an Italian internee here because they thought he was too friendly with the guards." The fight spread and more anti-fascists in the camp were attacked. The first indication the guards had of trouble was when 500 excited Italians gathered at the main gate.

Sirens blared and off-duty guards rushed to the camp with Thompson submachine guns in their hands. "We didn't know what was going on," said Moe. "They were complaining about all kinds of things at that time." One nervous guard accidentally set off a tear gas grenade inside a car, starting a fire. John Moe grabbed a fire extinguisher and put the fire out, but received a "snootful of tear gas." To make matters worse, "We had given Leonard Kuka in the tower a gun, and he decided to check it out and he shot himself in the foot. Then the Italians retreated. They said 'these guys are armed and dangerous.' And we had no further riots."[4]

Five Italians were hospitalized after this incident, and some of the communists were removed from the camp to keep the peace. Eighteen anti-fascists were sent to Townsend, where they lived in an abandoned hotel. Others were sent to Frenchtown and Stevensville to cultivate sugar beets. Despite some tensions, the remaining detainees led a somewhat idyllic existence. Cipolato remembered that, "life in Montana was calm and the food excellent, even though the camp was surrounded by a high wire fence and guards. There was a beautiful library, tennis courts, and other athletic facilities. We were never bothered."

Breakfast in the Italian mess hall featured Kellogg's Rice Flakes on this morning.
HMFM Peter Fortune Collection 2001.048.028

Restaurants and hotels around the country wanted to hire the chefs and the waiters from the Italian Village and *Il Conte Biancamano*. Instead, the chefs were in charge of preparing food for the internees, who enjoyed a variety of Italian and American food as well as fresh-baked bread. They sat at long tables in the mess hall, decorated with flags of the Italian empire. Alcohol was forbidden at first, but the enterprising internees made their own wine from raisins, figs, and local fruit under the noses of the INS inspectors who roamed the camp. John Moe remembered, "We provided them with raisins, and they made wine. Then we provided them with fruit, and they made wine." Eventually the detainees were allowed to buy locally brewed Highlander Beer at the Post Exchange. The chefs produced special meals at Thanksgiving, Christmas, Easter, and the Fourth of July, and the Italian Cruise Line donated cases of wine to the camp before Christmas in 1942. It arrived late, and was confiscated by the State Liquor Control Board, although some accounts indicate the detainees enjoyed it on Easter 1943. The Catholic Church was instrumental in advocating for the rights of the detained seamen. Local priests and the Archdiocese in Helena helped with legal matters, arranged proxy marriages to girls back home, advocated for work release, helped obtain a radio and a piano, and provided the detainees with a direct communication link to the Vatican in Rome, and ultimately to their families in Italy.

Movies were shown twice a week, and the detainees were provided with musical instruments and art supplies. They were also allowed to listen to the radio, purchased by the Archdiocese of Helena. "They would cheer when the Italians were making gains in the war, but later when we began to win some, their attitude changed and they became much more cooperative," recalled Moe.

There were numerous recreational opportunities available at the fort. The Italians played cards, board games, soccer, bocci ball, and tennis. Classes in foreign languages and navigation were offered for detainees, featuring textbooks written at Fort Missoula. Several of the Italian seamen built two large rowboats which were used on the adjacent Bitterroot River. Building wooden models of their ships (some are displayed today at the Historical Museum at Fort Missoula) became a popular pastime. Religious services were held on Sundays, and in an effort to increase attendance, the weekly ration of tobacco was given out at the end of the church services, resulting in an attendance of nearly 100 percent. Sunday mass was held at 9:00 a.m., and the band performed for the detainees after the service. The more artistic among the internees decorated the chapel with religious paintings and exhibited their paintings in downtown Missoula.

Led by Maestro Graziani, the tuxedo-clad performers from the *Il Conte Biancamano* included a string quartet, a musical trio, and a full-fledged symphony. They entertained their fellow prisoners and soon held regular public concerts for a small fee. They also performed at the Masonic Hall, churches, and private homes in Missoula, and gave music lessons to interested citizens. The string quartet once performed for 1,000 local residents.

Mass was celebrated in front of one of the concrete barracks buildings. The Catholic Church was instrumental in helping the Italian detainees keep in touch with their families.
HMFM Peter Fortune Collection 2001.048.219

The fort's brand new log recreation hall had a basketball court, boxing ring, bowling alley, restaurant and a theater that could seat 800 people. Alfredo Cipolato and ship's cabinetmaker Umberto Benedetti built sets for the stage plays. One of the productions put on by the detainees was a satirical play called *La Fiaccola*, about their life in the camp, which opened to decidedly mixed reviews. Ten percent of their performance earnings were donated to a Missoula charity. Cipolato remembered, "We put on concerts and theatrical productions, and I participated in these. Later we had to stop because the musician's union in Missoula said that the city's programs were being hurt by this."

As their first winter in Missoula approached, five of the interred Italian officers occupied their time repairing toys to be given as Christmas presents to local children. Mrs. Russell Neal, the Community Chest officer who organized the repairs, thought the seamen were doing a "splendid and careful job." The Missoula YMCA also donated 1,000 small Christmas gifts to the Italians, which were distributed via a lottery system.

Arrival of the Issei

The Japanese attack on Pearl Harbor on December 7, 1941 had profound implications for Fort Missoula. Within hours after the attack the FBI began arresting Italian, German, and Japanese aliens living in the US, even though the country would not be at war with Italy or Germany for several days. There were 600,000 Italians, 260,000 Germans, and 40,000 Japanese residents living in the United States in 1940, and many of them had been in the country for decades. During the next few months 31,000 enemy aliens were arrested by FBI agents, including more than 250 additional Italians picked up on the West Coast and sent to the fort in the two months following the attack on Pearl Harbor. Those detained included Italian veterans of World War I, leaders of Italian clubs and societies, radio announcers, and those who had publicly expressed support for Mussolini or fascism. The Italian detainees held at the fort, most of whom had been arrested for visa violations, were now reclassified as enemy aliens.

Discriminatory immigration laws prevented Japanese citizens who arrived in the US later than 1913 from owning land, and those who arrived after 1924 were prohibited from becoming US citizens. Many of these Issei (first generation) were successful businessmen who had been in America for decades. Beginning in 1939, the FBI's Enemy Alien Control Unit began compiling a Custodial Detention Index, which identified potential enemy aliens living in the US. Immediately after the attack on Pearl Harbor, FBI agents and local policemen, armed with blanket arrest warrants and 3 x 5 index cards on each suspect, fanned out across the country to pick up everyone listed on the FBI's Custodial Detention list. The 770 Issei on the list had already been classified according to their perceived threat. Diplomats, fishermen and fish producers, Shinto and Buddhist priests, importers, and community leaders were designated "A" or Most Dangerous. Others who might be dangerous but who had not yet been fully investigated were given a "B" rating. Japanese language teachers, editors, and martial arts instructors were classified "C" or possibly dangerous.[5] There seemed to be an effort to round up well-known and successful business and community leaders in an attempt to intimidate the Japanese-American population, even though most of the men interned posed absolutely no threat. Japanese leaders in Hawaii, California, Washington, and Oregon were arrested immediately, and approximately 1,200 Japanese, and 500 Germans and Italians were in custody within 24 hours of the attack on Pearl Harbor. While most of the Issei were arrested in Hawaii and the West Coast, Montana was not immune. Jean H. Maillet remembered, "My father was the general foreman for the Northern Pacific Railroad in Livingston. The railroad employed Japanese people, and my father was their supervisor... The man in charge of them was named Mr. Naudyee. When war was declared, the FBI in Butte called our home, ordering my father to have Mr. Naudyee at our home, as they were ordered to pick him up for questioning. I can still hear him say, 'What's going to happen to me, I don't understand. I worked here for many years with my friends.'" Maillet recalled the last time she saw Mr. Naudyee, "they hand-cuffed him and drove away. We never heard from him again."

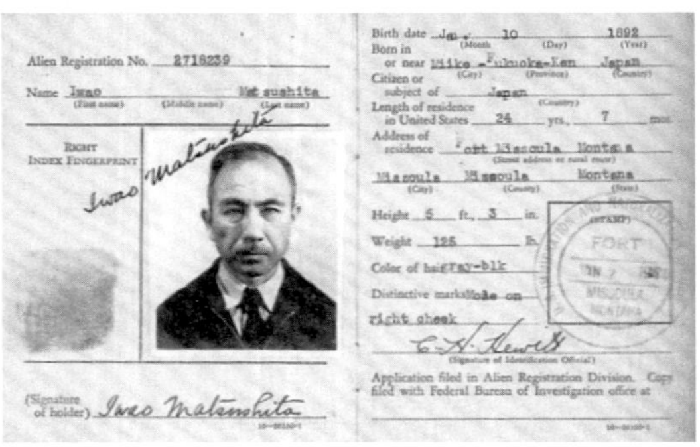
Alien Registration No. 2718239
Name Iwao (First name) (Middle name) Matsushita (Last name)
Right Index Fingerprint
(Signature of holder) Iwao Matsushita
Birth date Jan. (Month) 10 (Day) 1892 (Year)
Born in or near Mikke -Fukuoka-Ken (City) (Province) Japan (Country)
Citizen or subject of Japan (Country)
Length of residence in United States 24 yrs., 7 mos.
Address of residence Fort Missoula Montana (Street address or rural route)
Missoula (City) Missoula (County) Montana (State)
Height 5 ft., 3 in.
Weight 125 lb.
Color of hair gray-blk
Distinctive marks Mole on right cheek
C. H. Hewitt (Signature of Identification Official)
Application filed in Alien Registration Division. Copy filed with Federal Bureau of Investigation office at

Most of the Issei languished in jail cells with common criminals for a week or two before being herded aboard ships or trains. Warren Watanabe of San Francisco, a trade association official who had been in the US for more than 30 years, was one of those arrested.

He watched as his import-export business, which he would never see again, was padlocked. Tarao Takahashi, who spent two years at Fort Missoula, was arrested when his fishing boat docked at Terminal Island, California. He became one of 364 Japanese, 110 Germans and 25 Italians in custody at Terminal Island. The Italians and Japanese were soon sent by train to the Immigration and Naturalization Service's Alien Detention Center at Fort Missoula, and the first contingent arrived at the post eleven days after Pearl Harbor, escorted by three Border Patrolmen sent from the fort. Like many of the Japanese, Italian Filippo Molinari was arrested late on December 7 in California, wearing only pajamas and slippers, which he was still wearing when he arrived in Missoula in sub-zero weather.[6] One despondent Issei prisoner attempted to commit suicide on the train, but was saved by his fellow inmates. (He was later killed in an escape attempt at Fort Sill, Oklahoma.) The roundup continued, and dozens of Japanese copper miners from Nevada were also shipped to Missoula.

The first Issei reached Fort Missoula on December 18th, 1941, with a second train arriving on the following day. A Korean man who planned to enlist in the Army had the misfortune of traveling on the same train as the first Japanese, and was beaten at the Missoula train depot because he was Asian. Several other racially motivated attacks against anyone suspected of being Japanese occurred in the weeks after Pearl Harbor, until the state Attorney General finally warned Montanans to be tolerant of the estimated 17,000 foreign nationals living in the state.

Y. Kato wrote home as soon as he arrived in Missoula. "Officers here are very kind especially Mr. Collaer and Mr. McLaughlin who welcomed us in the American spirit." In the next few weeks hundreds of Japanese men arrived, as well as a few more Italian nationals who had been rounded up. The Issei were also allowed a degree of self-rule at Fort Missoula, and were responsible for their own cooking and cleaning.

According to Katsuma Mukaeda, "We formed a self-governing body among ourselves and I took charge of the supply office. I helped supply clothes and shoes and shirts and all the wearings, you know. We didn't have very many good things there for supplies. The detainees had what they brought from their homes. They didn't suffer. Of course, it was a very cold country. So most of the time we stayed in the barracks." The men slept on straw mattresses in wooden barracks heated by wood, and often complained of the cold. The Japanese men had their own mess hall, showers, and latrines. Some of the Japanese who had been common laborers and miners said they preferred life at Fort Missoula to the work they had been doing before the war. Like some of the Italians, Katsuro Miho described his days interned at Fort Missoula as, "a vacation at government expense."

They built Japanese baths, formed a baseball team, built a small golf course, and fished in the nearby Bitterroot River. The canteen at Fort Missoula provided toiletries, personal items, and tobacco. There was little for the prisoners to do at Fort Missoula, and many of the Issei spent their time gathering tiny rounded pebbles from the river bank and cementing them into vases and bowls in a hobby that came to be known as "stone fever." The arts and crafts of the detained Japanese came to be known as "Gaman," which meant "enduring the seemingly unbearable with patience and dignity"[7] Some of the Japanese internees served as volunteers with the

Many of the Japanese men occupied their time in captivity creating a variety of small arts and craft objects out of cement and small rounded rocks collected from the banks of the Bitterroot River. "Stone fever" was apparently contagious, and many of the detainees sent this type of artwork back to their families.
MHS 84-34

Missoula rural fire district, and in October 1943 six of them successfully extinguished a house fire in the Orchard Homes area.

Both the Italians and the Japanese were eventually allowed passes to shop in Missoula, although they were always accompanied by guards during the first months. Captain Bert Fraser was known to buy ice cream for the detainees during these outings. On one of these excursions in 1943 several Japanese men discovered the well-tended graves of 50 Japanese railroad workers who had died in Missoula in the first decade of the 20th century. The men were impressed that the community took care of the graves, and organized a Buddhist ceremony at the cemetery.[8]

By early 1942 Fort Missoula was the largest internment camp in the US and held nearly 1,000 men of Japanese ancestry and an equal number of Italians. The Missoula Chamber of Commerce formally requested that additional housing be added to the camp. Security measures tightened, and the Italians and Japanese at first shunned each other, but as time went on the fence between the compounds was removed and the men began to mingle. Japanese men learned to play soccer, and taught the Italians judo. Evelyn King, a young reporter for the *Daily Missoulian*, was given a tour of the camp, and was struck by the disparity between the quarters occupied by the neat and tidy Japanese, and the Italians. "The Italian barracks looked like some teen-ager's room or a college dormitory with clothes, bedding, and personal items scattered helter-skelter." She also reported that the elderly Japanese were polite and deferential, while the younger Italian sailors were, "sassy, teasing, boldly eyeing [*sic*] the girl reporter and making remarks (in Italian of course)."[9]

As soon as the first Issei arrived in Montana, the Japanese government accused the US of abusing the Japanese citizens in custody. In response Superintendent Collaer forwarded to INS headquarters what he described as "selected at random" excerpts from letters written by the internees. The excerpts, all written on December 20, 1941 were highly complimentary of the camp. F. Fukuda reported "Food and warm beds make this a vacation I have not had in 40 years." I. Oka declared "We are treated very kindly and everydays [*sic*] food is 1st class. US Government treat us like gentlemen."[10] By the end of December, 650 Japanese citizens from western states were being held at Fort Missoula.

The first Japanese internees who arrived at Fort Missoula were mostly elderly, with the average age over 60. A few suffered from dementia or mental illness, and three detainees died during the first four months in the camp. The first, who suffered from "severe senility" and pneumonia, died on his initial day in camp. Another suffered from both dementia and pneumonia, and succumbed to a heart attack. The third man died from terminal colon cancer in a Missoula hospital. These deaths would soon provoke a diplomatic incident.

The detainees could receive visitors at any time as long as they spoke in English, and could write daily letters to their families, although censors examined every letter. Japanese interpreter Paul Kashino arrived at the camp several weeks after the first Issei. Part of his job was to censor any letters written in Japanese, and to report any signs of subversiveness back to headquarters in Washington DC. Kashino sent in few letters showing signs of subversiveness, and W.F. Kelly, Chief of the Border Patrol, suspected he was not "doing his work properly." After an investigation other interpreters confirmed they could find little evidence of disloyalty among the Japanese internees as well.[11] The internees were eventually allowed to make phone calls and send telegrams, but some had little contact with their families for months.

Japanese detainees prepare the gardens at Fort Missoula.
HMFM Peter Fortune Collection

The Japanese were supplied with adequate supplies of food, but most of it was standard American fare with some rice, soy and fish thrown in. Just a few days after he arrived at Fort Missoula, E. Akutagawa wrote home, "Here we get turkey, beef, ham and ice cream every day. I hope I stay all my life."[12] At the request of the Japanese, the camp officials eventually found suppliers who could provide traditional Japanese foods, including tea, dried mushrooms, soy, seaweed, dried shrimp and squid, rice flour, and udon noodles. The Japanese Relief Fund, operating through the Red Cross, also sent much appreciated food and books to the internees.

A few Japanese men lived outside the wire and raised thousands of chickens at a small farm. The chickens were for their own consumption and for sale in the local markets. Fort Missoula internees (both Japanese and Italians) also planted huge Victory Gardens beginning in 1942, including 30 acres of vegetables, 25 acres of potatoes and 60 acres of wheat. The wheat was used primarily to feed the chickens. The Italians prepared the ground and were in charge of landscaping the gardens, while the Japanese proved considerably better at working with the plants.

Abuse and Injustice

Alien Enemy Hearings Boards for the Issei detainees were authorized by US Attorney General Francis Biddle just days after December 7, 1941 and more than 100 of these boards were eventually formed, one for each of the federal judicial districts in the US. The western Montana board was comprised of Missoula attorney Ed Mulroney, a young university professor named Mike Mansfield, and C.W. Leaphart, the dean of the University Law School. They were tasked with determining the immigration status and loyalty of the Issei living in their district. The Japanese men were supposed to be interviewed by Hearing Boards from their home states, and boards from Washington, Oregon, California, Utah, and Nevada traveled to Fort Missoula, however the Montana board wound up doing many of the interviews for the Issei from these states and others. The hearings at Fort Missoula were held in a formal courtroom built inside the newly restored Post Headquarters.

The Japanese men were afforded few of the rights enjoyed by US citizens. They did not have the right to be represented by an attorney, although they could present an affidavit and have friends and relatives testify to their character. They also could not see the evidence against them or call witnesses for the defense, and were not allowed to confront their accusers, who were often overzealous FBI agents or military men. Although the boards were later provided with FBI files on the detainees, during the initial hearings one board member reported he was not given any reports on the detainees, and only knew what the FBI or military told him about why the men had been detained. Besides the detainee and the members of the board, each hearing was attended by an interpreter (usually Korean), stenographer, prosecuting attorney, INS representative, and an FBI agent. Agents from the Internal Revenue Service interviewed the detainees to determine whether they had been paying taxes. Added to the indignity of being detained, some of the men were dunned for as much as $12,000 in back taxes.[13]

The post headquarters (T-1) served as administrative headquarters and courtroom for the Alien Detention Center and the Disciplinary Barracks. The foreign detainees were subjected to perfunctory trials to decide their fate.
Courtesy of Stan Cohen

Like the Italian side of the camp, there was a

wide disparity of political beliefs among the Japanese. Some openly cheered victories of the Japanese military, while others felt loyal to America. The deferential Japanese often told the inspectors what they thought they wanted to hear, and a few of the Issei tried to protect each other by claiming that their friends had arrived in the country before 1924, when Japanese immigration had been halted. This led to conflicting stories told by some of the internees and caused hard feelings among the prisoners when some were accused of perjury. Inspectors claimed that the Japanese were conspiring among themselves to lie to the Board, and Assistant US Attorney Gerald Hile declared that even though most of the Japanese posed no threat to the United States, "a few of them are not hesitant to let it be known that they hope Japan wins the war."[14] The men were particularly questioned about their involvement with various Japanese social clubs. Even membership in a judo or fencing club was viewed with suspicion, as the clubs were deemed subversive and were vigorously investigated by the FBI. Also under increased scrutiny were those who had visited Japan or entertained visitors from Japan.

Suyoichi Okamura raised seven children during his 36 years in California. Sent to Fort Missoula, he was "found to be a dangerous alien enemy," and was eventually transferred to an Army detention camp at Fort Sill, Oklahoma. The hearing board cited his three trips to Japan and his memberships in the Japanese Association of San Francisco and Togo Kai, a support group of the Japanese Navy.[15] Many of his fellow detainees were members of similar groups. The board recommended that Okamura be detained for the duration of the war. Even if a hearing board recommended that a detainee be released, Attorney General Biddle had the final say, and often overruled the boards that conducted the hearings.

The first hearings were perfunctory affairs, rarely taking more than a few hours, and the various boards wrapped up their work at the fort by mid-June 1942, by which time many of the Japanese men had been transferred to other camps. Ken Nakazawa was one of the first released in February when it was determined he had diplomatic immunity, and he was sent to West Virginia to await repatriation. American authorities were anxious to exchange the Issei men for Americans civilians held by Japan, and encouraged the detainees to voluntarily return to Japan. The INS tried to involuntarily deport many others as illegal aliens, but most of these detainees had established lives and families in the US, and vigorously resisted being sent to Japan. Others, bitter over having had their property seized, accepted repatriation to Japan. Warren Watanabe, a successful businessman in California for 30 years who had watched as his business was padlocked, was one of those who chose Japan over America. When they arrived in Japan, some of these men revealed they had been abused at Fort Missoula.

INS inspectors at Fort Missoula were responsible for interrogating the Issei men and had been told to adhere scrupulously to the Geneva Convention and to treat the detainees humanely, so it came as a surprise when Inspector Herman Schwandt overheard one of his colleagues cursing and threatening an internee in March 1942. He reported it and the INS launched an internal investigation, but word of abuses at Fort Missoula had already reached the outside world. Japanese ambassador Kichisaburo Nomura, detained in West Virginia, had also heard allegations of physical abuse, as well as the deaths of the three elderly Japanese men in the camp. Nomura asked the Spanish Consulate in San Francisco to investigate. The Spanish Consulate, which represented Japanese interests in the US, filed a formal complaint with the State Department in June, alleging that detainees had been, "beaten, kicked, forced to keep standing for hours running, and given no food." The subsequent investigation revealed that at least half a dozen detainees had been physically abused by Korean interpreters and several of the INS inspectors in the interrogation section. Inspector Walter Bliss, in charge of the interrogations, had previously worked in Los Angeles, and was familiar with many of the Japanese men when he arrived. From the start he suspected the Japanese were not only lying, but were conspiring among themselves to deceive the authorities. Despite the Geneva Convention clause ensuring detainees, "respect for their persons and honour," several INS inspectors and Korean interpreters slapped, kicked, bit, and hit the Japanese detainees. Verbal abuse was routine. Elderly Japanese men were threatened and forced to stand outside in subzero weather for hours as they waited for their hearings. Many were detained in tiny cells for long periods.

Katsuma Mukaeda explained the origins of the allegations of abuse. "An immigration officer started to question some of the people who were suspected for spying, or something. He was being rough with the detainees there. Finally, they found out that he was beating up some of the detainees and I think the main office in Washington called him back and he got discharged. He was one of the inspectors named Mr. Bliss. He wasn't on very good terms with the Japanese here in Los Angeles. He had a grudge against them, I guess. It is very seldom that you find that kind of person." Concerned about the fate of thousands of American civilians and soldiers being held by the Japanese in the Philippines, the State Department acted quickly to investigate the allegations, and released their report on August 6, 1942. Rather than being dismissed, Inspectors Bliss, Martin Herstrom, Jr., and Harold Brown were demoted and suspended for 90 days. Two Korean interpreters were fired, and Supervisor Collaer was transferred to Crystal City, Texas that same month to oversee establishment of a new detention camp, at least in part as a response to the allegations.

Despite the actions of the INS inspectors, some of the Japanese leaders wrote to Supervisor Collaer telling him how much they missed Missoula, and to thank him for his efforts on their behalf. Katsuma Mukaeda remembered that, "Mr. Collaer was head of the detention camp at Missoula, Montana, and he treated us very nicely." Collaer was soon replaced by Captain Robert Fraser, and Italian detainee Umberto Benedetti felt the camp administration improved thereafter.

The Spanish Consulate had also heard about the deaths of three elderly Issei men just after they arrived at Fort Missoula and formally complained to the State Department on October 27, 1942 of the "most inhuman cruelty and insult inflicted upon [Japanese nationals] by the United States Authorities in the course of their arrest, examination, internment and transport." An investigation into the deaths revealed that the three elderly men who died had received adequate medical care. After examining the medical records of the deceased and speaking to witnesses, the investigators concluded that three Japanese doctors in the camp had appropriately cared for one of the deceased men, and relatives of the other two sent letters thanking INS authorities for the care given their loved ones. This information was transmitted to the Japanese government almost a year after the initial allegations, although the report failed to address the question of why old and terminally ill men were interned in the first place.

Both the Italians and Japanese participated in theater productions held at the log recreation center. Two Japanese men portrayed a married couple in this play.
HMFM Peter Fortune Collection 2001.048.028

After the completion of the initial hearings, 673 Japanese men were transferred from Fort Missoula. Those deemed to be "dangerous enemy aliens" were sent to US Army Detention Centers at Camp Livingston, Louisiana, Fort Sill, Oklahoma, Fort Sam Houston, Texas, or the Lordsburg camp in New Mexico. At some of these camps the internee's families were allowed to join them. Despite their continued detention, none of the men held at Fort Missoula were prosecuted for espionage or disloyal conduct.

Some of the other men were lucky enough to be paroled to their families, who by this time were living in the internment camps run by the War Relocation Authority (WRA), as mandated by President Roosevelt's orders of February 19, 1942 to remove Japanese-Americans from their homes on the West Coast. The WRA camps soon held 107,000 men, women and children. Ironically, the detainees at Fort Missoula had fallen under the Geneva Convention, which mandated better conditions and better food than their wives and children, most of whom were American citizens, received in the camps run by the WRA. The men from Fort Missoula immediately noticed the difference in the quality of food when they arrived at the WRA camps. Ruth Hoshimiya, interned at Santa Anita, California, wrote to her father of the released men. "They tell me that they got good food, especially coffee. They want to go back to Montana again - just for the food."[16]

There were only 109 Issei left at the fort by August 1942, but new detainees were transferred in on a regular basis, and the detainee population remained steady. The Issei men gradually became aware of their rights under the Geneva Convention. Most requested rehearings, which allowed them time to arrange for witnesses who could travel to testify on their behalf. The next time a representative of the Spanish government visited in December 1943 there was a noticeable increase in complaints from the Japanese who now understood their rights. A worried Fraser wrote to his department heads, "I believe we are taking too much for granted and paying too little attention to this internee group." He further instructed that, "...every employee should keep in mind that the fate of thousands of Americans yet in Japan may very definitely depend on our actions right at Fort Missoula. One wrong act may undo all that we have done and prove disastrous..."[17]

The War Department transferred their remaining civilian detainees to the INS at Fort Missoula in May 1943 in order to make room for German prisoners of war. Late in the year, 258 more Japanese were transferred to the fort, where they remained until March 1944. Some of these men were residents of Peru, Bolivia, Panama, or Cuba, and had been interned at the request of the US. Fifteen South American countries, acting at the request of the US, rounded up 6,600 German, Italian, and Japanese civilians and sent them to American detention camps. The Issei from South America were not allowed hearings, and many were not released until more than a year after the war's end. The fort became something of a transit camp and temporary holding facility for Japanese, Italian, and a few German citizens, as most of the new arrivals spent only a few months in Missoula. Additional hearings were held as needed until the camp was closed.

A number of German internees were also housed at Fort Missoula at various time during the war. Some were seamen from two German merchant ships seized in American ports in 1940. Border Patrolman John Moe reported that a handful of German Luftwaffe pilots were held at the fort in late April or early May, 1941. These were probably men who had escaped from Canadian prisoner-of-war camps and sought asylum in the then neutral United States. Approximately 100 German civilians were present at the fort when the camp was ordered closed in 1944. Spokane farmer Karl Vogt, born in Germany and arrested two days after Pearl Harbor, was sent to the fort in March 1943 to await what he thought would be a swift decision handed down from Washington DC regarding his parole. He wound up staying at Fort Missoula until August. He was the only German interned there at the time, but soon made friends with the Japanese and Italian detainees. Family members were allowed to visit at any time, and his children visited monthly, with his 6-year-old son proudly wearing a US Army uniform. Armin Vogt later recalled, "When I wore this uniform, every soldier that I met, there were lots of them in Missoula, gave me a salute. This was a big deal for a six year old kid!"[18]

Work Release

When the camp was first established the INS asked the Public Health Service to take over medical care for the detainees. The Health Service was willing to provide advice and consultation but was not willing to staff the hospital without compensation. The Fort Missoula hospital, which had been damaged by fire, was repaired and by December 1941 the Health Service agreed to staff it, as long as the INS paid the bills and was responsible for administration. Many of the Italian seamen were infected with syphilis, while the Japanese suffered from age-related diseases. The major problem reported among the detainees was inactivity, and the camp doctor reported a significant rise in "neuroses" or "barbed wire fever" due to the boredom of incarceration. While there were numerous activities at the camp, not everyone took advantage of them. Several depressed men committed suicide, one by leaping from the third story of the hospital. Aurelio Mariani left a note that read "I kill myself because I am tired, tired of being closed in a cage."[19] By the end of 1942 the fort's medical officer wrote, "if the men are not furnished more work and liberties, I dread conditions a year from now."

Early on the Immigration and Naturalization Service hired detainees to do construction work, weaving, sewing, furniture making, and blacksmithing around the fort, and paid them 80 cents a day. Sugar farmers were desperate to harvest their crops during the fall of 1942, and at least 65 of the fort Missoula internees volunteered to work the fields. Alfredo Cipolato was one of the first group of 13 sent to pick beets in the Missoula Valley. "They took us to the fields by truck with more guards and machine guns than prisoners. When we said we would not work under such conditions they agreed to take us back and forth without heavy guard. We made thirty dollars a month, although we never saw the money. Instead they issued us requisitions for purchases at clothing stores and so forth."

Cipolato's crew was later sent to pick beets near Gold Creek, where they were quartered in an old chicken house. "We made the place livable by first cleaning it, then hanging sheets for curtains and making a table. On Thanksgiving Day that year we invited the Italian families from Butte and we cooked a wonderful dinner."

During the fall many of the Japanese were trucked to the Bitterroot Valley to help pick the apple crop. They returned with their clothes stuffed full of apples for their friends.

John Rehder, whose father had a contract to haul coal from the Post Siding to the fort, remembered that one of the Issei detainees told him, "The army was very odd, because over at the fort they had guns and barbed wire, then they bring them to the fields and give them big knives and go away, and leave them with women and children." Rehder also recalled the cook for the sugar beet crews. "Mr. Watanaube dug a hole in our backyard and lined it with stones, and made a fire pit, he then placed a large washtub over it and boiled rice in it, he also roasted corn and fried and boiled meat."

The severe shortage of able-bodied workers prompted Representative Mike Mansfield to forward the names of nine Italian men to the Justice Department in early January 1943 as candidates for parole by an Alien Hearing Board, similar to the ones the Japanese detainees had gone through the previous year. A week later Edward J. Ennis, the Director of the Alien Enemy Control Unit in Washington thanked Mansfield for his recommendations. Ennis wrote, "As soon as this board can be appointed, we hope to conduct hearings and arrange for the release on parole of a considerable number of these Italians in order to put that manpower to work in the factories and in the fields where it belongs."

Most of the Italians had been behind bars for two years, and they were anxious for approval to work outside the camp. The Florence Hotel in Missoula hired two Italian chefs and several busboys once they were granted parole. Other men worked as gardeners for local citizens. Father Alfredo Bruno was paroled in 1943 but was allowed to move into the fort's recreation hall so he could continue to minister to the detainees. Alfredo Cipolato and several of his comrades worked at St. Patrick Hospital in Missoula as orderlies and maintenance men, but were restricted to a one-block radius around the hospital. They were supposed to check in at the fort once a week. Cipolato remembered, "I was trained as an orderly, since most of the orderlies and doctors were in the service." John Moe recalled, "They weren't supervised hardly at all. The sheriff of Missoula County, Bob McLean, was sitting in his office at the courthouse one day, and seven of the Italians were working on the lawn, unsupervised. Well the bell at St. Francis Xavier rang, and they dropped everything and left. He didn't know

Italians who volunteered to pick sugar beets relax at a makeshift camp after work.
MHS PAC 84 - 34F3

where they were going, and he called the camp and they sent a Border Patrolman, and they found them all sitting in the back row of St. Francis Church. They had gone to mass."

Sixteen of the Fort Missoula detainees found employment in Great Falls. A majority, including Umberto Benedetti, worked at Columbus Hospital, while others worked at the Coca-Cola bottling plant. John Paolillo, worked at the Saint Thomas orphanage in Great Falls from 1942 until 1944. By the end of July 1943, two-thirds of the Italians were on work release.

Many of the Italians and some of the Japanese men were immediately hired by the Northern Pacific, the Milwaukee Road, and the Great Northern railroad. Forty of the Italian detainees worked on the construction of a new 3,105 foot tunnel underneath the Bozeman Hill. Due to a serious shortage of housing in the area, they lived in rail cars until the project was completed in December of 1944. The Northern Pacific employed as many as 250 Italians, including 18 carpenters who built bridges and worked on construction crews. The Italian detainees were paid the same rate as regular employees, but they were only allowed a small stipend at one time and the rest of their pay was sent to Fort Missoula, where it was saved for them. They were however, allowed to withdraw up to $500 from their accounts to pay expenses incurred by their families. Under the Geneva Convention detainees were not supposed to have more than $10 in their possession at one time, so the men were issued meal tickets redeemable at local restaurants.

The Forest Service employed 360 of the Italians, and paid them according to the Army pay scale ($50 per month). They fought fires, piled slash and built trails in the Kaniksu, Coeur d'Alene, Clearwater, and Kootenai National Forests. According to Axel Lindh, Assistant Regional Forester, "the Italians are doing their work well, with enthusiasm for outdoor life despite the different environment under which they are living in the woods." Foresters considered the Italians much better workers than the high school students who were also working in the woods. Many of the young Italian men managed to become friends with local girls, and there were several weddings. One of the Italian ship captains married Wilma Jacobson, the INS's chief clerk at the fort. The effort to parole the detainees on work release got another boost in February 1943 when Bert Fraser examined Canyon Creek Prison camp in Idaho to see if the INS could use the facility for a satellite work camp for highway construction. Fraser approved the location and several hundred detained Issei men from around the country volunteered for jobs at at the Kooskia Internment Camp. These men worked on the construction of Highway 12 in heavily timbered and very rough country. Fort Missoula served as the administration and supply center for the Kooskia camp, and sent guards, administrators and secretaries, as well as shipments of clothes, shoes, towels, food, beer and other supplies.

These Italian men were employed on the Musselshell road project near Pierce, Idaho.
Courtesy of Stan Cohen

Closure of the Alien Detention Center

Hundreds of Italian detainees and 293 of the remaining Japanese had been paroled on work release when Captain Fraser announced that the Fort Missoula Alien Detention Center would be formally closed during the spring of 1944. Most of the 310 Italians still interned in the camp left town by train on April 3, 1944, although a few remained behind to help close the facility. One hundred recently arrived German civilians were sent to work for the Forest Service, while most of the remaining Japanese detainees were sent to camps in the South. The Japanese food stockpiled in the warehouse was sent to the Kooskia Internment Camp.

The war in Europe ended in May 1945, and the Italian internees who had previously been held at Fort Missoula received word that they were free to return home. On May 30 the Red Cross ship SS *Gripsholm* set sail for Europe with 1,150 aliens, including many of the Italian seamen. More of the Italians were sent to Ellis Island in July and September, where they boarded the SS *Gripsholm* and SD *Drottningholm*. Some of the Italians had saved up to $2,000 of their wages, and they bought scarce items to take home to Italy. Most had been away from home for nearly six years.

Several former detainees were drafted or volunteered to serve in the US military. John Paolillo was drafted in 1944, and served two years as a military policeman in France and post-war Germany. Agostino Ronzitti, one of the workers from the 1939 World's Fair in New York, spent three years with the US Army in England. A few Italians chose to stay in the US, although most moved to large cities with a sizable Italian population. Butte and Spokane also attracted men who had worked there during the war.

Umberto Benedetti, the *Il Conte Biancamano's* cabinetmaker, served in the US Army from 1943 to 1947, yet was still considered an alien after four years of service. Benedetti served again during the Korean War, and was one of several Italians internees who returned to Missoula after the war. He earned a Master's Degree from the University of Montana, and wrote a book entitled "Italian Boys At Fort Missoula, Montana 1941-1943." Benedetti donated his tools, photos, letters, paintings, and other memorabilia to the Historical Museum at Fort Missoula before his death in 2009 at age 97.

Alfredo Cipolato, who worked as a sugar beet picker, hospital orderly, and railroad construction crewman while an internee, also sang in the church choir. "...Some of the Italians working at the hospital were musicians from their merchant ships, and the rest of us had good to great singing voices, and so we were allowed to join the church choir." He met a local girl from an Italian family in the choir, and Alfredo and Anna Cipolato were married in 1943. The INS attempted to deport him in 1945, but the order was stayed after an appeal to Representative Mike Mansfield, who suggested that Cipolato immediately apply for citizenship, which was granted in 1948. Alfredo and Anna raised five children in Missoula, and operated the Broadway Market from 1957 until 2004. Alfredo helped found the Missoula Mendelssohn Club and sang with them for 63 years. He passed away in 2008 at age 95.

The US Disciplinary Barracks, Northwestern Branch

Community leaders worried that the loss of jobs from the detention camp would hurt the local economy, but Representative Mansfield managed to pull some strings and soon notified the local Chamber of Commerce that Fort Missoula would be turned back over to the Army to be used as a detention camp for medium-security military prisoners who had been sentenced to terms ranging from two to 30 years.

The Immigration and Naturalization Service formally transferred Fort Missoula back to the US Army in July 1944, and the Fort Missoula camp was renamed the US Disciplinary Barracks, Northwestern Branch. The prison was activated June 25, 1944, and the first prisoners soon arrived. The fence was strengthened and rerouted behind the two Mission-style barracks, which became housing for guards. The prefabricated barracks were divided into two

Security was tightened when the disciplinary barracks was created, with double fences, additional guard boxes, and sirens. A fence also surrounded the post hospital, (background).
Courtesy of Stan Cohen

fenced off compounds (B & C). A single but much larger barracks was fenced off into a separate Compound D. Five smaller guard boxes were added around the perimeter, and guard boxes were installed just outside each residential compound. A three-story frame recreation hall and gymnasium (T-150) was built inside the fence south of the Mission-style barracks. (It was later used by the Army Reserve as a warehouse, and now houses the US Forest Service's Materials Testing Laboratory.) Two large concrete cell-block buildings (buildings 156 and 157) were built on the southeast side of the camp, a Provost Marshall's office (building 63) was built near the fort's guardhouse, and a new boiler plant was built on the west side of the post.

Colonel Alexander M. Weyand commanded the 1969th Service Command Unit. A total of 2,000 inmates were held at the fort over the years, and at its peak the camp had 560 officers, 576 enlisted men, and 171 civilian employees, a massive increase from the staffing of the Alien Detention Center, and the largest Army contingent ever stationed at the fort.[20] The staff members, when they weren't tracking down escaped criminals, found time to field a baseball team in 1945 and 1946. They played teams from the local area and from military installations at Fort Harrison, the Great Falls Army Air Base, and Fort Douglas, Utah.

More than 1,000 medium-security disciplinary prisoners were transported by rail from Fort Leavenworth, Kansas to Missoula during the late summer of 1944. The prisoners were primarily deserters and men absent without leave (AWOL), but some had also been convicted of rape, theft and assault. Two of the prisoners had been found guilty of a rape in California and had been given death sentences. Their scheduled execution date was set for August, 1945 but they were given a last-minute stay, and the executions never took place. The purpose of the Disciplinary Barracks was to confine and rehabilitate general army prisoners who had been court-martialed. First Lieutenant Stanley Levin, the judge advocate of the camp, declared the aim was to restore the prisoners to active duty or discharge them, "as better citizens." Apparently the way to do that was to make prisoners break rocks with heavy hammers and dig mock graves. Some of the luckier inmates were put to work in the camp print shop, which produced several books as well as the newspaper *Fort Missoula Spotlight*.

These guards were members of a Disciplinary Company at Fort Missoula in 1945. The presence of several African-American soldiers indicates the Fort Missoula garrison was desegregated several years before the Army was officially desegregated by President Harry Truman in 1948.
Charles Patton Collection HMFM 2006.007.162

The large contingent of guards was needed, and authorities in Missoula soon learned that 1,250 American Army prisoners presented far more problems than the Italian and Japanese civilians had. The prisoners quickly demonstrated that the Fort Missoula facility was not totally secure. During the first week of October, 1944 eight prisoners escaped from the camp, including one who was described as particularly dangerous. One of these escapees burglarized the nearby house of rancher David Maclay and got away with a considerable amount of cash. He was apprehended in Iowa six weeks later and given a six-year sentence for the escape and theft. There were still five escapees at large when three more scaled the wire in a flurry of gunfire at 9:30 pm on the night of October 16, 1944. Another prisoner successfully scaled the wire later that night.

Three days later, Gerald Jellvik and two companions decided to escape. Jellvik had already successfully escaped earlier in the month, and had been apprehended just four days earlier by a former Highway Patrolman while walking down a road near Dixon. Jellvik and Jack Adams led the way. They cleared the fence and were running for their lives when they were hit by a "fusillade" of gunfire about 25 feet from the fence. Jellvik was killed and Adams critically wounded. At the first shot the third would-be escapee stopped short of the fence, and was recaptured.

Ten more prisoners escaped from Fort Missoula on November 27, although three were soon recaptured near Noxon. Six others stole a car but were caught near Polson after a 90-mile-an-hour chase in which police fired repeatedly at their fleeing car. The last escapee was captured in Missoula a few days later. At the request of irate citizens, a siren was installed to warn residents when an escape attempt was underway. The siren blew frequently, but didn't stop the escapes. Three more men got away during the first week of December after scaling the fence while guards fired at them. Two of these men were captured near Lolo, and the other one, who had escaped once before, was apprehended near St. Ignatius. Eight of the recaptured prisoners were sentenced to an average of 17 years behind bars.

Still, the prisoners kept trying. Two men escaped from Fort Missoula in late May of 1945 but were recaptured in the Bitterroot Valley on the following day. Later in the summer a disturbance left one prisoner stabbed to death, another seriously injured and several others hurt in a free-for-all in the camp. Charles Goddard was charged with the fatal stabbing. Another rash of escapes occurred in late August 1945. Two inmates stole an army truck, which was later found abandoned at Lolo. Perhaps inspired by their success, 11 additional prisoners escaped within the week. One was eventually recaptured in Los Angeles. Five more internees escaped from a Spokane hospital where they had been taken for medical treatment. Two were immediately recaptured and a third was found dead after he hid in a house that was being fumigated with cyanide.

The most dramatic incident in the history of the Disciplinary Barracks occurred on July 4, 1946 when the prisoners rioted throughout the day. They burned one of the wooden barracks to the ground, and four other barracks were badly damaged before the guards and the Missoula Fire Department restored order.

Later that month three prisoners took advantage of a wild lightning and wind storm to escape the wire, and then on August 2 prisoner Paul Kelly slipped away from a nearby farm where he was on a crew working under the supervision of armed guards. There were 110 escapes from the fort out of a total of 2,000 inmates, although all of the escaped convicts were eventually recaptured. Five train cars of new prisoners arrived at Fort Missoula from the West Coast on August 2, 1946 but word soon arrived that the Disciplinary Barracks was slated to close due to the postwar reduction in the size of the military. A train carrying 100 prisoners left for Fort Leavenworth on October 17, 1946, and by the end of the year nearly all of the prisoners had been shipped elsewhere. The Fort Missoula Disciplinary Barracks officially closed at midnight April 18, 1947 with the departure of the last of the staff.

Most of the temporary barracks from the Alien Detention Center were sold to local farmers and businesses and moved away by 1947, although one has since been returned to the fort and restored by the Historical Museum at Fort Missoula. Dr. L.E. Hall and his wife Venna paid $500 for one of the barracks for use as a horse barn. Many years later Venna recalled dismantling the prefabricated barracks into 4x8 foot sections. "My 6-year-old gathered up all the bolts and nuts and put them in boxes. My eighth-grader and I would haul them over here and stack this one or that one."[21]

Despite the prison just yards away, the staff of the Disciplinary Barracks found time to celebrate the birthday of Virginia Johns Johnson (center) in 1945.
HMFM 1990.053.010

The NCO Quarters

Construction of Fort Missoula's oldest remaining building was started late in 1877 and finished the following year. It is a T-shaped duplex designed to house two families, and was built of western larch logs cut in Pattee Canyon. Officers and their families lived there until 1879. After that the building was designated for the fort's ordnance and commissary sergeants.

Ordnance sergeants reported to the post commander and were in charge of securing and maintaining all arms and ordnance on the post. They also supervised soldiers in reloading cartridges. Typically they were dropped from the rolls of the regiment and assigned to the post. The families of Sergeant Horace W. Bivins and Sergeant Alexander Pillow, both Buffalo Soldiers, lived in this building. Commissary sergeants were also assigned to the post, and were responsible for the proper storage and issuance of all food stocks at the fort, although they were not responsible for food preparation.

During World War II, civilian employees of the Immigration and Naturalization Service lived in the building from 1941 to 1944, and it was then occupied by Regular Army soldiers from 1944 to 1947. The families of university faculty members lived there until the 1950s.

The General Services Administration planned to destroy the building in the 1960s, but Captain Herman Wittman of the Army Reserve was persuaded to bid on the building. He submitted the winning bid and was required to move the building from the site within 90 days. In preparation for the move, Wittman removed the clapboard siding and discovered that he had bought one of the fort's original log buildings. Wittman then enlisted Donovan Worden Jr. and Brigadier General Walter Johnson, and the three men formed the Fort Missoula Historical Society, which persuaded the GSA to leave the building on the grounds. A local Boy Scout troop helped landscape the grounds, and the Exchange Club volunteered to put a new roof on the building. The newly formed Western Montana Ghost Town Preservation Society bought the building for $1 from the Fort Missoula Historical Society in 1972. The Ghost Town Society undertook major restoration work on the building with help from Green Thumb workers and Army Reservists. A stone foundation was placed under the building in 1974 and vintage windows were obtained during the demolition of the Eddy/Hammond house in downtown Missoula, as well as from the fort's deteriorating log officer's club. Restoration of the NCO quarters eventually spurred formation of the Historical Museum at Fort Missoula, which now owns the building.

The green carriage house in the rear of the building, built in 1880, was sold to Ed Hogan and moved off-site in 1959, but Hogan agreed to donate the building, and it was returned to its original stone foundation once the NCO quarters was restored.

9

For Sale: Fort Missoula

"The integrity of the fort complex, even with the removal of the earliest buildings, remains extraordinarily high."

National Register of Historic Places nomination

The Army Pulls Out

Closure of the Army's Disciplinary Barracks in 1947 marked the end of 70 years of Army control of Fort Missoula. The Army was interested in retaining only five small parcels at the fort, comprising 45.19 acres. This included the 1911 officer's row, one barracks, some of the warehouses, the headquarters building, the Reserve armory and garages. The Fort was to be used primarily for the use of the National Guard and Reserve units, and the armory became home to the Montana Military District, which moved from Fort Harrison after World War II. An Army Reserve training center of several thousand acres was established on Blue Mountain in 1947, just west of the fort. The area was transferred to the Forest Service by Executive Order in 1952, but it was leased to the National Guard, which used it for live ammunition training until 1992. William Maclay recalled, "When they practiced with artillery, the shells would go from Target Range right over the Butte and land on Blue Mountain. Clyde [Maclay] rented that land for a nominal amount. He had to vacate the cows from the land with a few hours notice when they were going to fire artillery."[1] Montana's National Guard's 443rd Field Artillery Battalion was headquartered at the Fort beginning in 1947, with companies in Missoula, Kalispell, and Deer Lodge. The unit was equipped with 105 millimeter self-propelled howitzers and towed guns, and was led by Colonel M.Y. "Bo" Foster.

The Department of Defense declared in June 1947 that nearly all of the rest of the land at Fort Missoula, some 1,383.52 acres, was "excess." Since the Army had no further use for the fort, the land and buildings at Fort Missoula fell under the auspices of the War Assets Administration, which was charged with disposing or leasing excess land.

The center of the fort was sought by several different entities. The Flathead tribe expressed interest in owning much of the fort, but found they did not have the same rights to excess Federal land which some other tribes had been granted. James McCain, the president of the University of Montana, also wanted to obtain the fort buildings. He wrote to Senator Burton K. Wheeler and asked him to help the university buy most of the fort buildings, while Governor Sam Ford asked Montana's Congressional delegation to support the university's bid for the land.

Missoula County also offered to buy the historic fort and surrounding land, with the enthusiastic support of the local Chamber of Commerce. Many county residents believed the fort had a great deal of potential. Moving the fairgrounds to the fort would free up land in the center of town. The fort's stable was perfect for 4-H and FFA (Future Farmer of America) events. The hospital was available for medical care or to house juvenile offenders. The fort's cell-blocks could replace the aging county jail (city police liked the idea of a modern jail, but thought the fort was inconveniently far from the courthouse, and warned that one police car would have to be taken off patrol to transport prisoners to and from arraignments).

The War Assets Administration refused to give the fort away, but did eventually agree to a lease-sale agreement with Missoula County in 1948. The county agreed to buy most of the fort (822 acres and 110 buildings) for $153,733, with an annual payment of $9,900. The agreement was to be reviewed by both parties every five years.

University enrollment grew rapidly after the war, creating a housing shortage, and for a ten-year span starting in 1947 University of Montana faculty members and their families rented county buildings at the fort. There were 24 housing units available in the original Officers Row and the NCO quarters south of the detention center (Buildings 14 and 16). Many of these were duplexes. The rental program ended in 1957 when adequate housing became available closer to the university.

The War Assets Administration was merged into the General Services Administration (GSA) in 1949, and the GSA was directed to lease or sell off the fort's remaining buildings and land. By 1950 the GSA decided to dispose of 160 acres north of South Avenue to the county, 200 acres to the state Department of Natural Resources and Conservation (DNRC), the State Tree Nursery, and Fish, Wildlife and Parks. The US Forest Service received 40 acres. The GSA also granted the Veteran's Administration two 40-acre plots and one 80-acre plot for veteran's housing in 1951.

When the County's five-year lease on the historic fort came up for renewal in 1953, the Montana Legislature passed a bill requesting that the GSA give the fort to Missoula County "without consideration," and Senators Mansfield and Murray introduced an unsuccessful bill to that effect in the US Senate. The county continued to make annual payments of $9,900 until the Army announced in early 1955 that it wanted to cancel the lease.

The Montana Military District had moved from Fort Harrison to Fort Missoula after World War II, and soon realized that Fort Missoula would make an excellent training and supply center for the Army Reserve and National Guard. The District wanted to use the fort's buildings for a Reserve training center. The new program was intended to bring 1,203 Reserve trainees to the fort for six weeks each summer, as well as 987 National Guard troops. Citizens were told they could expect to see troops marching to and from Pattee Canyon as part of their drills. Plans also called for an air strip at the fort designed for small observation planes. Target Range School District objected to having an airstrip so near the school, but the army assured them the planes would be small and far from the school.

Local citizens had fought for decades to keep the Army at the fort, but now there was immediate opposition to returning county land to the Army. The Chamber of Commerce had spearheaded the effort to acquire the land for the county after the Army left in 1947, and the Chamber's President John H. Toole led the opposition to returning the land. The city had been expanding westward, and Toole estimated the current worth of the land at the fort was now $1,200 to $2,000 per acre. He questioned why the army needed such expensive land for armored vehicle training. The discussions did not go well, and County Commission Chairman Thomas W. Duncan declared on February 10, 1955, "Negotiations on returning Ft. Missoula to the Army have collapsed completely and we are proceeding on the assumption that Missoula County will have control of the property for a long, long time."

Nevertheless, Lieutenant Colonel M.Y. "Bo" Foster requested the Chamber change its position because the proposed expansion of the National Guard and Reserve activities at the fort would benefit the community. The Chamber then asked Senator Mike Mansfield to confirm with Secretary of the Army Robert T. Stevens whether the rumors about Fort Missoula being reactivated were true. The Chamber eventually stated they would support the Pentagon regaining the land, but only if the, "Army can assure full usage of fort property with accompanying payroll…"[2] On July 27, 1955 representatives of the Sixth Army from San Francisco and several Army engineers from the Walla Walla District arrived in Missoula to restart the stalled negotiations. The Army delegates stated that they had spent $263,000 at the fort in 1954 for military services, but planned to double that amount by 1956 if the land was reclaimed. The Army also planned to spend another $90,000 to refurbish the barracks, and announced plans to add 25 to 30 civilian employees with a payroll of $200,000 per year.

The county eventually proposed a compromise where the fort would be divided, with the county retaining a portion of the land in exchange for the lease payments already paid. Meetings between the Army and Missoula County took place in mid-October 1955 and by November an agreement was reached giving the Army 545 acres of the fort while the county would retain 302 acres on the east side of Section 31. County Commission Chair Duncan wanted Guardsman Lane from the fort to South Avenue closed, but the Army insisted it stay open. The county received title to the land after a final payment of $24 per acre in 1956. As part of the agreement, the county gifted a couple of acres to the Missoula Country Club because a small portion of the golf course had been inadvertently built on government property. The county also agreed to give 20 acres to Target Range School. When the deal was completed the county retained possession of 278 acres on the east end of the fort. This land includes what is now Larchmont Golf Course, Community Hospital, and the Rural Fire Station. The National Guard was given 17.62 acres for vehicle storage and shops, and the military regained control over the Fort Missoula cemetery.

Once the Army reclaimed most of the fort, Army Reservists constructed an extensive training ground in 1956. They built a confidence course, a mortar range, a grenade practice area, a camouflage training site, a rappelling tower, and a communications site that featured pole climbing and practice in stringing telephone wire. Army engineers repeatedly built temporary bridges over the Bitterroot River, and the west side of the fort became a "tank trap," a training area for drivers of wheeled and tracked vehicles. One of the barracks was remodeled to house 600 men, while the other barracks was converted into a school, with a rifle range installed in the basement. The large recreation hall and gymnasium south of the company barracks (T-150) was turned into an Army Reserve warehouse with workshops and the capability to store up to 3,500 different types of military supplies.

Many men trained at the fort on weekends and summers, and there were numerous civilian employees, but only 10 full-time Army officers and 11 enlisted men were present in 1956. During the summer of 1957 Montana's National Guardsmen from the 96th Division did their summer training at the Yakima Training Center in Washington, rather than at Fort Missoula. The new Army Reserve Center in Barracks 26 was dedicated Veuve Hall on November 23, 1957, in honor of Medal of Honor winner Ernest Veuve, but the Army continued to re-evaluate facilities and reorganize units. The fort was designated as an evacuation center if the West Coast had to be evacuated due to war or natural disaster, but its usefulness to the military seemed to be at an end by 1958 when the Army announced plans to eliminate the Montana Military District and consolidate headquarters of the 10th Corps at Fort Lawton, Washington. The Army once again declared that most of Fort Missoula was "excess" property. Senator Mike Mansfield and Governor J. Hugo Aronson objected to the change, and asked that Fort Missoula at least be designated headquarters of the 96th Infantry Reserve Division. The state legislature passed a resolution in 1959 calling for reactivation of the post, and the Secretary of the Army requested the General Services Administration withdraw plans to dispose of surplus land at Fort Missoula on December 18, 1959. Nevertheless, there was no clear military purpose for the fort and the GSA once again made plans to dispose of 523 acres of surplus land.

The 1960s and 70s

Only a few National Guard and Reserve units used the fort during the early 1960s, and the headquarters company of the 443rd Artillery Battalion was nearly transferred elsewhere. A new unit arrived on May 1, 1963 when Company C of the 19th Special Forces Group (a National Guard unit) was headquartered in one of the former CCC buildings on the western side of the fort. Special Forces units from around the country traveled to Fort Missoula to train for a wide variety of missions. Parachute training was held at the Forest Service's Smoke-jumper Center, and ski training and winter survival were taught at Snowbowl, just north of town. The

National Guard and Reserve training activities did not require much land, and were concentrated on the western edge of the fort, so the GSA began a concerted effort to sell, lease or demolish many of the historic buildings at the fort. Barracks 24 was leased out for office space. The Missoula County Search and Rescue group kept their horses and equipment in the stables, while the US Fish and Wildlife Service used one of the cell block buildings for storage. The University of Montana used the fort's root cellar for storage, while the city wanted to use the quartermaster's warehouse (now the headquarters of the Historical Museum at Fort Missoula) for the same purpose. The Missoula Community Theater group expressed interest in using the carpenter's shop, while the Missoula Gun Club requested that the lease on their long-time shooting range near the cemetery be renewed.

The fort buildings were inventoried, photographed, and evaluated for their condition. The General Services Administration then proceeded to remove many of the historic buildings at the fort, including the remaining structures of the original Officer's Row (built between 1879 and 1894). The old log officers club (T-3) was temporarily spared, although it burned January 11, 1972. While the destruction of historic buildings apparently received little notice from the public, the prospect of the Army selling off hundreds of acres alarmed some of the fort's long-time neighbors. On July 9, 1963, James C. McCauley, a descendant of Colonel McCauley, declared he would challenge title to Section 36, since his ancestor had claimed the land before the Army arrived. (Colonel McCauley had never been able to file on the land since it had been granted to the state for support of schools in 1864.)

The Maclay family had leased most of the fort land north of South Avenue for many years for grazing and irrigated cropland, and W.C. Maclay renewed the agricultural lease in 1947, agreeing to pay $605 annually for grazing rights. Harry Maclay, who had operated a grocery store on former fort land just north of the post's main gate since 1931, wrote countless letters and worked tirelessly to secure a future for Fort Missoula. He proposed

Brigadier General M.Y. "Bo" Foster

As a child, Bo Foster spent summers on his family's ranch on the Blackfeet Reservation. After graduating from Yale University in the middle of the Great Depression, he hitchhiked to Montana and joined the Forest Service. When the US entered World War II Foster joined the Army Air Corps and learned to pilot a light observation plane. He won the Silver Star for his reconnaissance flights during the landings in Southern France in 1944, and had flown 70 missions by war's end. Nazi Reichsmarshall Hermann Goering, once Hitler's chosen successor, surrendered to the US 7th Army in Austria in May 1945, and Bo Foster was chosen to fly Goering back to Germany in a two-seat L-5 Stinson. During his flight into captivity, a seemingly jovial Goering pointed out the landmarks below to Foster.

Major Foster returned to Missoula after the war, and was appointed a lieutenant colonel in the National Guard. He helped form the 443rd Field Artillery Battalion at Fort Missoula, and eventually commanded the 154th Artillery Group. Promoted to Brigadier General in 1963, he retired in 1971 as Assistant Adjutant of the Montana National Guard. He remained active at the fort and was instrumental in the formation of the Northern Rockies Heritage Center and the Rocky Mountain Museum of Military History. Building 30 in Officer's Row, the former Commanding Officer's quarters, was dedicated to Foster in 2003. Foster passed away in Missoula at age 99 in 2011.

Bo Foster looks over his L-4 Piper Cub, nicknamed "Hunch n' Pray." Foster won the Silver Star and French Legion of Honor for his bravery in the skies over southern France.

Courtesy of M.Y. Foster.

that the county courthouse and fairgrounds be sold and new facilities be built at the fort. Maclay hoped the government would commit to a permanent presence at the fort, and planned to build a large shopping center on his land at South and Reserve.

Instead the Army's remaining 558 acres were divided into a confusing patchwork of parcels among the University of Montana, the Bureau of Land Management, the US Forest Service, and the state of Montana. The Target Range was leased to the state, and the county road department was allocated 60 acres south of old Highway 93 South.

The University of Montana had tried to acquire land at the fort in 1902 and again in the late 1940s. In 1964 the university began sounding out the Army regarding 245 acres of the excess land, and two years later the university was given the choice of buying 300 acres for the appraised value of $177,000, or a promise that title would be granted if the university used the land for research and educational purposes for 20 years. University administrators knew the prospect of getting funding from the state legislature was slim, and agreed to the conditions of research and education for 20 years. As a result, the university took control of eight buildings, including the historic stables and the cell-block buildings from the Disciplinary Barracks. This land would become the center of much controversy in the 1990s.

By 1973 the city, county, Missoula High School District, Missoula Community Hospital, and the University of Montana either owned or leased Fort Missoula lands. The GSA leased the large company barracks (Building 24) and four smaller buildings to the Forest Service for the Lolo Forest and Missoula Ranger District headquarters in the early 1970s. The fort's original entrance at South and Reserve was closed in 1974, and the Missoula Rural Fire Department built a station on South Avenue. A National Guard Armory was constructed on 4.7 acres of land at the entrance in 1977, and the Guard also improved their facilities on the west end of the fort. The Army acted as landlord to other entities, and continued to maintain an aging electrical grid, leaky water pipes, substandard sewer lines, and crumbling roads. The fort's sewer system in particular was not adequately treating the sewage, and the Army had to install a new sewage force main in 1973 which connected with the city sewer on Reserve Street. The new system still relied on the clay tile pipes laid down more than 60 years before.

Birth of a Museum

The Historical Museum at Fort Missoula can trace its roots back to the efforts of a small group of volunteers known as the Fort Missoula Historical Society to preserve the log NCO building, one of the fort's earliest structures. The short-lived Fort Missoula Historical Society soon went defunct, and the log NCO building was sold to the Western Montana Ghost Town Preservation Society for one dollar. The Ghost Town Society had been formed in December 1971, with original board members including Don Miller, K. Ross Toole, Jim McDonald, and Dale Johnson. At about the same time, the GSA leased the land now owned by the historical museum to the Forest Service, and the Ghost Town Society received a permit to keep the NCO building on site. A group of volunteers poured a concrete floor in the NCO quarters, replaced rotted logs and windows, and put a new roof on the building.

This homestead cabin was moved to the museum from the Potomac Valley in the mid-1970s with the help of students from Sentinel High School.

The city of Missoula made an application for excess land at the fort, and the Secretary of the Interior granted the city

28.82 acres for a Fort Missoula Park in December 1972. This land included the site of the original Officer's Row and parade ground, the brick quartermaster warehouse (T-322), root cellar (T-323), and Army garage (T-203). Once the city owned the land, the Western Montana Ghost Town Preservation Society was given authority to move other historic structures to the fort in 1973. The Grant Creek School was moved to the museum in 1974, and restored with the assistance of the teacher sorority Delta Kappa Gamma. Although the city of Missoula owned the land, there was no money available for the operation of a museum, so in September 1974 the county agreed to impose a mill levy on property tax, with the income to be shared with the Missoula Art Museum. A county board of trustees was established to govern both museums.

Stan Cohen, who had been involved with the repair of the NCO quarters, was hired in October 1974 as a temporary director of the Fort Missoula Historic Park on a monthly contract. He was paid $600 per month and submitted regular reports. Cohen bought a tractor and moved his workbench and tools into the old brick quartermaster's warehouse. The interior of the warehouse was a total mess, but a wood stove was installed to heat it during the winter months. Cohen set about trying to preserve as much local history as possible before buildings crumbled into dust. He had a vision to create a pioneer town using old buildings from around the area, and numerous volunteers helped with development of the museum. Army Reserve troops were instrumental in moving buildings and earth-moving. A Green Thumb crew also assisted with several projects. One of the first tasks was to build a fire station to house a 1918 American-LaFrance fire engine donated by the Missoula Fire Department. The Missoula Exchange Club provided money and volunteers, and the Army Reserve poured the station's foundation. While the firehouse was being built, Cohen dug a foundation for a gas station next door, and built a bandstand to the south, which he envisioned as the center of the historic town. An old homestead cabin had been brought from the Potomac Valley with help from students at Sentinel High School and the Army Reserve. Cohen found an old outhouse at Clearwater Junction and installed it behind the homestead cabin.

The early spring of 1975 brought a flurry of activity. Two buildings were moved from a motor court near Hellgate Canyon, and turned into a law office and a newspaper office. They sat near where the Drummond Depot is today. That spring the top of a Forest Service lookout was brought to the museum (the lookout would not be erected until 1983). A shed was also built over the Missoula County gallows (last used in 1943).

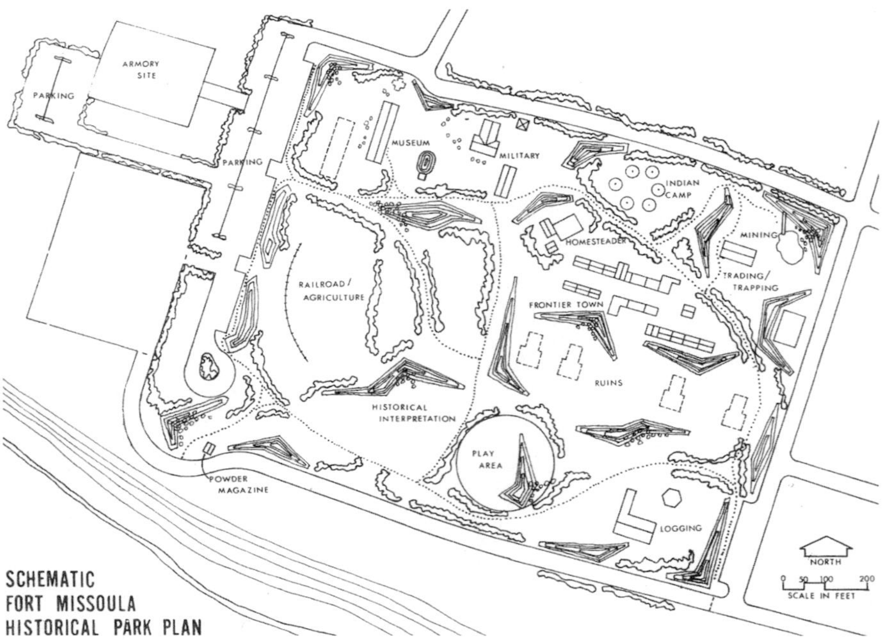

The Historical Museum at Fort Missoula looks much different today than what was envisioned in 1973.

Missoula's last remaining electric streetcar was donated to the fledgling museum (see Page 80) and the Northern Pacific Railroad donated tracks, ties, and trucks to put the trolley on tracks. Archie Roemer provided equipment to lift the trolley, and also sandblasted it. A local Girl Scout troop received a $500 grant from *Reader's Digest* to paint the trolley. Cohen tarred the trolley's roof, repaired the floor, and built a replica cowcatcher. With railroad tracks in place, the Anaconda Copper Mining Co. moved a donated logging flatcar to the museum, and the Northern Pacific Railroad offered to donate the

Frenchtown Depot. (The Milwaukee Road Depot from Drummond was eventually moved to the museum in 1982). Cohen obtained permission to move a school from Woodworth, and also received permission from the Catholic Diocese in Helena to move St. Michaels Church from Hellgate to the museum. The Army Reserve agreed to tear the church down, mark the logs for reassembly and move it to the museum to preserve it. This plan fell apart when a local resident filed a restraining order and stopped the dismantling. The church was eventually moved to the museum in 1981.

The speed with which changes were occurring at the fort concerned some board members of the Ghost Town Society and the county museum board. "I scared a few people because I was going too fast," Cohen recalled. The museum board decided to advertise for a full-time museum professional who could serve as permanent director in early 1975, and several of the 25 applicants were brought in for interviews. Cohen thought he had the inside track and was stunned when he was told during the summer of 1975 that he was being replaced. (Cohen would later be instrumental in the formation of the Museum of Mountain Flying and the Rocky Mountain Museum of Military History.)

Geoff Hunt was hired as the historical museum's new director and curator. Shortly thereafter, the members of the Western Montana Ghost Town Society decided to get out of the museum business in order to concentrate on ghost town preservation (although the society retained ownership of the NCO quarters until 2007, when it was deeded to the museum). A public meeting was held in the fall of 1975 which led to the formation of the Friends of the Historical Museum at Fort Missoula, and by April 1976 the City Council decided to deed the 28 acres to Missoula County.

Director Hunt announced that the grand opening of the museum would be July 4, 1976, and the museum received a $2,250 grant from the Montana Bicentennial Committee to put on the celebration. This inaugural 4th of July celebration became an annual affair that continues to attract thousands of participants each year. The Fort Missoula area was also placed on the National Register of Historic Places in 1976. The nomination read, "The integrity of the fort complex, even with the removal of the earliest buildings, remains extraordinarily high, weathering both ownership changes and adaptive reuse of the individual buildings."

Community Hospital

For many years Community Hospital (originally founded as the Thornton Hospital in 1922) was located in downtown Missoula. Beginning in the late 1960s, board president E.W. Lister led an effort to build a new hospital on a 45-acre campus at Fort Missoula. It was an ambitious project, with initial construction costing $4.6 million, but the new 105-bed Community Hospital opened in 1972. The campus soon grew to include the Village Health Care Center and Senior Center, Community Nursing and Rehab, Missoula Medical Arts, and eventually the Ronald McDonald House. In order to extend sewer lines that far west, the city annexed the hospital and land near the main entrance to the fort, including the Union Square Apartments built by A.W. Fetscher.

The Post Hospital

The first hospital at Fort Missoula consisted of two tents and a shanty set up by the 3rd Infantry in November 1877. The following year construction on a large L-shaped frame building with accommodations for 12 patients was begun. The building had plaster walls and a stone cellar. Dr. Robert Mills Whitefoot, a Civil War veteran who had previously served at Fort Ellis and Camp Baker was the post surgeon from 1880 to 1881. The post was quarantined in 1882 to prevent the spread of smallpox. Prisoners who needed medical care were shackled to their beds, although one escaped anyway. The hospital was expanded again in 1888 by local contractor A. Swartz. A new three-and-a-half story post hospital (T-9) was built near the riverbank in 1911 in accordance with the Surgeon General's recommendations for a regimental post. The plans called for a Mission-style building with two patient ward wings, each with a capacity of 30 patients. The plans also called for an annex in the rear with quarters for 22 hospital corps privates and 5 NCOs. The 16,000 square foot hospital was built with only one ward at first. There were plans to add a second ward as well as the rear annex in 1913, but Congress declined to appropriate the $40,000 requested for these improvements. The hospital was overwhelmed during the Spanish influenza outbreak in 1918, and treated an outbreak of polio among the children living at the fort during 1934 and 1935. Mumps and flu struck the fort in early 1936. The building was damaged by fire prior to World War II, but was repaired in December 1941.

The hospital was deactivated in 1947 after serving soldiers and their families, student trainees, CCC men, foreign detainees, and Army prisoners. It sat vacant until 1962 and was frequently targeted by vandals during this time. The Army estimated it would take $50,000 to put it in good repair, and it was declared to be federal surplus property. The Western Montana Youth Guidance Corporation applied for ownership in 1959. Harry Maclay, who favored construction of a 200-bed Veterans Administration hospital at the fort, led the opposition to that plan and declared that giving away the hospital would rip the heart out of the historic fort. Nevertheless, Senators Mike Mansfield and James Murray introduced a bill to transfer the hospital, two outbuildings (T-12 & T-14), and 6.03 acres of land on the river bank to the corporation in 1963.

The former Post Hospital has served as the administration and accounting offices of the Western Montana Mental Health Center for more than 50 years. A staff of 760 spread throughout 15 counties in western Montana provides numerous programs related to mental health and addiction services. The center announced plans in 2012 to build a 4,600 square foot addition on the northwest side of the Post Hospital to house a 38-bed inpatient center for addiction treatment, although the center estimated that construction would not begin for several years.

The Mission-style Post Hospital built in 1911 (left) was originally supposed to have a second patient ward built on the right side of the main entrance. From 1941 to 1947 the hospital was surrounded by a double fence with a guard tower. An Italian detainee committed suicide during World War II by leaping from the roof. The building is now owned by the Western Montana Mental Health Center. The original post hospital (right) was located just west of the current headquarters of the Lolo National Forest.

10

The Battle of Fort Missoula

"I don't think anyone at the time anticipated the public reaction that would occur."
Leroy Schramm, *Missoulian,* August 18, 1995

The Army entered into an agreement with the University of Montana in 1966 to transfer title of several tracts of land at Fort Missoula to the university in 20 years on the condition that the land was used for educational and research purposes during that period. The university did use the cell block buildings for animal research labs, and botany professor James Habeck and his students used the land south of the Bitterroot River for research, at least until a neighbor cut off land access. Habeck then informed university president James Koch in writing that his research had been curtailed by lack of access and warned that his work should not be used to claim the fort lands were being used for educational purposes. The university made little further effort to utilize the Fort Missoula land and buildings for educational or research purposes. The university did consider building a football stadium and a separate graduate campus at the fort, but nothing came of either proposal.

The Fort Missoula Steering Committee was formed in 1972 to create a plan to guide development at the fort. Over the next year the committee, which was composed of area landowners, worked with the City-County Planning Board and local citizens to create a land-use plan for the former military reservation. The plan envisioned the fort complex to be "...an entity, usable in many ways for public service..."[1] The plan recommended putting in place the administrative structure, policies, and inter-local agreements to create "... a recreation area, an historical landmark, a nature education area and an administrative public service center."[2]

Although the university had made only minimal efforts to meet the conditions of education and research, the US Government granted the Board of Regents a conditional deed for the property in 1986. Shortly thereafter the university declared the land a "dormant asset" and made plans to transfer the 300 acres to the University of Montana Foundation, a private non-profit support group. Chronically underfunded by the state legislature, the university saw the surplus Army land as a wonderful opportunity to raise money and to build up the foundation, which intended to sell off all of the land. The most valuable portion of the land was directly adjacent to the Missoula Country Club and the Bitterroot River, and was perfect for a high-end housing development. It was also part of the historic fort, and included the area formerly occupied by the Alien Detention Center, the historic stables, the two cell-block buildings constructed for the Army Disciplinary Barracks, and two early NCO quarters (Buildings 14 and 16).

University president James Koch declared in a 1987 memo that the best way to avoid controversy over the proposed sale was to earmark the proceeds for student scholarships. Unfortunately, top-ranking university officials seriously underestimated the Missoula community's attachment to the historic fort, and while the motives of the university administrators may have been pure, their methods were not. They failed to adequately follow a number of state laws that governed selling state-owned lands, which ultimately led to the formation of an opposition group, a lawsuit, a citizen's initiative to reverse a controversial rezoning of the land in question, scrutiny by the state Land Board and Board of Regents, and ultimately a 10-month long investigation by the Montana Attorney General.

A consultant recommended in 1988 that the university get legislative approval before any sale, to file the environmental reports required by state law, to extensively advertise the sale, and to get written confirmation from the federal government that any deed restrictions had lapsed. His advice was ignored. President Koch did intend to seek legislative approval for the sale, but was advised against it by Leroy Schramm, the university's attorney, who pointed out that the State Board of Regents had authority over all university activities. President Koch sent a memo to top administrators in 1988 asking them to minimize publicity about the sale.

An attorney acting for the university wrote a memo in 1988 that set specific conditions for transfer of the land in order to comply with state law and protect state residents. The conditions specified the sale of the land at the highest market price feasible in a public bidding process, that the land be returned to the university upon demand or in case of a change in circumstances or a court order, allowed for inspection of UM Foundation records at the request of the university or the regents, and termination of the deal if the foundation defaulted. Sherman Lohn, the foundation's attorney, called those conditions, "totally unacceptable."[3]

The attorney general's report indicated that some administrators and consultants urged the university to make sure that it was a public process and that all of the legal procedures were followed. George Mitchell, a university administrator and former UM lawyer wrote a memo in 1989 stating that in his opinion the transfer of land from the university to the foundation was an attempt to avoid state regulations, politics and the laws that govern state lands.[4] His advice, and the advice of others, was also ignored.

Ray Nicolet was hired to appraise the university's fort property in 1989, but was hampered by the lack of a modern survey or title insurance on the land. He also discovered 135 easements on the property, and made his appraisal assuming that the land would remain under the current zoning. Nicolet valued the university's 300 acres at $396,000. He dropped off his appraisal at President Koch's office in Main Hall and returned to his office downtown a few minutes later, only to find a livid President Koch on the phone. According to Nicolet in a 1995 *Missoulian* article, "He [Koch] exploded. He told me I was incompetent, that the land was worth $1 to $3 million. I told him he couldn't have possibly scanned my report, much less read it, in that time."[5]

Using the endangered historic stable as a background, this editorial cartoon from the *Missoula Independent* reflected the desire of many local residents to prevent the commercial development of Fort Missoula.
Courtesy of Greg Siple

A vice-president of the university later threatened to withhold more than $6,000 of Nicolet's fee unless he changed his appraisal to reflect the value of the land once the zoning was changed. Nicolet explained that it would be illegal to base an appraisal on speculation that the zoning might be changed sometime in the future, but he ultimately submitted an "evaluation of potential values," which established a conditional value of the land at $1.57 million. Nicolet later recalled, "What they wanted, they figured they'd slide this thing through real quick... the university stonewalled my appraisal, they hid it."[6]

The University commissioned a different firm to conduct a second appraisal later in 1989. Stevens, Stuckey & Company determined the land had a value of $500,000, but was potentially worth $1 million if it was split into 20-acre lots. The 15 most desirable acres were excluded from this appraisal.

University President James Koch and Carrol Krause, Commissioner of Higher Education, signed a warranty deed transferring ownership of 300 acres from UM to the University Foundation on June 6, 1990, but the Missoula County Assessor questioned whether the deed properly showed that the land belonged to the state, and insisted the deed must be changed. Joan Newman, the university's attorney at the time, then changed some of the language in the document as well as the name of the "Grantor," and attached the revised version as page one, with the original document comprising pages two and three. She refiled it on August 23, 1990 without noting that it was a corrected document. The revised document still had the signatures of President Koch and Commissioner Krause, although both of them had left state employment by the time the revised document was filed. State Attorney General Joe Mazurek eventually ruled that the sale was not legally recorded because the filed document did not reflect the changes.

Nevertheless, the University Foundation believed it had received a valid title to the land, and prepared to sell the most desirable portion near the river. The WGM Group, a local planning and engineering firm, was chosen to assist with the process. WGM, at no charge to the foundation, proceeded to hold a series of meetings in early 1991 with public agencies and others who owned land at the fort, but did not publicly notice the meetings as would have been required had the university still owned the land. George Dennison, the university's new president, wrote a memo about the sale, and sent it to foundation board member and attorney Tom Boone for review. Boone suggested leaving off the line, "all decisions will be made public."[7] Gerard Berens of the Save the Fort group would later charge that there was no public notice of the sale by the foundation.

The foundation also ignored a request from the State Historic Preservation Officer to assess the historic properties of the site before selling it. The university had already fielded numerous queries from out-of-state land developers who had their eye on this parcel when a Foundation board member and a representative of the WGM Group compiled a list of interested parties to be notified about the sale in October 1991. Notably absent from the list were the names of eight parties who had previously expressed interest in the land, including those wealthy out-of-state investors.

Divot Development, a partnership between several prominent Missoula businessmen, seemed to have the inside track on buying the land. Bob Brugh of Divot had learned that the land might be available while golfing with a former UM faculty member at the Missoula Country Club. Divot was also a client of the WGM Group which had consulted with the university and the foundation on how to market the property.[8] On October 9, 1991 Brugh sent a letter seeking potential investors for a high-end housing development at Fort Missoula. According to a *Missoulian* article just after the sale, Brugh had begun developing a plan for the property 11 months before the foundation released a Request for Proposal, and had obtained written commitments from potential home buyers two months before the land was made available for sale.[9] This led to charges that Divot Development had cut a back-room deal for the historic land. "In short, Divot was taking reservations for the future sale of UM, public land that was not yet even offered for sale," claimed Gerard Berens of the Save the Fort organization.[10]

Buildings 14 and 16 were built as NCO quarters in 1910, and were used as UM faculty housing from 1947 to 1957. The Montana Department of Institutions operated a Life-Skills Center there from 1966 to 1982. They were originally slated for demolition if a housing development was approved. Owned by UM, they now sit vacant.

Divot requested that a third appraisal of the 83 most sought-after acres near the river and the

Missoula Country Club be conducted in 1992, and the foundation hired the Hall-Widdoss Company to re-evaluate the land. Taking account of the lack of infrastructure, the current zoning, and the use of the land for storage, the new appraisal valued this smaller parcel at $340,000 despite the premium location. Earl Pruyn, one of the principals of Divot Development, then agreed to pay $375,000 for the 83 acres in September 1992. Pruyn also received a right of first refusal on purchasing the rest of the 217 acres of fort lands owned by the foundation. Foundation Board member Tom Boone called the offer from Divot Development of $4,096 per acre "a good price."[11] (At about the same time the Five Valleys Lutheran Retirement Center made an offer to pay $13,000 per acre for up to 24 acres of the foundation's land. Although the price was accepted, the sale never occurred and their $10,000 deposit was later returned once controversy erupted.)

As a response to changes in ownership at the fort and changes in the goals of land owners, a new steering committee was convened in 1993 to update the 1973 Fort Missoula Plan. The committee was made up of community members and fort landowners (including representatives from Divot and the UM Foundation), and 10 committee meetings and two public meetings were held during the fall of 1993. The committee recommended five goals: protection of the historical and cultural values of the fort, conservation of native plants and animals, maintenance of open space for parkland, trails, urban forests, and agriculture, ensuring that new developments met community needs and respected the distinctiveness of the fort area, and coordination among the entities represented at the fort on the construction of new buildings and infrastructure. This revised Fort Missoula Plan was adopted by the City Council early in 1994.

The Board of Regents finally approved a buy-sell agreement with local builder Mark Fisher, another of the Divot partners, on March 22, 1993. Fisher agreed to pay $450,000 for title to 83 acres, and Divot was given a year to pay. The buy-sell agreement also stated that the foundation would help Divot get the property rezoned and that Divot could walk away from the deal if the rezoning did not occur within one year. The Foundation also took responsibility for obtaining title insurance and getting permission from the state so that Divot could demolish historic buildings, and assured Divot that environmental cleanup costs would not exceed $50,000. Divot's purchase was also conditioned on receiving utility contracts at the price and capacity they had specified, along with their preferred traffic access.

Divot would later claim that 110 meetings were held on the project between May and December 1993, and that 95 of those were public meetings. A city planner who worked extensively on the project thought that number was greatly inflated. Doris Fischer said, "I think they really mixed things up. I think [the Divot partners] put their calendars together and they just duplicated things, perhaps inadvertently."[12]

T-156 is one of two cell-block buildings built in 1945 as part of the Army Disciplinary Barracks. The cell-blocks originally had flat roofs and an open courtyard in the middle of each building. Both buildings were slated for demolition by Divot Development in the 1990s. T-156 is now used by UM's Geosciences Department, and was renovated during the fall of 2007 for $600,000. The adjacent T-157 (not shown) is used for storage by UM's Fine Arts Department.

One of the first obstacles faced by the Divot partners and the foundation was getting the land rezoned for a housing development, but that hit a roadblock when Ginny Cass, the chair of the Missoula Consolidated Planning Board, broke a tie vote and rejected rezoning of the land on November 17, 1993. Cass thought the development was troubling due to the loss of open space, destruction of historic buildings, and lack of affordable housing. "I basically wanted to send a message to the council that the Planning Board was very concerned about this project and that a number of things needed some very careful review."[13]

This sent the decision to the City Council, which needed to change the zoning before the sale could go through. It also spurred other opponents of the project to come forward. Alfredo Cipolato, a former detainee of the Alien Detention Center said, "I wish they would leave the place alone and make a nice beautiful park there."[14] Allan Mathews, Missoula's Historic Preservation Officer, called the plan to build housing at the fort, "an attempt to deny the history there. The camps provide a lesson that we can still learn from, a lesson about freedom, and how easily freedom can be taken away, even in this country."[15]

With opposition mounting, Divot renamed the project "The Greens," and proposed donating the 25-acre Slevin's Island in the Bitterroot River to Five Valleys Land Trust for open space. The Greens housing project was to encircle the historic fort on the west and south. Despite the name, Divot Development still intended to destroy the historic stables and the cell-block buildings from the Disciplinary Barracks at this time.[16]

The Missoula Office of Community Development wanted the developers to save the historic stables and some of the foundations of the Alien Detention Center, and establish a 250 foot greewnway through the middle of the development.[17] During a four-and-a-half hour meeting on December 6 1993, the City Council, with the County Commissioners in attendance, held a public hearing on whether or not to create a Special Historic District Overlay zone around Fort Missoula to protect the historic buildings. Ted Delaney of the University Foundation protested that it, "would place undue hardship and restriction upon our ability to market and develop our property."[18] Nevertheless, the City Council created a special Fort Missoula Historic Overlay to protect 1,700 acres and 29 historic buildings at the fort.

With the historic overlay in place, the City Council voted (by a two to one margin) to rezone the Fort Missoula land to allow for up to 303 homes on December 20, 1993. Immediately after the vote a group of citizens formed an advocacy group named Save the Fort and launched a massive petition drive to put the City Council's zoning decision up for a public vote. Spokesman Gerard Berens said "Our feelings are that this land belongs in the public domain, and Divot represents privatization. We won't give it up without public debate."[19] Save the Fort gathered signatures all over town and citizens flocked to sign the petition.[20] Volunteers needed to gather 4,849 signatures by January 18, and instead turned in 12,500 signatures. The public vote on whether or not to overturn the zoning was set for June 7, 1994.

Shortly thereafter, community activist Ross Best threatened to sue unless the foundation released their records on the property, which the foundation reluctantly did in February 1994, although Attorney General Joe Mazurek later ruled that, "A number of significant documents were not made available to the public."[21]

Given the uncertainty over the zoning, the Divot partners (now comprised of Bob Brugh, Mark Fisher, and James Hoffman) asked for an extension to buy the land, which was turned down by the foundation. Divot Development then waived all of their previous conditions for the sale, including that of zoning, and officially bought the 83 acres on March 3, 1994 for

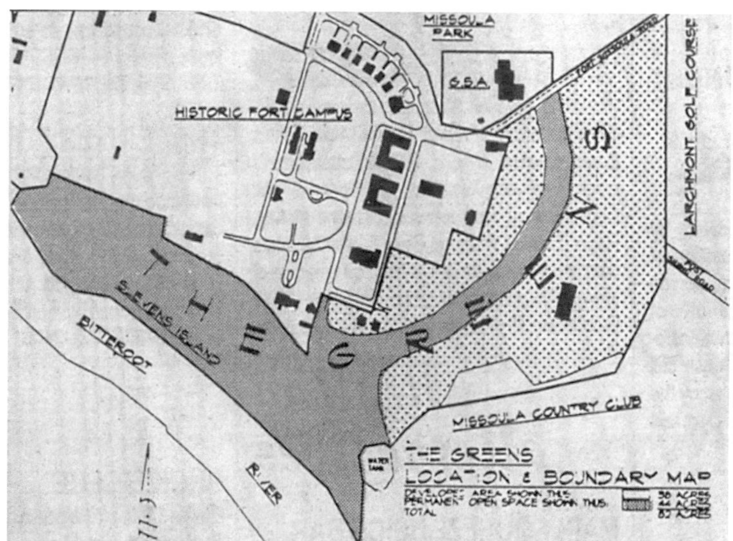

Divot Development originally planned to build 303 housing units at the fort. After a public outcry they agreed to reduce the number to 212 units with a greenway through the center of the development allowing public access to 44 acres of open space on the riverbank and Slevin's Island. The revamped project was known as "The Greens."

$450,000. The State Attorney General ruled in 1995 that the transfer of state land to the foundation and subsequent sale to Divot, "was not in compliance with state law."[22]

With an upcoming public election on the zoning, Divot made changes to the plan in order to placate opponents. The number of housing units was reduced to 212, covering 38 acres of the former internment camp. The plan also called for a medical facility, professional offices, and single and multiple housing units. Divot offered to give the stables to the Historical Museum at Fort Missoula, provided the museum could raise the money to move the massive concrete building. Divot also offered to give Five Valley Land Trust a 25-acre easement on Slevin's Island, and to leave a greenway through the center of the development for public access to the river. They promised to renovate the old NCO quarters (Buildings 14 and 16), and they promised not to destroy any historic buildings. (The two cell block buildings from the Disciplinary Barracks were not considered historic.)

On March 11, one week after the sale, Divot sued the City of Missoula in hopes of preventing the citizen's vote, claiming that rezoning did not qualify as a citizen initiative. On May 13 Judge Jeffrey Langton ruled that the voting could proceed. Representatives of Save the Fort in late May 1994 presented the Board of Regents, Governor Marc Racicot, and others with a voluminous collection of memos and letters purporting to show a conflict of interest, and charged that members of the UM Foundation Board and the principals of Divot had socialized together at the Missoula Country Club, where a sweetheart deal was reached before the land was publicly offered for sale. Gerard Berens also alleged the land was sold for substantially less than it was worth. The report accused several prominent local businessmen and women of having a conflict of interest.

Despite an advertising campaign financed by Divot, the voters in June rejected the City Council's zoning change 55 to 45 percent. Divot, which by this time had 40 prospective buyers interested in living at Fort Missoula, then appealed Judge Langton's decision to the Montana Supreme Court.

Save the Fort asked the State Land Board in August 1994 to decide whether the Regents or the Land Board had authority to sell state land. State law was vague on the topic, and the State Land Board asked the Board of Regents to cancel the sale to Divot on October 17, 1994 until a policy could be developed over who had the right to sell state lands. Faced with a potential lawsuit from the Land Board, the Regents agreed in November to cancel the sale. The Divot principals then asked to be reimbursed not only for the purchase price but also for the several hundred thousand dollars in costs they had incurred since the sale for architectural plans, legal fees, zoning expenses and permit fees.[23] Divot wanted $847,000 in exchange for return of the land. Foundation director Larry Morlan said in November 1994 that the foundation could pay only $450,000, plus interest, to purchase the land back from Divot, and that other entities would have to come up with any additional funds.

Once public outrage grew over the planned destruction of the historic stables, the partners of Divot Development offered to give the building to the Historical Museum at Fort Missoula, provided the museum pay to move the massive concrete building off-site. The museum trustees, already struggling to keep the doors open, were unwilling to go into debt just to bail out the developers.

Given the lingering questions over the sale, State Attorney General Joe Mazurek mounted an investigation late in 1994. The 10-month-long investigation culminated on August 17, 1995, when the 31-page report found that the Board of Regents ignored state law, avoided public scrutiny, and sold the land for less than market value. "Fort Sale Called Illegal" screamed the front page banner headline of the *Missoulian* the next morning. Mazurek wrote, "The Board of Regents and the University did not desire to be constrained by the requirements of the Montana Antiquities Act and Montana Environmental

Policy Act, legislative audit procedures, and public bidding principles."

The findings of State Attorney General Joe Mazurek were summed up in his report, "The University of Montana and the state Board of Regents illegally gave public land at Fort Missoula to the UM Foundation, which then ignored state law and its own policies, actively avoided public scrutiny and sold the land for less than full market value..."[24] Leroy Schramm, the university's lawyer, replied, "We can maintain until the cows come home that we were right, but we recognize... it has caused a rift in the community."[25]

The Board of Regents eventually agreed on September 29, 1995 to pay $790,000 to reacquire the 83 acres from the Divot partners. The money came from the original purchase price, $65,000 in interest earned on that money, plus $275,000 borrowed from a university fund meant to pay accrued vacation time for visiting professors and researchers. President George Dennison thought it was, "the best resolution that we could make." He finally acknowledged the Missoula community's desire to protect the fort. "It's quite clear, given the attitudes within the community, that this is an issue that had to be resolved."[26]

Round Two

The Western Montana Mental Health Center (WMMHC), which had coordinated regional mental health and addictions services from the historic but decaying post hospital since the early 1960s, decided to move their administrative offices to downtown Missoula in order to combine several different programs under one roof. The agency entered into an agreement in August 1996 to sell the post hospital and 4.88 acres of land along the riverbank to a land developer for $505,000. Pacific Harbor Capital intended to use federal tax credits to build 70 units of low-income housing for the elderly along the river bank. The second phase of the project entailed remodeling the historic post hospital into 22 additional housing units. The company agreed that ownership of the housing would revert to the Missoula Housing Authority after 15 years. Paul Meyer, the Center's Director, was fully aware of the controversy generated by the proposed housing development on the university lands, but stated, "We tried to get a feel for who might shoot at this project, and we haven't found any wild opposition."[27]

The project nonetheless generated considerable controversy, and Gerard Berens and the Save the Fort organization once again led the opposition. The city had annexed the Western Montana Health Center property in May 1996, and at that time the land was automatically rezoned with a designation of a public lands and institutions district. Save the Fort accused the City Council of not giving adequate public notice of the rezoning in order to avoid public scrutiny on the project, and asked the council to rezone the land as open space. The City Council took the request up in November, and agreed to hold a public hearing, however just hours after that decision was made Save the Fort filed suit to have the zoning changed. The Western Montana Health Center then threatened to sue the city if the council changed the zoning of the six acres.

The tax credits that Pacific Harbor Capital planned to use expired at the end of the year, and with time running out the company pulled out of the agreement with the Western Montana Mental Health Center in hopes of finding other land to build on. City Councilman Jim McGrath observed, "Clearly our community needs low-income senior housing. And we have this special place, the fort, that we want to save... We have not come together as a community."[28] Although the deal was dead, the City Council held a public hearing on December 23, 1996, and two weeks later a divided City Council voted to retain the controversial zoning. Mayor Mike Kadas wanted to swap land with the mental health center in exchange for the 4.88 acres at the fort, but nothing came of it and the center's administrative offices remained at thc fort.

Save the Fort eventually dropped the lawsuit, but Patty Kent of the Western Montana Mental Health Center observed, "The harassment and the methods that have been employed by the Save the Fort to kill this have been completely inappropriate and a disservice to the community."[29]

Parks and Recreation at Fort Missoula

Sports and recreation have always been an important part of life at Fort Missoula. The historic fort had a baseball diamond, basketball court, boxing ring, swimming pool, tennis courts, and ice-skating rink. The Army and CCC men fielded numerous boxing and baseball teams. The Italian detainees during World War II engaged in spirited soccer matches, while the Japanese detainees practiced judo and built their own golf course. The Missoula Gun Club operated just south of the cemetery and the fort's Timber Reserve eventually became the Pattee Canyon Recreation Area.

When the Army began to dispose of excess fort land north of South Avenue, title was transferred to the State of Montana and Missoula County. The state built offices for the state Fish, Wildlife and Parks and the Department of Natural Resources and Conservation. Other county land in Section 25 sat vacant, and in 1982 Rita Baumgardner convinced the County Commissioners that 60 acres of former fort land would make a good equestrian park. The Missoula Horseman's Council signed a lease in 1983 and began to develop the park.

Danielle Boulais of the Montana Conservation Corps and CCC veteran John Phillips celebrate cutting the ribbon on the proposed Fort Missoula Regional Park in 2012.

The area west of Community Hospital was acquired by Missoula County in the 1950s, and was eventually turned into a 63-acre park, with baseball fields, soccer fields, tennis courts and other amenities. City voters passed a $5 million open space bond in 1995 intended for the purchase of park land at Fort Missoula, and in 1997 the city began negotiations to buy 100 acres owned by the University of Montana. The state Board of Regents sold the land to the city in return for $700,000 from the open space bond fund in 1998. By 2001 the City Parks and Recreation Department began a master planning process for design and construction of a new recreational facility north and west of the historical center of Fort Missoula. This plan was approved by the City Council and County Commissioners in 2002. That same year the JTL Group Inc., operators of a gravel pit just west of the Fort Missoula boundary, donated 82 acres to the city, and agreed to help the City Parks Department develop the park. JTL agreed to remove gravel from the city land in exchange for more than $300,000 in construction credits. Voters rejected a bond to pay for the regional park in November 2002, and the project languished until 2008, when the Friends of the Fort Missoula Regional Park mounted a fresh campaign. Archaeological studies were done of the historic areas, and a detailed plan based on the 2002 Master Plan was approved by the city in 2008. JTL removed huge amounts of gravel from much of the site, which created a sunken, level area that will eventually become playing fields. The former JTL gravel pit will be transformed into a fishing pond with a dock for non-motorized watercraft. The regional park will be developed in phases as funding becomes available, and is expected to cost $28 million to complete. The Department of Interior designated the regional park as one of 101 signature projects of the America's Great Outdoor Initiative in 2011. On September 29, 2012 (National Public Lands Day) a formal ribbon cutting ceremony was held at the park. Two months later County Commissioners approved a comprehensive plan for redevelopment of the county's 63 acres at the east end of the regional park. The revamped county portion of the park will cost $16.1 million, and will include five lighted softball fields suitable for tournament play, two additional softball fields, four parking lots, and a dog park. Upon completion, the Fort Missoula Regional Park will eventually cover 246 acres, most of it formerly part of the Fort Missoula Military Reservation.

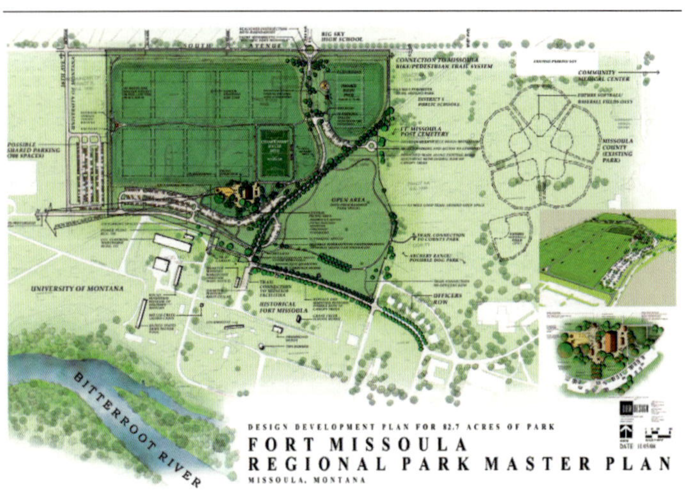

11
The Modern Fort

Fort Missoula has... evolved to a point where it now accomodates an uncommon blend of rich history, traditional military base activity, unspoiled natural features, and a wide spectrum of community affairs."

1993 Fort Missoula Plan

The nature of the fort has changed dramatically in the last 40 years as an increasing number of public agencies and non-profit groups have moved to the fort. In 1975 the Child Development Center (CDC) moved into Building T-214, a one-story frame structure built as quarters for CCC workers in 1938. The CDC offers services to those with developmental disabilities. Building T-210 serves as the CDC respite house to provide short-term housing for children with severe developmental disabilities. Located just north of the Bitterroot River, the CDC buildings look out upon the original parade ground where Lt. Colonel Charles C. Gilbert planted a flag to mark the fort's location in 1876.

The Bureau of Land Management's Missoula office was built just north of the firehouse/guardhouse (Building 46) in 1984. It was designed with white stucco and a red-tiled roof in imitation of the fort's numerous mission-style buildings.

For more than 80 years Missoula high school students have raised alfalfa, cattle, sheep, and pigs at what is now Big Sky High School's 100-acre Agricultural Educational Center, headquartered near the fort's original Target Range, with additional acreage east of the post cemetery. Big Sky High School was built a few blocks east of the farm in 1980. The school district's Vocational-Technical program built the Department of Industrial Technology adjacent to the farm in the 1970s. Administration of the Missoula Vo-Tech and 13 acres was transferred to the State Board of Regents in 1988, and it is now known as the West Campus of Missoula College. The Fort Missoula site has also been identified as a site for future expansion of the Missoula College facilities.

Diners enjoy a gourmet salmon dinner at a fund-raising event at the historical museum in 2004. A spectacular iris garden and gazebo make the west lawn a favorite place for weddings and community events, including Missoula's Fourth of July celebration, which has been held at the museum annually since 1976.

University of Montana President George Dennison appointed a committee of 12 university administrators and faculty members to draw up a master plan for the university lands at Fort Missoula. The university sold 100 acres to the city for a park, and agreed to preserve land on the riverbank and south of the river for research. Various university departments utilize the fort's historic stables (see page 78) and the Army cell blocks (see page 122), as well as surrounding land for storage and research.

The Fort Missoula Native Plant Garden is located on land owned by the university just south of the former Alien Detention Center, and is operated by the Montana Natural History Center. One of the barracks buildings from the Alien Detention Center will be moved from the Yellow Bay Biological Station on Flathead Lake and placed near the community gardens south of Buildings 14 and 16.

A group of Missoula military veterans began lobbying for a veteran's cemetery in western Montana beginning in 2001. The Federal government eventually approved construction on a 23-acre site of former sort land land north of Big Sky High School in 2007. The US Department of Veteran's Affairs agreed to pay for construction of the $4.15 million dollar cemetery. Administered by the State of Montana, the Western Montana State Veteran's Cemetery was dedicated and opened on September 11, 2008. Over 700 veterans had been interred there by 2013.

Base Realignment and Closure

The Regular US Army had not had troops stationed at Fort Missoula since 1947, but the Army still owned 52 acres in six different parcels and was responsible for maintaining the fort's electrical, water, sewer, and phone infrastructure as well as the roads. In 1990 Congress passed the Defense Base Closure and Realignment Act (BRAC), and two years later the Army announced that due to budget cuts their property at Fort Missoula would be disposed of. Details were left up to the 1995 Defense Base Closure and Realignment Commission, which recommended transferring four buildings and 13 acres, including the Post Cemetery and Veuve Hall (Barracks 26) to the Army Reserve's 96th Regional Support Command. The Montana National Guard received ownership of several former CCC buildings plus their training site and shops on the west side of the post. The Guard still had three units stationed at the fort, including a mechanized infantry company equipped with M2A2 Bradley armored fighting vehicles. The Army Reserve and National Guard eventually decided to relocate to a location west of Missoula on Highway 93 North. The National Guard armory on Reserve Street was sold to a private developer in 2007 for $3.5 million, although the Guard retained a three-year lease on the building. The building was eventually purchased by Goodwill Industries in 2013. The National Guard retained their shops on

The Fort's Golf Courses

The **Missoula Country Club** built a golf course at the base of Mount Sentinel in 1917 on land owned by the Alumni Challenge Athletic Field Corp, but members decided they needed to buy land of their own in order to fully develop the golf course. After Congress decided in 1918 that Fort land could be leased or sold, members negotiated a number of trades, leases, and purchases for land at the southeast end of Fort Missoula. With the help of the Chamber of Commerce they arranged to buy land on a 20-year lease-sale agreement in 1922. Construction of a nine-hole golf course at Fort Missoula began shortly thereafter, with the course opening a year later. Post commander Colonel P.H. Mullay declared it was, "a golf course with a setting more lovely than any other in the country."[1] Both officers and enlisted men were allowed to use the club, and soldiers were issued, "good golf clubs." On September 2, 1942 the Army officially deeded 91.52 acres to the Missoula Country Club. When the course was expanded to 18 holes, part of Hole 17 intruded on government land, and in 1955 Missoula County agreed to give the Country Club several additional acres. Today the Country Club covers 111 acres of former Fort land. Besides the 18-hole golf course, the club offers a dining room, lounge, clubhouse, pro shop, and swimming pool.

Just across Post Siding Road from the Country Club, the County-owned **Larchmont Golf Course** occupies 153 acres in the center of the original fort. Although the 1973 Fort Missoula Plan recommended building the golf course at Maclay Flats, the 18-hole public course was constructed at Fort Missoula in 1981 and opened for business during the spring of 1982. It is governed by a County board and run by a private management committee.

the west end of the fort. The Army Reserve has left the fort, but still owns Veuve Hall (Barracks 26) and the old post bakery. The Forest Service was granted eight acres, headquarters of the Lolo National Forest (Barracks 24), the Materials Testing facility in T-150, the firehouse/guardhouse (Building 46) and the former Post Headquarters (T-1), which was used as the Technology and Development Center.

The BRAC Commission recommended disposing of the rest of the Army property at Fort Missoula, including the seven historic buildings of officer's row, the carriage houses behind them, the Post Exchange (T-2) and the 1878 Powder Magazine. At the urging of local citizens, Senator Max Baucus worked to prevent the General Services Administration from taking over those historic buildings, and instead sought out a local group to take responsibility for them. County Commissioner Ann Mary Dussault declared that the county was willing to take ownership of the buildings but could not afford the maintenance and any plan would have to be self-funded.

The Northern Rockies Heritage Center

The idea of a Heritage Center in Missoula (sometimes dubbed the Smithsonian of the West) had been talked about since 1985. The vision was to build a center with artist and music studios, museums, and educational space. The historic Officer's Row buildings at Fort Missoula seemed an ideal use for the long-talked about center, and the Northern Rockies Heritage Center (NRHC) was organized as a non-profit group in 1993, with General Bo Foster one of the founding members. The following year Congress allowed the new Heritage Center to take over administration of 16 acres of Army land, including the six-acre parade ground, the seven Mission-style buildings of Officer's Row, the carriage houses, the Post Exchange (T-2, see page 74), the powder magazine (see page 28) and the water tower (see page 73). The NRHC operation's plan was approved by the State Historic Preservation Office (SHPO) in 1995, and SHPO also provided a $10,000 matching grant to repair the roofs of Officer's Row as well as the large open-air front porch of Building 32. Once the fort was formally deactivated in 2000, the NRHC was authorized to manage 16 acres and 13 buildings for, "historical, cultural or educational purposes." The Heritage Center is today headquartered in Building 30, also known as the M.Y. "Bo" Foster Building. The Heritage Center rents out office space in Heritage Hall (T-2) and the buildings of Officer's Row to non-profit groups and other organizations. The carriage houses behind Officer's Row are used for studio space by local artists and musicians. Heritage Hall is also rented out for many community events, while the scenic parade ground is a popular spot for outdoor weddings.

The Fort's Infrastructure

With the Army preparing to leave, the question of who would take over the fort's infrastructure remained unresolved. Given the patchwork of ownership among several public agencies, no one was sure who was responsible for future maintenance of the roads and utilities at Fort Missoula, but the Army wanted a resolution to the problem by September 1997. The Army wanted to transfer the water system, electrical system, sewer, natural gas system, telecommunications system, and some of the roads to other government entities. Fort Missoula was 120 years old in 1997, and the Army wanted to leave the fort by September of that year, although the final deadline was 2001. (The fort was officially decommissioned in 1999.) Even though the historic fort was within city limits, Missoula Public Works Director Bruce Bender stated that the city had no obligation to take control of the aging roads and sewer system, particularly given the lack of curbs and sidewalks. Missoula County indicated that it was only willing to pave one-half mile of roads at the fort. In the meantime the infrastructure continued to deteriorate since no one felt responsible for making repairs. The sewer system in particular suffered from antique pipes and an old pump that was at risk for failure. The roads were eventually transferred to the NRHC, the National Guard, the Army Reserve, and the City of Missoula. The city and Army eventually entered into an infrastructure maintenance agreement, with the Army providing the city with annual grants for maintenance.

The Rocky Mountain Museum of Military History

The military museum has existed since 1985 when Tom Wilkins of the Missoula Chamber of Commerce identified the need to preserve America's military history. He approached local collector Hayes Otoupalik as well as veterans like Brigadier General M.Y. Bo Foster, seeking their help in forming a military museum. Wilkins formed the Rocky Mountain Military Museum and served as the museum's original director from 1985 to 1992. Warren Wilcox provided a substantial donation to ensure the Otoupalik collection remained in Montana, and in 1992 the museum claimed to have the largest military collection in the northern Rockies. The military museum, led by director Tate Jones, now occupies Buildings T-310 and T-316 on the western edge of Fort Missoula under a special arrangement with the Montana National Guard. The museum's collection is housed in T-316, the former CCC administrative building renamed the Parrish Building after local Medal of Honor recipient Laverne Parrish. The museum features exhibits dating from the frontier era up to the Iraq and Afghanistan wars, and also has a research library and an extensive collection of historic Montana documents donated by Robert Svoboda in 2003. Outside exhibits include the M-7 105mm self-propelled howitzer which sat in front of the National Guard Armory on Reserve street for many years, as well as a Bell UH-1H helicopter gunship which saw combat in the Central Highlands of Vietnam in the late 1960s.

The Rocky Mountain Museum of Military History exhibits an extensive collection of military artifacts, including this "Huey" helicopter from the Vietnam War.

The Historical Museum at Fort Missoula

The historical museum focuses on the history of the city and county of Missoula, the history of Fort Missoula and the importance of forest management and the wood products industry in western Montana. After its founding in the 1970s, the historical museum experienced a second building boom in the early 1980s when a number of additional historic buildings were moved to the grounds. St. Michael's Church was moved from Hellgate in 1981, and a Milwaukee Road railroad depot was moved to the historical museum from Drummond in 1982. The US Forest Service's Sliderock Mountain fire lookout, parts of which had been moved to the museum years earlier, was erected in 1983 with the help of the Society of American Foresters. That same year a Forest Service guard cabin, built in 1910, was moved from Miller Creek and placed near the foot of the lookout.

Wes Hardin, the historical museum's director in 1990 focused on building the infrastructure of the museum and help increased the professionalism of the governing County Board of Trustees and the Friends of the Historical Museum at Fort Missoula, the non-profit support group. When Hardin left in 1991, the Trustees advertised the director position nationally, and the notice caught the eye of Dr. Robert M. Brown, a self-described "fort guy" who was working at the Museum of American Textile History in North Andover, Massachusetts at the time. Brown was granted an interview, and recalled, "I came out here in early March. There was beautiful snow and I fell in love with it. I was one of two finalists. The other was a local guy and I figured I didn't have a shot at it, but they offered me the job and I took it on the spot."[2] Brown took charge of a museum with plenty of history, land, buildings, and artifacts, but little money. The Historical Museum at Fort Missoula had three full-time staff members at the time, and shared a 1.33 mill property-tax levy with the Missoula Art Museum. The county funds were barely enough to pay salaries and left little for collections care or routine maintenance. A 1993 update of the original Fort Missoula plan reported that the museum had made, "modest progress in developing a historic park on 32 acres of fort land deeded originally to the City and subsequently acquired by the County."[3]

The Save the Fort organization had identified seven former barracks buildings of the Alien Detention Center camp located around the Missoula Valley, and one of those barracks buildings was eventually moved from the University Golf Course to the grounds of the historical museum in 1995. The building now houses an exhibit on the Alien Detention Center and also serves as storage space for the historical museum.

The archives of Missoula County High School from 1904 to 1955, which included 65 trophies, numerous photos, and other memorabilia were moved to the historical museum in 1996. This project was spearheaded by the Golden M Club, which raised $3,000 to care for the collection. Some of the trophies were won by local sports heroes Greg Rice, "Wild Bill" Kelly, and Guy Rogers.[4]

Diane Sands, the museum's development director, advocated that the museum purchase the former Post Headquarters (Building T-1, see page 91) which sat just across the street from the eastern edge of the museum. Owned by the Forest Service, the building had the potential for vastly increased office space and collections storage. The building was appraised for $480,000 in 2008 and the museum formally purchased it in 2009. Remodeling of the building revealed that it was much older than assumed. A little research brought to light the fact that it once been the post's chapel, built in 1883, which had been moved and remodeled in 1940. Another discovery came when the carpet was pulled back in one room, revealing the outline of a judge's bench. During World War II the post headquarters served as a courtroom for Alien Detention Hearings, and also for the inmates of the Disciplinary Barracks. Director Brown remembered, "We didn't know the courtroom was there. We didn't know it was the church. We just loved the basement."[5]

Despite the museum's uncertain funding and

Top - The Fort's former quartermaster warehouse (T-322) received little maintenance after World War II, and by 1973 it was in bad shape. After extensive cleanup and renovation the warehouse became the headquarters of the Historical Museum at Fort Missoula in 1974. The building now has exhibit space, staff offices, and collection storage.

Bottom - The Grant Creek Schoolhouse (left) and the Drummond Depot are only two of the relocated buildings at the Historical Museum. The schoolhouse has been fully restored with the help of the Delta Kappa Gamma teacher sorority, and each spring local schoolchildren are treated to a one-room schoolhouse experience. The Missoula Model Railroad Club uses the Drummond Depot, which has a fully restored ticket office and a model train display.

future, during the late 1990s the museum sought professional accreditation from the American Association of Museums (AAM). "The achievement of accreditation is recognition of a museum's commitment to excellence and high professional standards of operation."[6] It was a rigorous, years-long process that demanded a major effort from the director, staff, and boards. AAM granted accreditation in 2000, and declared the museum was, "a well-organized, smoothly functioning organization. The staff are professional, competent and enthusiastic, as are the volunteers. Indeed, a great deal of work that would be handled by staff in a larger museum, from lawn-mowing to collections care and demonstration, is very well done by enthusiastic volunteers. It is a credit to the director, the board and the Friends that so many volunteers, both organizations and individuals, are found to meet the museum's many needs."[7] The museum's accreditation was renewed in 2010 after a second rigorous examination of every aspect of the operation.

During the late 1990s Missoula County faced serious budget deficits, and by 1999 the historical museum was on the brink of closure. County officials made it clear that passage of a permanent mill levy was the only way to ensure an adequate and stable source of funding for the museum. In response, the Friends of the Historical Museum teamed up with the Missoula Art Museum to form the "Yes to Museums" campaign to seek voter approval for a shared three-mill property tax levy. The vote was held in June 2000, and while city residents generally supported it, many county residents did not. The measure was defeated, and museum director Dr. Robert M. Brown later remembered, "The fact that we lost in 2000, that hurt."[8] Undeterred, two years later the Friends of the Historical Museum mounted the "Yes to History" campaign, seeking a dedicated two-mill levy for the historical museum. Increased outreach to rural areas of Missoula County resulted in a successful vote in June 2002, and the future of the historical museum was assured. Brown recalled, "I remembered [County Commissioner] Fern Hart telling me, 'you have no idea how this is going to change your job.' And it has." He added, "if I had to pick one accomplishment it would be getting the mill levy, because that has made everything else possible. Before we could do incremental steps along the way, but now we have taken huge jumps. The increase in staff, and the increase in professionalism among the staff was made possible by that. The pathways, the trolley and all that became possible because suddenly we were free from that enormous burden of survival."[9]

The Army retained the right to retake control of the fort if needed for national defense, but, "effective 30 September 1999 the United States Army Garrison at Fort Missoula, Montana... is discontinued as an active Army organization in accordance with the Defense Base Closure and Realignment Act of 1990,"[10] Unlike most historic forts, abandonment by the Army did not mean a long slide into obsolescence. A remarkable transformation has taken place since the 1960s, and the once remote military post is now a cherished community asset, home to dozens of vibrant businesses and organizations, cultural and educational groups, western Montana's largest medical complex, two golf courses and a developing regional park. Numerous governmental agencies such as the US Forest Service, Bureau of Land Management, State of Montana, Montana National Guard, and University of Montana also have a presence at the fort.

The 379th Engineer Battalion, the last Army Reserve unit stationed at the fort, was deactivated on the parade ground at Fort Missoula in August, 2010, and the detachment's commander, Captain Charlie Cromwell, paid fitting tribute to the fort's long history when he wrote, "To the honorable soldiers stationed at Fort Missoula over the past 133 years - I salute you."[11]

The Forestry Interpretive Area

The historical museum's mission includes a provision to interpret and preserve the history of forest management and the wood products industry in western Montana. The museum's Forestry Interpretive Area features a variety of antique logging equipment, including a working steam sawmill, a tipi burner, the Sliderock Mountain lookout tower, a 1910 Forest Service guard cabin moved from Miller Creek, and a logging train with a Shay locomotive, slide jammer, flatcars, a crummy car (used to transport loggers), and a library car used by the Anaconda Company at remote logging camps. The Society of American Foresters has been instrumental in helping the museum fulfill its mission, and also exhibits a collection of antique logging equipment, including a restored horse-drawn logging high wheels.

Since 1994 the museum has hosted Forestry Day each spring in conjunction with the Society of American Foresters and the University of Montana's Woodsman team. Then annual college and Pro-am logging sports competition attracts athletes in events such as ax throwing, pole climbing, log rolling, springboard, and "hot saws."

The centerpiece of the Forestry Interpretive Area is the operational steam-powered sawmill. The orange teepee-burner in the background was built in 1946 and was moved from the Bitterroot Valley in 2006 by the Society of American Foresters.

A "Jack and Jill" team competes in the crosscut saw event at Forestry Days.

The US Forest Service's Sliderock Mountain Fire Lookout, built in 1934 from prefabricated components, was originally located in the Rock Creek drainage southeast of Missoula. Part of the lookout was moved to the museum in the 1970s, and it was erected in 1983 with the assistance of the Society of American Foresters. The interior of the lookout has been fully restored.

The United People's Federation Powwow

The fort's original parade ground, long abandoned and infested with weeds, became home to the United People's Federation powwow for several days each summer beginning in 1989. Missoula resident Chris Roberts organized the powwow during the early years. A dance arbor was built not far from where Lt. Colonel Charles C. Gilbert had planted a flag in 1876 to mark the location of Fort Missoula. The powwow traditionally attracted Nez Percé, Assiniboine, Gros Ventre, Blackfeet, Salish, Chippewa, Cree and Navajo dancers. Participants often camped on the grounds during the three-day event. The powwow featured a traditional Plains-style of dancing, where the dancers traveled in a clockwise direction, rather than the counterclockwise dancing typical in the Pacific Northwest. Although the powwow continued until 2000, the high point may have come in 1995, when 8,000 people attended, and the event gave out $15,000 in prizes. Native American students from the university have since erected traditional sweat lodges near the riverbank south of the water tower.

The Fort Missoula Amphitheater

The Fort Missoula Theatre Company, a collaboration between actor Deny Staggs and investor Mike Bragg, produced and performed "Cowboy: Charlie Russell's Montana" during the summer months from 1998 to 2000. Volunteers from the Friends of the Historical Museum plus members of the 279th Engineering Detachment of the Army National Guard and workers from the Missoula Community Service Program began construction on the Fort Missoula Amphitheater beginning in 1997. The project was assisted by several corporate donors and a great deal of community support. The Theatre Company kicked off the fund-raising campaign with a production of "A 1940s Christmas Carol." "Cowboy" opened in 1998 and the 6,000 spectators who attended the first season were treated to a western barbecue before the play, then thrilled to the magic of live theater on summer evenings at the Fort. The musical on the life on artist Charlie Russell was written by R. Richard Riddle and featured cowboys, Indians, dance-hall girls, shootouts and horses. Dr. Brown remembered the project as, "a fun, exasperating three years."

Other groups that have performed at Fort Missoula include Willie Nelson, the University's Young Rep theatre, the Big Sky Mudflaps, Rob Quist and the Big Sky Singers, the dancers of the United Peoples Federation Powwow, and Rocky Mountain Ballet Theatre.

Fort Missoula fiction

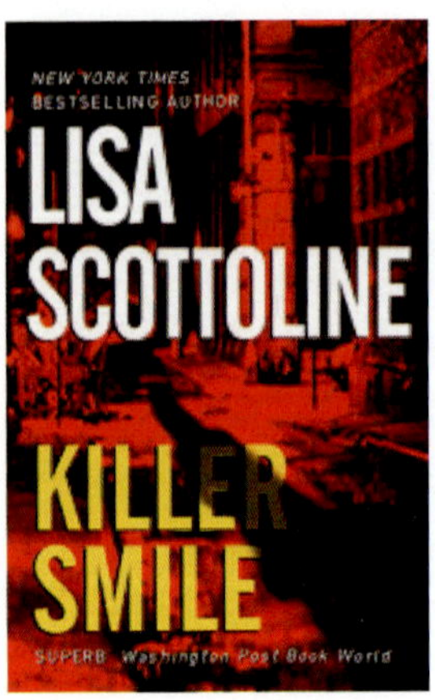

Fort Missoula has inspired at least two novels. **Killer Smile** by Lisa Scottoline (Harper 2004) is a thriller about Mary DiNunzio a young Philadelphia lawyer who investigates the suicide of an Italian detainee at the Alien Detention Center. It is based on the experiences of the author's Italian grandparents who were forced to register as enemy aliens in 1942. **First Reveille** by Pat Rahmann (Trafford Publishing Ltd. 2004) tells the story of eleven-year-old Maggie Blanchard, whose father was a captain in the 4th Infantry stationed at the Fort in 1939. It is a snapshot of what life was like for the families of the soldiers, and takes place in the area bounded by officers row, the parade ground, and the WPA recreation center.

Chapter Notes

Chapter 1 - Missoula Has Got That Post at Last

1. *Roundup Record Tribune and Winnett Times*, Jan. 9, 1941.
2. Father Adrian Hoecken letter to Fr. Joseph Joset, Aug. 1, 1855
3. *Weekly Missoulian*, April 26, 1876
4. Harding, E.F. 2nd Lt. 4th Infantry, *History of Fort Missoula*.
5. Miller, D. and Cohen, S., *Military & Trading Posts of Montana*
6. *Weekly Missoulian*, June 1, 1877

Chapter 2 - The Most Extraordinary of Indian Wars

1. Quoted in Cozzens, Peter. *Eyewitness to the Indian Wars 1865-1890. Vol. II: The Wars For the Pacific Northwest.*
2. Capt. Charles Rawn letter to the Acting Adjutant General at Fort Shaw, July 3, 1877
3. Leeson, Michael A. *History of Montana, 1739-1885*
4. *Diary of Wilson Barber Harlan* p., quoted in West p.173
5. *Helena Daily Herald*, July 30, 1877
6. Chauncey Barbour letter to Gov. Potts, July 31, 1877
7. The *New Northwest*, Aug. 10, 1877 p. 18
8. Quoted in Cozzens, Peter. *Eyewitness to the Indian Wars 1865-1890. Vol. II*
9. W.B. Harlan letter to *New Northwest*, Aug. 4, 1877
10. Shields, G.O. *The Battle of the Big Hole: a history of General Gibbon's engagement with Nez Percés Indians in the Big Hole Valley, Montana, August 9th, 1877* (1889)
11. Edgar I., ed. "Letters from the Big Hole." *Montana: The Magazine of Western History* 2 (Oct. 1952)
12. Henry Buck, quoted in Cozzens, Peter. *Eyewitness History of the Indian Wars 1865-1890. Vol. II.*
13. "Algonquin, An Underdog View," undated *Missoulian* article in the Historical Museum at Fort Missoula (HMFM) archives

Chapter 3 - Building the Fort

1. Report of the General of the Army, Nov. 7, 1877
2. Capt. Rawn letter to Dept. of Dakota, Sept. 30, 1877
3. *History of Fort Missoula, Montana: This History was found in the Adjutant's Desk at Fort Missoula, Montana by Capt. E. E. Ely, 4th Infantry, March 7, 1931.* Missoula Public Library
4. Ibid.
5. Ibid.
6. Ibid.
7. Ibid.
8. Capt. Penrose to Headquarters of the Army, Sept. 25, 1879
9. F.P. Avery personal letter, April 5, 1879. HMFM archives
10. *Detroit Post*, Jan. 11, 1879
11. Lt. Col Gibson letter to War Department, Nov. 8, 1885
12. *History of Fort Missoula, Montana: This History was found in the Adjutant's Desk at Fort Missoula, Montana by Capt. E. E. Ely, 4th Infantry, March 7, 1931.*
13. Minnie Spurgin letter to Missoula citizens, 1925. Courtesy of Kris Crawford.
14. Frieda Klapwyck letter, 1976. Courtesy of Kris Crawford.
15. Antonio Bertapelle letter, 1994. Courtesy of Kris Crawford.
16. William Maclay interviewed by his son Walter Maclay, 2008. Courtesy of Kris Crawford.
17. Ray Rademacher letter, 1993. Courtesy of Kris Crawford.
18. Warren, *Affray at Brownsville*

Chapter 4 - The Buffalo Soldiers

1. *Missoula Gazette*, June 2, 1888. HMFM archives
2. Burt, Elizabeth, "An Army Wife's Forty Years in the Service, 1862-1902.
3. Ibid.
4. *Weekly Missoulian*, Dec. 11, 1889
5. Bigart, Robert J. *Getting Good Crops: Economic and Diplomatic Survival Strategies of the Montana Bitterroot Salish Indians 1870-1891.* University of Oklahoma Press, Norman. 2010.
6. Mary Ronan in letter to her son, quoted in *Spokesman Review*.
7. *Anaconda Standard*, Aug 6, 1894
8. Ibid.
9. Ibid.
10. Ibid.
11. *Anaconda Standard*, Aug. 3, 1895
12. Burt, Elizabeth.
13. Mark Twain quoted in *New York Times*, Aug. 17, 1895

Chapter 5 - The Bicycle Corps

1. Lt. James Moss letter to War Dept., April 13, 1896
2. Edward Boos quoted in Sorensen, George N. *Iron Riders*, p.57
3. *St. Louis Globe-Democrat*
4. Edward Boos quoted in Sorensen, p.57
5. *St. Louis Globe-Democrat*, July 28, 1897
6. *Daily Missoulian*, June 29, 1897
7. Quoted in Koelbel, Lenora. *Missoula the Way It Was*, p.66
8. *Daily Missoulian*, June 29, 1897
9. *New York Times*, Sept. 21, 1897
10. Ibid.
11. *St. Louis Dispatch*, July 28, 1897
12. *Daily Missoulian*, April 11, 1898
13. Steward, T. G. *The Colored Regulars in the United States Army*
14. Warren. *Affray at Brownsville*
15. Ibid.
16. *Worthington Herald*, May 29, 1898

Chapter 6 - The Early Twentieth Century

1. General Orders No. 14, Adjutant General's Office March 30, 1898
2. Sen. Thomas Carter to Secretary of War, April 27 1899
3. Gen Nelson A. Miles letter to Headquarters of the Army, Aug. 20, 1900
4. Major Geo. E. Pond letter to Dept. Dakota June 11, 1901
5. Nelson Miles to Headquarters of the Army, June 24, 1901
6. *Daily Missoulian*, Sept. 11, 1928
7. Maj. Geo. E. Pond to Quartermaster General of the Army, Oct 26, 1900
8. Annual Report of Secretary of War Vol. 1, 1912, Washington, 1913
9. Ibid.
10. *Montana Kaiman*, Aug. 16, 1918.
11. Mullay, Col. P.H. "History of Fort Missoula, Montana," *US Army Recruiting News*, Feb.1, 1924.
12. Koelbel, *Missoula the Way it Was*
13. Vecchia, Alice Della, letter to HMFM June 14, 1995

Chapter 7 - The Civilian Conservation Corps

1. Vecchia, Alice Della, letter to HMFM June 14, 1995.
2. Robert Fechner quoted in Salmond, *The Civilian Conservation Corps, 1933-1942*. p.138
3. Cohen, Stan. *The Tree Army: A Pictorial History of the Civiilian Conservation Corps, 1933-1942.*
4. Otis, Alison T., et al. *The Forest Service and the Civilian Conservation Corps: 1933-42.*
5. *Daily Missoulian*, Oct. 25, 1940
6. *St. Petersburg Times*, Oct. 1, 1918.
7. Dr. Robert M. Brown, interviewed by the author, Feb. 21, 2013

Chapter 8 - The Prisoners of Bella Vista

1. US Department of Justice, INS. *Instructions Concerning the Treatment of Alien Enemy Detainees.* April 28, 1942
2. *Time Magazine*, Aug. 18, 1941
3. Van Valkenburg, Carol. *An Alien Place: the Fort Missoula, Montana, Detention Camp, 1941-1944*, p21.
4. John Moe speech at Fort Missoula, Nov. 3, 2001
5. Van Valkenburg, Carol. p35
6. DiStasi. Lawrence. *Una Segretia*, p13
7. Hirasuna, Delphine, et al. *The Art of Gaman: Arts and Crafts from the Japanese American Internment Camps, 1942-1946.*

Berkeley, Ca.: Ten Speed Press. 2005
8. Saiki, Patsy Sumie. *Ganbare! An Example of Japanese Spirit*. Kisaku Inc. Honolulu. 1982
9. *Missoulian*. Jan. 29, 1995, pE3
10. Missoula INS office letter from to W.F. Kelly, Chief Supervisor of Border Patrol, Washington, DC. Dec. 29, 1941
11. Wegars, Priscilla. *Imprisoned in Paradise: Japanese Internee Road Workers at the World War II Kooskia Internment Camp*. p129
12. Letter from Missoula INS office to W.F. Kelly, Chief Supervisor of Border Patrol, Washington, DC. Dec. 29, 1941
13. Van Valkenburg, Carol
14. Ibid.
15. *Report of the Northern California Alien Hearings Board at Fort Missoula for Suyoichi Okamura, Feb. 9, 1942*
16. Ruth Hoshimiya to father Toske Hoshimiya, May 21, 1942 Quoted in *Imprisoned in Paradise*, p49
17. Bert Fraser memo to ADC staff, Dec. 20, 1943
18. Potter, Ursula Vogt, ed. *The Misplaced American*.
19. DiStasi, *Una Storia Segreta*. p39
20. Long, Wally. *The Military History of Ft. Missoula*, p.16-17
21. Sullivan, Patricia. *Missoulian*, July 17, 1994

Chapter 9 - For Sale: Fort Missoula

1. Maclay, William. Interview by Walter Maclay, 2008.
2. Missoula Chamber of Commerce telegram to Sen. Mike Mansfield, June 14, 1955.

Chapter 10 - The Battle of Fort Missoula

1. Fort Missoula Plan. 1973, p.23
2. Ibid.
3. Sullivan, P. *Missoulian*, "Selling the Fort," Aug. 20, 1995
4. Ibid.
5. Ibid.
6. Ibid.
7. George Dennison memo, Oct. 11, 1990. Quoted in "Selling the Fort" by Patricia Sullivan. *Missoulian*, Aug 20, 1995
8. Sullivan, Patricia. "Fort Sale Called Illegal" *Missoulian* Aug. 18, 1995
9. Sullivan, Patricia. "Report Faults Fort Dealings" *Missoulian*, May 20, 1994
10. Ibid.
11. Ibid.
12. *Missoula Independent*, April 1, 1994
13. *Missoula Independent*, Nov. 11, 1993
14. *Missoula Independent*, Dec. 3, 1993
15. Ibid.
16. *Missoula Independent*, Dec. 10, 1993
17. Ibid.
18. Ibid.
19. Reese, Joel, "Citizens Petition to Save the Fort." *Missoula Independent*, Jan. 14, 1994
20. Ibid.
21. Sullivan, P. *Missoulian*, Aug. 18, 1995
22. Ibid.
23. Sullivan, P. *Missoulian*, Aug. 20, 1995
24. Sullivan, P. *Missoulian*, Aug. 18, 1995
25. Ibid.
26. *Missoulian*, Sept. 29, 1995
27. Merriam, Ginny. "Affordable Housing," *Missoulian*, Aug. 3, 1996
28. Nailen, Dan. "Save the Fort Wants its Day in Court," *Missoula Independent*, Dec. 5, 1996
29. *Missoulian*, Dec. 12, 1996

Chapter 11 - The Modern Fort

1. Mullay, Col. P.H.
2. Dr. Robert M. Brown, interviewed by the author Feb. 21, 2013.
3. 1993 Fort Missoula plan
4. Jahrig, Gary. "Group rescuing, restoring history of MCHS" *Missoulian*, Sept. 26, 1996
5. Brown, Dr. Robert M. interview
6. American Association of Museums (http://www.aam-us.org)
7. American Association of Museums report on the Historical Museum at Fort Missoula, 2000
8. Brown, Dr. Robert M. interview
9. Ibid.
10. Headquarters: Department of the Army, Washington DC, "General Order No. 8 Fort Missoula, Montana Base Closure Action, Sept. 30 1999."
11. *Missoulian* letters, Aug. 29, 2010

Select Bibliography

Agnew, Jeremy. *Life of a Soldier on the Western Frontier*. Missoula: Mountain Press Publishing Co., 2008.

Anaconda Standard, Aug. 3-6, 1894

Author unknown. *Historical Museum at Fort Missoula*. Pamphlet in the archives of the Historical Museum at Fort Missoula.

Author unknown. *History of Fort Missoula, Montana: This History was found in the Adjutant's Desk at Fort Missoula, Montana by Capt. E. E. Ely, 4th Infantry, March 7, 1931.* Missoula Public Library.

Bailey, Linda. *Fort Missoula's Military Cyclists: The Story of the 25th U.S. Infantry Bicycle Corps.* Missoula: Friends of the Historical Museum at Fort Missoula, 1997.

Bigart, Robert J. *Getting Good Crops: Economic and Diplomatic Survival Strategies of the Montana Bitterroot Salish Indians 1870-1891.* Norman, Ok.: University of Oklahoma Press, 2010.

Billings Gazette, June 28, 1942

Brown, Dee. *Bury My Heart At Wounded Knee*. New York: Holt, Rinehart and Winston Inc., 1971.

Brown, Dr. Robert M. Interviewed by the author Feb. 21, 2013.

Burt, Elizabeth. *An Army Wife's Forty Years in the Service 1862-1902.* Unpublished manuscript, 1912.

Civilian Conservation Corps. *Pictorial Review of Civilian Conservation Corps in Montana. That the work of Young America May be Recorded.* Spokane. Aug. 15, 1937.

"Civilian Conservation Corps News from the Fort Missoula District." *The Green Guidon: Number sixty-three.* Sept. 1934

Carroll, John M., Ed. *The Black Military experience in the American West.* New York: Liverlight Publishing Corporation, 1971.

Cohen, Stan. *The Tree Army: A Pictorial History of the Civilian Conservation Corps, 1933-1943.* Missoula, Mt.: Pictorial Histories Publishing Co., 1980.

Cohen, Stan. Personal interview by the author, Nov. 16, 2012.

Cozzens, Peter. *Eyewitness to the Indian Wars, 1865-1890: Vol. II. The Wars For the Pacific Northwest.* Mechanicsburg, PA: Stackpole Books, 2002.

Detroit Post, Jan. 11 & 13, 1879.

Devlin, Sherry. "A Place to Rest." *Missoulian*, May 28, 1995.

DiStasi, Lawrence, ed. *Una Storia Segreta: The Secret History of Italian American Evacuation and Internment during World War II.* Berkeley, Ca.: Heyday Books, 2001.

Electric Railway Journal, 1918-1920.

E.R.A. Headlights, Vol. 8, No. 2. Feb. 1946.
Federal Writers Project. *The WPA Guide to 1930s Montana*. Works Project Administration. Tucson and London: University of Arizona Press, 1994.
Fiset, Louis. "Medical Care for Interned Enemy Aliens: A Role for the US Public Health Service in World War II." *American Journal of Public Health*. 2003. October; 93(10): 1644–1654.
Fort Missoula Regional Park Master Plan. Missoula. 2008.
"Fort Missoula Plan - 1993: A revision and update of the 1973 Fort Missoula Guidelines For Development." Adopted by the Missoula City Council, January 1994.
Fowler, Arlen. *The African American Experience: Black Infantry in the West 1869-1891*. Norman and London: University of Oklahoma Press, 1996.
Frenchtown Historical Society. *Frenchtown Valley Footprints*. Missoula: Mountain Press, 1976.
Great Falls Tribune, Dec. 24, 1944-Feb. 11, 1945
Greene, Jerome A., and Josephy, Alvin M. *Nez Perce Summer, 1877: The U.S. Army and the Nee-Me-Poo-Crisis*. Helena: Montana Historical Society Press, 2000.
Habeck, Dr. James R. A. *Compilation of Documentation of Cultural and Natural History Information for the former Fort Missoula Timber Reserve in Pattee Canyon, Missoula County*. Missoula: University of Montana, 2003.
Haines, Aubrey. *An Elusive Victory: The Battle of the Big Hole*. West Glacier, Mt.: Glacier Natural History Association, 1991.
Haines, Francis. *The Nez Perce: Tribesmen of the Columbia Plateau*. Norman, Ok.: University of Oklahoma Press, 1955.
Helena Daily Herald, July 30, 1877
Johnson, Dale. "Western Montana Ghost Town Preservation Society." Unpublished manuscript.
Koelbel, Lenora. *Missoula: The Way It Was*. Missoula: Pictorial Histories Publishing Company, 1972.
Koury, Michael J. *Military Posts of Montana*. Johnstone, Co: Old Army Press, 1970.
Lacey, Richard H. *The Montana Militia: A History of Montana's Volunteer Forces 1867-1976*. Dillon, Mt.: Dillon Tribune Examiner Press, 1976.
Leckie, Robert. *The Buffalo Soldiers*. Norman, OK: University of Oklahoma Press, 1967.
Leeson, Michael A. *History of Montana 1739-1885*. Chicago: Warner, Beers & Co., 1885.
Lolo History Committee. *Lolo Creek Reflections*. No publisher or date listed.
Long, Wallace J. *The Military History of Fort Missoula*. Missoula: Friends of the Historical Museum at Fort Missoula, 1983.
— *McCauley Bluff Target Range*, Nov. 1, 1985.
— *History of the Fort Missoula Cemetery*.
— *Sgt. Ernest Veuve, Medal of Honor Winner*. May 15, 1980.
Luppi, Robert. "Captain William Logan: A 'Brave and Sagacious Officer' Who Died at the Big Hole, Leaving a Prominent and Enduring Montana Legacy." 2009. Available at http://www.friendsnezpercebattlefields.org/captainwilliamlogan.htm.
McDonald, James R., Long, Wally, and Hardin, Wes. *Fort Missoula Historic Resources: An Architectural and Historical Resource Survey of the Fort Missoula Complex*. Missoula: June, 1984.
Miller, Don and Cohen, Stan. *Military and Trading Posts of Montana*. Missoula: Pictorial Histories Publishing Co., 1978.
Missoula Gazette, June 2, 1888
Missoula Independent, Nov. 11, 1993, Nov., 19, 1993, Dec. 3, 1993, Dec. 10, 1993, Dec. 30, 1993, Jan.14, 1994, April 1, 1994, Apr. 20, 1994, Dec. 5, 1996
Missoulian, June 13, 1974. June 15, 1974, July 26, 1974, May 20, 1994, July 17, 1994, Jan. 29, 1995, Aug. 18-20, 1995, Sept. 29, 1995, Sept. 26, 1996, Dec.17, 1996
Daily Missoulian, June 14 1897, June 16 1897, June 29 1897, July 3 1897, July 7 1897, July 10 1897, July 17 1897, July 24 1897, April 23, 1898. Sept. 11, 1928, Oct. 25, 1940
Weekly Missoulian, Apr. 26, 1876, June 1, 1877, July-Aug. 1877, Dec. 11, 1889
Missoulian-Sentinel, July, 27, 1960. 100 Years of Progress Centennial Edition
Moe, John. Presentation at the Historical Museum at Fort Missoula, Nov. 3, 2001.
Montana Kaiman, Aug. 16, 1918
Mudd, Robert,and Nolan, John. Compiled by Sharon Garner. *The 24th Infantry Buffalo Soldiers, Spanish American War and WWI*. Historical Museum at Fort Missoula archives. 2007.
Mullen, Robert W. *Blacks in America's Wars: The Shift in Attitudes From the Revolutionary War to Vietnam*. New York: A Pathfinder Book, Anchor Foundation, 1973.
Mukaeda, Katsuma. Interview by Paul F. Clark for the Japanese American Project of the California State University, Fullerton, Oral History Program, at Mr. Mukaeda's office on 125 Weller Street in Los Angeles, California, on May 22, 1975 at 3:30 p.m.
Nankivell, John H. *Buffalo Soldier Regiment: History of the Twenty-fifth United States Infantry, 1869-1926*. Lincoln, Ne.: Bison Books, University of Nebraska Press, 2001.
New Northwest, Aug. 10, 1877
New York Times, July 26, 1897
Otis, Alison T. and William D. Honey, Thomas C. Hogg, and Kimberly K. Lakin. *The Forest Service and The Civilian Conservation Corps: 1933-42*. USDA Forest Service, August 1986.
Palladino, Father L.B. *Indian and White in the Northwest, A History of Catholicity in Montana 1831-1891*. Wickersham Publishing Co., 1922.
Pond, Maj. J.B. *Eccentricities of Genius*. New York: G. W. Dillingham Company, 1900.
Porter, Marcia. "History of the Fort Missoula Post Cemetery: Stories in Stones." Historical Museum at Fort Missoula Archives.
Potter, Ursula Vogt ed. *The Misplaced American*. Bloomington, IN: AuthorHouse,2003.
Rockwell, Ronald V. *The U.S. Army in Frontier Montana*. Helena, Mt: Sweetgrass Books, 2009.
Ronan, Margaret. *Frontier Woman: the Story of Mary Ronan*, as told to Margaret Ronan, ed by H.G. Merriam. Missoula: University of Montana Publications in History, 1973.
Rothermich, Capt. A.E., ed. "Early Days at Fort Missoula. Missoula." *Frontier and Midland*. Vol. XVI #3 Spring, 1936.
Saiki, Patsy Sumie. *Ganbare! An Example of Japanese Spirit*. Honolulu: Kisaku Inc., 1982.
Salmond, John. *The Civilian Conservation Corps, 1933-1942: A New Deal Case Study*. Durham, NC: Duke University Press, 1967.

Sorensen, George Niels. *Iron Riders: Story of the 1890s Fort Missoula Buffalo Soldiers Bicycle Corps*. Missoula: Pictorial Histories Publishing Co., 2000.
St. Louis Globe-Democrat, July 28, 1897
St. Louis Post Dispatch, July 28, 1897
St. Petersburg Times, Oct. 1, 1918
Steward, T. G. *The Colored Regulars in the United States Army.* Philadelphia: A.M.E. Book Concern, 1904.
Swett, Ira L. "Montana's Trolleys III." *Interurbans Magazine: Interurbans Special 51.* Southgate, California, 1970.
Tackett, Amy. "Detained at Fort Missoula: Application of International Law on Italian and Japanese Internees." Senior Thesis. Billings: Montana State University Billings, Dec. 14, 2012.
Time Magazine, Aug. 18, 1941
Toole, John H. *Red Ribbons: A Story of Missoula and Its Newspaper.* Missoula: Lee Enterprises, 1989.
Utley, Robert M. *Frontier Regulars: The United States Army and the Indian, 1866-1890.* New York: MacMillan Publishing Co., 1973.
— *The Indian Frontier of the American West 1846-1890.* Albuquerque, NM: University of New Mexico Press, 1984.
Van Valkenburg, Carol. *An Alien Place: the Fort Missoula, Montana, Detention Camp, 1941-1944.* Missoula: Pictorial Histories Publishing Co., 1995.
Warren, Francis Emroy. *Affray at Brownsville, Texas.* US Congress, Senate Committee on Military Affairs, United States Army. 60th Congress, 1st session, 1907-1908.
Wegars, Priscilla. *Imprisoned in Paradise: Japanese Internee Road Workers at the World War II Kooskia Internment Camp.* Moscow, ID: Asian American Comparative Collection, University of Idaho, 2010.
West, Elliott. *The Last Indian War.* New York: Oxford University Press, 2009.
Woody, Frank H. *History of Missoula (city & county) from data furnished principally by Hon. Frank H. Woody.* Compiled and edited by W.E. Ellsworth. Missoula: *Democrat-Messenger*, 1897.
Works Progress Administration. "Completion Report: Official Project No. 13-3-91-123, Fort Missoula, Montana." Sept. 15, 1939.
Worthington Herald, May 29, 1898

Alphabetical Index